Ritual and Symbol
in Peacebuilding

Ritual and Symbol in Peacebuilding

Lisa Schirch

Kumarian
Press, Inc.

Ritual and Symbol in Peacebuilding
Published 2005 in the United States of America by Kumarian Press, Inc.
1294 Blue Hills Avenue, Bloomfield, CT 06002 USA

Production and design by Rosanne Pignone, Pro Production
Copyedited by Beth Richards
Proofread by Jody El-Assadi, A Proofer's Touch
Index by Barbara DeGennaro

The text for *Ritual and Symbol in Peacebuilding* is set in Janson 10/12.
Printed in the United States of America on acid-free paper by Thomson-Shore, Inc.
Text printed with vegetable oil-based ink.

∞ The paper used in this publication meets the minimum requirements of the American National Standard for Information Sciences—Permanence of Paper for printed Library Materials, ANSI Z39.48-1984

Library of Congress Cataloging-in-Publication Data
Schirch, Lisa.
Ritual and symbol in peacebuilding / Lisa Schirch.
    p. cm.
    Includes bibliographical references.
    ISBN 1-56549-194-7 (pbk. : alk. paper) — ISBN 1-56549-195-5
    (cloth : alk. paper)
    1. Peace-building. 2. Conflict management. 3. Ritual—Political aspects.
4. Symbolism in politics. 5. Nonverbal communication—Political aspects.
6. Communication in politics. I. Title.
JZ5538.S36 2005
    399—dc22

                                                2004018655

14 13 12 11 10 09 08   10 9 8 7 6 5 4 3 2   First Printing 2005

Table of Contents

List of Illustrations

Boxes

Tables

Figures

Acknowledgments

Many people and organizations contributed to this book. First, my husband William H. Goldberg edited and critiqued my work, asked for clarification when my thoughts were cloudy, cooked, and cleaned the house while I was tied to the computer. My parents, Verne and Carol Schirch, provided moral and financial support so that I could take a year without working and conduct the research for this book with minimal interruptions. Jayne Seminare Docherty and Galey Modan shared many cups of coffee and listened to me try to articulate what I was learning. Cynthia Sampson and Rabbi Marc Gopin encouraged and supported me in the publishing process. Mary Frederick edited the manuscript for grammatical and compositional errors.

A number of organizations and individuals also contributed to this work by allowing me to study their rituals. I first discovered my interest in studying peacebuilding rituals while working with Louise Diamond and Ambassador John McDonald at the Washington, DC–based Institute for Multi-Track Diplomacy. I want to thank each of them for telling me many of their stories and sharing my interest in ritual. I would also like to thank the First Nations community in Ontario, particularly the Native Canadian Centre in Toronto, the Spirit of the People program in Toronto, and the Weejeendimin Native Resource Centre in Waterloo, Ontario. Finally, I deeply appreciate the Women's Alliance for Theology, Ethics, and Ritual in Silver Spring, Maryland, for opening their doors to me as I studied feminist rituals. In particular, thanks to Diann Neu for allowing me to see the inside process of developing feminist rituals.

This book began while I was completing my Ph.D. in Conflict Resolution at George Mason University. I would like to thank my professors there, particularly Mary Catherine Bateson, Tamra Pearson D'Estree, Michelle LeBaron, Sara Looney, and Hamdesa Tuso for their support and interest in my work. I completed the book while teaching at the Conflict Transformation Program (CTP) at Eastern Mennonite University (EMU).

I appreciate Ruth Zimmerman and Howard Zehr, CTP co-directors, and the EMU administration for their support of my leave of absence to finish this book and their feedback on its contents. In spring 2004, I taught my first class on "Ritual, Theater, and Peacebuilding" using this book as a text. I am grateful for the feedback students gave to me on the draft of this book and for the new stories of ritual peacebuilding they shared.

Finally, thanks to Jim Lance and all the staff at Kumarian Press for believing in the importance of this book and for leading me through the publishing process.

Introduction

. . . to study humanity is to study ritual . . . to ponder the future of humanity is to consider the future of ritual.[1]

C onflict is dramatic. All theater, literature, and good storytelling revolve around some form of conflict. John Wayne, Rambo, and their video descendants attest to the magnetic attraction of the drama of violent conflict. Peacebuilding can and needs to be equally dramatic to capture people's imagination and interest. Imagine CNN and other news networks giving half their air time to showing the dramas and symbols of peacebuilding processes to balance the barrage of violent images used to invoke the emotions and senses of television viewers.

Scholars and practitioners of peacebuilding do not often articulate the importance of ritual or symbol in solving complex, deep-rooted conflicts. Instead, students in conflict studies are accustomed to hearing of serious negotiations, rational discussion, and problem-solving efforts in conflict situations. Yet virtually all peacebuilders, whether they are government diplomats, nongovernmental organization (NGO) leaders, or grassroots mediators and activists, can tell stories about a meal, coffee break, handshake or other symbolic, physical act when adversaries made real progress toward peace. Peacebuilders are the choreographers, directors, and set designers of a drama centered on the visually engaging process of building peace. Peacebuilders need to see the place where peacebuilding occurs as a stage that must be constructed and set in a way that draws people to observe and take part in the peacebuilding drama. Peacebuilders should demonstrate a skilled capacity to choreograph bodies and movements on the peacebuilding stage to engage people's emotions, senses, and passions.

Ritual does not replace other tools for conflict transformation. Rather it is a supplement to traditional "front door" approaches to conflict that deal with issues in direct, rational, and linear modes. Ritual has three specific characteristics. First, ritual occurs in a unique social space, set aside from normal life. Second, ritual communicates through symbols, senses, and heightened emotions rather than relying heavily on the use of words. In ritual humans learn by doing. There is a preference for nonverbal communication using bodies, senses, and emotions rather than words or rational thought. Third, ritual both marks and assists in the process of change. It confirms and transforms people's worldviews, identities, and relationships with others.

The ideas in this book will be helpful to all people in the broad class of peacebuilders, including labor mediators, international diplomats, business negotiators, school-based conflict mediators, environmental mediators, community organizers, divorce mediators, nonviolent activists, domestic violence shelter workers, conflict resolution trainers and facilitators, and other people working for peace in their communities. Reading this book will enable both scholars and practitioners to articulate the need, functions, and dynamics of ritual in the drama of peacebuilding.

Note

1. Tom Faw Driver, *The Magic of Ritual: Our Need for Liberating Rites That Transform Our Lives and Our Communities* (San Francisco: Harper San Francisco, 1991).

CHAPTER 1

Peacebuilding Dramas

A dancer stands naked in line waiting for her turn to enter the gas chamber. We see a human being with its natural power to command space reduced to a body taking up space, passively submitting to the prospect of death. A guard tells her to step out of line and dance. She does, and carried away by her authoritative action and by her repossession of a self and a world, she dances up to the guard—now within the compass of her space—takes his gun and shoots him.[1]

This is a story of the profound ability of a symbolic act to transform space, to communicate nonverbally, and to transform worldviews, identities, and relationships. Unfortunately, Adolph Hitler understood the power of ritual as well and orchestrated enough emotion-whipping public rituals of booming drums, rhythmic marching, and swastika-laden soldiers before and during WWII to transform a nation and beyond.

In this story, the act of dancing becomes symbolic and changes the entire social context. The death camp becomes a dance floor. The dancer begins moving within the space in a way that is radically different than the solemn line where she had been standing. She transforms a rigid line of bystanders into a mesmerized audience of guards and prisoners circling around her. In the final moment, victim and killer change places. There is no peace here, but for a moment there is revolution.

The dancer responds to the guard's verbal command through nonverbal symbolic action. How could the dancer verbally communicate to herself and her captors that she was alive and free in any other way that would have been so believable? Her dancing says that she is indeed alive, human, vibrant, and an active participant rather than a helpless victim. The message is not only *transmitted* through her body. She *discovers* the message in the dancing. The dancer's body learns first that it is free. Her body recognizes its freedom and acts on that freedom by killing the soldier. In her shape-shifting she begins to see and feel the world around her in a new way. The dancer acts as if she is alive and powerful, and through dancing, she becomes alive and powerful. The dancer transforms her identity from a naked, helpless victim, subject of the guard, to a liberated, powerful dancer, master of the guard.

The guard is also magically transformed by her dancing. His world-view is penetrated and overwhelmed by her symbolic message of freedom. He stands unable to act or respond. If the guard had known what message the dance would bring and how that message would affect him, he likely would not have ordered the dancer to perform.

The relationship between guard and prisoner is reversed. The former imprisoned dancer transforms her relationship with the guard by moving close to him and then by killing him, a reversal of the hierarchy of their initial relationship. The strength of the dancer and the power of her dancing overwhelm the divisions between them. For that moment, they are all part of a ritual action, where human-to-human connection is real, if deadly.

While this story ends with death rather than peace, it attests to the surprising power of dancing to symbolize a message of freedom and the power to act. The dancer does not simply walk up to the guard, take his gun, and kill him. Without the symbolism of dancing, that direct method would not work to overcome the guard's sense of his role and desire to defend his life.

Humans are the only animals that use symbols. Symbols communicate indirectly; their message is unclear and flexible enough to allow for multiple interpretations. Dancing is a symbolic act because it represents or communicates more than one message. Depending on the context, the dancer, and the dance itself, the act of dancing could communicate beauty, anger, freedom, or any other idea.

The first step toward embracing the symbolic dimension of peacebuilding is recognizing the profound effects that symbolic acts have on humanity. Symbolic acts can penetrate the impenetrable, overwhelm the defensive, and convey complex messages without saying a single word. As with other human tools, their power can be used for good or evil. Clearly, the power of symbolic acts must be harnessed by those building peace in a terrorized world.

The stories in this chapter describe how people in conflict use symbolic acts to set the stage for peace. Some of the stories illustrate informal symbolic acts such as eating a meal, dancing, fishing, or looking at a photograph. Other stories illustrate more formal and traditional symbolic acts that are referred to here as rituals. This book covers the whole spectrum of symbolic acts: formal and informal, traditional and improvised, secular and religious. The examples here provide a foundation for theoretical exploration in future chapters.

Dinner Diplomacy:
From the Negotiation Table to the Dance Floor

The power of symbolic acts in the peacebuilding process first drew my attention in the early 1990s. Prior to 1974, Greek and Turkish Cypriots lived on both sides of the Mediterranean island of Cyprus. During the 1974 conflict, Turkish Cypriots in the south and Greek Cypriots in the north were forced to leave their homes. Since 1974, Greek and Turkish Cypriots have lived apart from each other, separated by the "Green Line," a UN-monitored buffer zone between the two ethnically divided communities. Turkish Cypriots now live on the northern side of the island and Greek Cypriots live in the south. Negotiations between the unrecognized Turkish Cypriot government and the recognized Greek Cypriot government have been unsuccessful in creating an agreement for the future of Cyprus.

In the 1990s, a group of American conflict resolution trainers began bringing Greek and Turkish Cypriots together for the first time in more than twenty years to talk about their conflict and the prospects for peace. In one of a series of ten-day workshops in 1994, conflict resolution trainers led participants through exercises in improving communication, problem solving, and negotiation skills. The focus was to build the capacity of the Turkish and Greek Cypriot participants to manage their conflict without violence and to encourage the development of Cypriot peacebuilders. Many evenings after the workshop, the Turkish and Greek Cypriots ate dinner together and occasionally danced and sang together in local restaurants. White tablecloths, candles, abundant dishes of food, guitars, and a dance floor set the stage for very different types of interaction between the workshop participants. The inclusion of these types of symbolic occasions is sometimes referred to as "dinner diplomacy."

In dinner diplomacy, participants do more than simply eat food to nourish their bodies or enjoy the pleasures of dancing. These acts become symbolic because the participants themselves are unusual. They come from opposing sides of a conflict. Eating and dancing take on new meanings when they are done in the company of enemies.

The symbolic acts of eating and dancing were essential to the success of transforming the participants' understanding of themselves, their "enemies," and the conflict as a whole. Instead of viewing each other by their ethnic identity as "Turkish Cypriot" or "Greek Cypriot," as they primarily did during the daytime training, during the evenings the participants seemed to view each other by other identities: mother, father, fellow victim of the war, teacher, musician, dancer, man, woman. One trainer noticed that the Greek and Turkish Cypriots would

> sing the same songs and dance the same way. Several of them said it brought them back to old times when they lived in the same village. And they knew they did the same things and were the same way. There's nothing on the island to reinforce that idea. I mean I can't think of any influence that would in any way suggest that the two sides are the same in any way. There's no contact, so there's no way of knowing.[2]

These activities emphasized their similarities rather than their differences. It strengthened their identity as Mediterranean islanders who had lived side by side for centuries. In addition, dancing requires individuals to play male and female roles, so gender identities became more salient in this atmosphere. The transformations that occurred between the Greek and Turkish Cypriot participants revealed new patterns in peacebuilding.

I began to wonder what was going on during these activities. The Greek and Turkish Cypriots were not just eating and dancing together. These social contexts had taken on a different ambience: significant symbolic, transforming actions were taking place. The idea that these symbolic actions may be important to the peacebuilding process came into focus. But what was going on during these festive evenings of glorious food and music?

As I attempted to make sense out of my Cypriot observations, I remembered rituals of First Nations peoples in Ontario, Canada, that I took part in while working on land claims issues from 1990–1992. I reflected on all the different ways people handled conflict in Native communities and began to see how culture shaped vastly different approaches to conflict. In Native communities, the rituals of smudging, passing the peace pipe, sweat lodges, and other ceremonies were a kind of "negotiating without words." Indigenous societies seem to prefer symbols and rituals as means of communication as opposed to Western industrialized societies, which prefer more direct communication modes. My Native friends rarely spoke directly of interpersonal conflict. Yet, drinking a cup of tea together, hunting moose out in the bush, or performing a ceremony together all were ways Native people handled conflicts and repaired relationships. In contrast to the direct forms of communication taught in most conflict resolution courses, the Native approach to conflict was avoidant and silent, yet effective. Why do many Native communities use symbols and rituals rather than verbal negotiation to transform conflicts?

A second memory of the role of ritual in peacebuilding surfaced. I recalled my experiences as an undergraduate student of feminist theology and women's spirituality. Many women theologians note the important role ritual plays in all of our lives. Feminist scholars talk about developing new, meaningful rituals and tell stories of how ritual transforms women's lives. How do women create their own rituals to deal with conflict? What lessons would this hold for peacebuilders?

Digging even further into my past, I remembered important rituals in the Mennonite Church in which I was raised—in particular, the memory of a foot-washing ceremony with a friend-turned-adversary. Our friendship had been damaged by a variety of unfortunate events. When she approached me to engage in the ritual of washing each other's feet during a church service, this symbol of forgiveness and grace became an awkward and difficult experience. Yet it marked the turning point when we began moving toward each other and our former friendship. While we eventually went to a mediator to help us talk about our conflict, the ritual pointed us down the road to reconciliation.

These personal experiences were foundational to my own interest in exploring the role of ritual and the symbolic dimension of peacebuilding. As I shared these experiences and my hypotheses of ritual's role in peacebuilding in other workshops and classrooms, I collected countless other stories.

Fishing for Trust

Allister Sparks tells a remarkable story in his book *Tomorrow is Another Country: The Inside Story of South Africa's Negotiated Revolution.*[3] Negotiations were under way in South Africa. The negotiator for the African National Congress, Cyril Ramaphosa, and his adversary, Roelf Meyer, Deputy Minister of Constitutional Development, were both invited to bring their families to a remote trout lodge for a relaxing weekend away from the negotiating tables. Neither was aware that the other had been invited.

To fill the uncomfortable time together, the whole group went fishing. Meyer admitted to his son that he did not know how to fish. When Ramaphosa heard Meyer's confession, he offered his expertise. As Meyer tried to cast his line, however, he accidentally embedded the fishing hook deep in his thumb. Meyer was at his adversary's mercy. Ramaphosa and his wife worked together to remove the barbed hook and finally succeeded. Meyer reportedly muttered, "Well . . . don't say I didn't trust you."[4] From that time on, the tone of the formal negotiations changed. The fishing accident seems to have provided a transformative ritual that built trust and changed the relationship between the two adversaries. These two key negotiators were central to creating the plan for national elections and the end of apartheid.

This story exemplifies the symbolic dimension of peacebuilding. These two men had spent countless hours at the negotiating table. They had nearly exhausted their ability to communicate directly through words designed to convince the other to trust and move forward with elections. Then the two men found themselves at a fishing lodge far from the negotiation tables. The context was unique, set apart, and unrelated to their professional lives. The communication at the pivotal moment was nonverbal and symbolic: Gently removing the barbed fishing hook from a finger was like turning a symbolic key that opened the door to their relationship. The situation was transformational and central to the design for elections.

Tennis, Horse Shoes, and Photos at Camp David

Former President Jimmy Carter brought Israeli Prime Minister Menachem Begin and Egyptian President Anwar Sadat to Camp David to discuss peace between Egypt and Israel specifically because of the atmosphere he thought the informal surroundings would create for the adversaries. Carter claimed Camp David was a "harmonious environment because Egyptians and Israelis who had been devoting their adult life to killing each other were required to swim in the same swimming pool, watch the same movies, play on the same tennis courts, throw horse-shoes together; sit on the same rock and talk. . . ."[5]

When asked about particular turning points in this peace process, Carter remembers a moment when sentiment and symbolism rather than words were the primary mode of communication. Prime Minister Begin had stopped interacting with President Sadat and had given up on the negotiation process. As he was preparing to leave, Begin asked Carter to sign pictures of himself, Sadat, and Carter for his eight grandchildren. At Carter's request, his secretary Susan Cloud obtained the names of each grandchild so that Carter could write a personal note to each of them. When Carter handed Begin the photographs, Begin's eyes watered. The photographs had triggered thoughts of his grandchildren and their future in a war-torn region. The tears expressed the emotional disappointment he felt over giving up on the peace process. According to Carter, a few minutes later Begin announced that he wanted to continue working. From that point on, they developed a proposal that could meet Begin's interests and needs while saving face for Sadat.[6] In this story, looking at the photographs became a transformative symbolic act. Although the verbal negotiations had failed, seeing a picture and thinking about grandchildren made all the difference in this peacebuilding effort.

Silent Poetry in the Norway Channel

The 1993 breakthrough negotiations between Israel and the Palestinian Liberation Organization (PLO) provide another clear example of the role of rituals in the peacebuilding process. While working with a variety of NGOs in the Middle East, a Norwegian couple, Terje and Mona Larson, developed a passion for creating a space where Israelis and Palestinians could meet together to build relationships without the pressure of the media, Americans, or any other outsiders. After developing important contacts on both sides, the Larsons invited Israeli and PLO representatives to a variety of different Norwegian country houses and mountain chalets for a series of meetings.

In *The Norway Channel: The Secret Talks That Led to the Middle East Peace Accord*, Jane Corbin notes that the Larsons paid meticulous attention to introducing a social element into the negotiations. She notes the importance of food, seating arrangements at meals, the ambience of beautifully decorated Nordic houses, good wine and whiskey, coffee, cigarettes, CNN, and gorgeous views of mountains and pine forests. According to Corbin, "Larson loved to place people in the right setting, to steer the conversation to create an ambience around the talks" creating a kind of "silent poetry" around the negotiations.[7]

This silent poetry around the negotiations also seemed to create room for the negotiators to make progress. During the meetings, a Palestinian negotiator exclaimed, "When I negotiate, I negotiate with my eyes, with my ears, with my nose, with my sense of smell, with my mouth. I use my whole body—everything!"[8] Larson made space for this holistic approach to the negotiations, which ended with the famous symbolic handshake between Israeli President Rabin and PLO leader Arafat. Instead of using a sterile negotiating room with a table and chairs and all the formalities of luxury hotels and capital cities, the Norwegians helped construct a context for the negotiations that would allow a variety of informal interactions to take place. They set the stage for peace, even though other events and people in the Middle East would cause the peace to be short term.

Somali Clan Peace Prize

In Northeastern Kenya, Somali clans battle over sovereignty issues in a European-created state that drew political lines without reference to ethnicity. In the Wajir district, a Peace and Development Committee was formed to respond to the severe clan violence. In addition to creating conflict resolution workshops for elders, youth, security forces, religious leaders, and local government officials, the Peace and Development Committee sponsored a peace festival and created a $200 peace prize for the chief who had made the largest contribution to peace in his location. According to Dekka Ibrahim and Jan Jenner, who documented these local efforts, "[t]he peace prize was such an honor that it was necessary to hold an unplanned workshop for chiefs the following day to instruct them in what they needed to do during the following year to win the prize at a subsequent peace festival."[9]

In the ceremonial setting of a peace festival, chiefs who were vital to the peacebuilding process were drawn to the symbolism of a peace prize and jointly recognized the value of working to stop violence. Awarding a yearly peace prize became a symbolic act that was far more powerful in contributing to peace in the region than many of the former negotiations between clan chiefs. Violence defined much of their lives in previous years, but the Peace and Development Committee succeeded in helping the community find a new focus for their relationships: celebrating peace.

Washing Out War

Both rebel and government forces in Mozambique used grotesque, violent rituals to terrorize the country during fifteen years of war. Traditional societies throughout Mozambique also used ritual in the healing process, helping local communities find a way forward beyond their trauma and the haunting memories of the past. While many Western forms of trauma healing focus on helping individuals come to terms with what happened and to return to "normal" through verbalizing painful experiences, many traditional and indigenous communities view trauma as a collective experience needing symbolic group healing and purification rituals. Mozambican anthropologist Alcinda Honwana describes the rituals of trauma healing in postwar Mozambique in her article "Sealing the Past, Facing the Future."[10] Mozambican communities used rituals to capture and put to rest the spirits of people who were not buried properly during the war. Other rituals cleansed and purified those who had been "tainted" by the war.

A nine-year-old boy who had been kidnapped by Renamo soldiers, for example, went through a purification ceremony when he returned home after eight months spent at a military base. The boy entered a special "house of the spirits" and took off his clothes as directed by a relative. The family member then set the hut on fire and helped the boy out. The boy was cleansed both internally and externally through breathing an herbal remedy, taking a ritual bath, and drinking medicine. Rather than urging the boy to talk about what happened in the past, the boy's family gave him a way of symbolically acknowledging it while also giving him a rite of passage into his future life.[11]

Many Renamo and government soldiers went through *timhamba* rituals of purification after the war. Family elders organized and conducted the ritual process. As the sun rose in the morning, an elder called the names of the relatives who died during the war and other ancestors, telling them about the current family matters and thanking them for protection and guidance during the war. Then a goat, ox, or chicken was sacrificed under a *gandzelo* tree as a symbolic bridge between the living and the dead. After eating the sacrificial animal, the family and community drummed, danced, and sang together.[12]

Honwana acknowledges that traditional trauma healing rituals can be problematic. They are subject to political motives of forgetting about the past at the expense of justice or human rights. In some communities, there were no respected elders to lead the processes, or the people were so impoverished that it was impossible to find the resources to conduct the rituals. Yet, Honwana argues, traditional rituals have had an unquestionably positive effect on Mozambique as a whole in the postconflict recovery period.[13] These traditional rituals communicated the complex message of recovery and rebirth, cleansing and forgiveness. They transformed individuals, communities, and the nation.

Hutus and Tutsis on a Kenyan Safari

These stories of the power of ritual in the peacebuilding process began to inspire my own work as a facilitator, trainer, and mediator. These last three stories come out of my own peacebuilding practice.

In late December 1997, I was part of a training team leading a two-week peacebuilding workshop for Hutu and Tutsi community workers from Rwanda, Burundi, and the Democratic Republic of Congo. The workshop was held in Nairobi, Kenya. Given the history of tensions and extreme violence between these two ethnic groups, leading this workshop was tremendously difficult for the entire training team. There were death threats among the participants, hostile interactions in the workshop, and a feeling that the workshop itself could easily fall apart.

On the workshop's sixth day, the local organizers took all the participants and trainers on an all-day safari into one of Kenya's national parks. It was a relief for everyone to be out of the training room after five long days of intense discussions. Excitement grew as participants started spotting lions, giraffes, ostriches, and other wildlife from the tour bus. On the way home from this long day at the park, all the participants started singing Christmas carols, as Christmas was just one week away. The bus ride was an oasis of harmony, socially and musically, in the midst of twelve very difficult days. The safari experience transformed the nature of the interaction between participants. The drama of spotting wildlife together and singing songs overcame, if only temporarily, the participants' deep tension and trauma. In hindsight, I wish we had spent more time as a group outside of the workshop. If a few hours on a safari can make people start singing together, what would a daily soccer game, night-time dancing, or other informal activities do if integrated into the daily workshop schedule?

Slavery Memorial and Weekend Retreats

Richmond, Virginia, is home to the international Hope in the Cities organization that began dialogues on race, economics, and jurisdiction issues in cities in North America and Europe in the early 1990s. Recognizing the need for rituals of healing between black and white Virginians in a city where the institutions of racism and slavery were born, Hope in the Cities held a Walk Through History in 1993. Large numbers of people made the solemn walk to the old docks for slave ships, slave auction blocks and holding cells, as well as sites significant in the Confederate history of those who fought for the continuation of slavery, in a spirit of honest, respectful, and inclusive history-telling. Flowers were released on the James River that flows through downtown Richmond in memory of Africans who perished on the hellish voyage from Africa to Virginia.

Continuing their tradition of mixing honest conversation with rituals of healing, Hope in the Cities began a series of weekend retreat dialogues for groups of twenty black, white, Latino, and Asian Richmonders in spring 2001. As a facilitator for many of these weekend retreats, I again noted the impact that eating meals together, sharing rooms with people of a different race, and relaxing in a recreational room had on participants who came to these dialogues. Most interracial dialogue models in the United States involve two- or three-hour sessions. The weekend retreat dialogue model allows for much deeper relationship building and a greater degree of transformation following the dialogue. Informal rituals of eating, drinking, walking, and relaxing together are essential to a process designed to transform awareness of issues of race, class, and politics—for they allow space for building relationships. Solid relationships between people in different economic and racial groups provide the fuel to move people into real action to bring about change in their communities.[14]

Fijian Kava Ceremony and Indian Dancing

In fall 2001, I cofacilitated a national peace workshop on the island of Fiji for members of the two major ethnic groups, Indigenous Fijians and Indo-Fijians who were brought to Fiji from India by British colonialists, as well as a rainbow mix of other ethnic groups from surrounding islands. A series of political coups and violent attacks in communities across Fiji led a local organization called the Ecumenical Center for Research, Education, and Advocacy (ECREA) to organize this weeklong workshop for key community leaders. As with the Cypriot workshop described earlier, the content of the peacebuilding workshop in Fiji included interethnic dialogue, problem-solving, and relationship-building components. During the evening social events, I again witnessed the dramatic power of ritual.

Indigenous Fijians shared their well-known kava or yaqona ceremony with the Indo-Fijians and other ethnic groups. Indo-Fijians sang and shared Indian dances. Laughter, music, and the soothing effects of the mildly sedating kava drink soon made it clear that solid relationships were being built in the evenings of this workshop. The quality of dialogue between ethnic groups progressed rapidly during the week and attested to the importance of the evening activities.

Legitimizing the Obvious?

These stories of the symbolic dimension of peacebuilding are emerging dramas on the global stage. While they are gaining attention within the peacebuilding community, the idea of using ritual and other symbolic acts raises some intriguing questions for peacebuilding theory and practice. In a field that has relied so heavily on verbal communication skills, can fishing, dancing, eating, and kava drinking find legitimacy as important aspects in the peacebuilding process? If these rituals and symbolic acts are important to building peace, what is the nature of conflict and peacebuilding? This book provides a link to the scholarly work done in the loosely defined fields of ritual and symbol studies that may help peacebuilders talk about ritual or symbolic acts in their work.

People who deal with conflict as part of their jobs often know intuitively that the symbolic dimension is important in their work. Yet scholars still use hushed tones or bumbling language when they talk about the role of ritual or symbolic acts in building peace. Many of the people interviewed for this book shared sophisticated opinions and theories about how ritual and other symbolic acts work, what they do, and how they relate to conflict. The idea of using ritual and symbolic acts in the process of peacebuilding is common sense for many people who know little about the academic field of conflict studies or peacebuilding. In casual conversations over the past years, children, grandmothers, and people from a variety of cultural backgrounds have inquired about my research on this topic. Their responses have been equally adamant. "Of course eating a meal together assists in the process of peacebuilding!" "Of course ritual is a transforming process!" "You mean nobody else has written about *that* yet!?" Sometimes I have felt a bit indulgent writing down the obvious. Perhaps the best of academia simply describes common sense—what we all know but rarely voice because it appears so self-evident—in theoretical terms.

Notes

1. Yi-Fu Tuan, "Space and Context," in *By Means of Performance*, ed. Richard Schechner and Willa Appel (New York: Cambridge University Press, 1993), 237.

2. Interview with James Notter, by Lisa Schirch (Institute for Multi-Track Diplomacy, Washington, DC, June 1995).

3. Allister Sparks, *Tomorrow is Another Country: The Inside Story of South Africa's Negotiated Revolution* (Johannesburg, South Africa: Struik Book Distributors, 1994).

4. Sparks, *Tomorrow is Another Country*.

5. James Laue, "Conversation on Peacemaking with Jimmy Carter: Interview with James Laue," paper presented at the National Conference on Peacemaking and Conflict Resolution, Charlotte, NC, June 1991, 3.

6. Laue, "Conversation on Peacemaking with Jimmy Carter," 4.

7. Jane Corbin, *The Norway Channel: The Secret Talks That Led to the Middle East Peace Accord* (New York: Atlantic Monthly Press, 1994), 139.

8. Corbin, *The Norway Channel*, 139.

9. Dekha Ibrahim and Jannice Jenner, "Breaking the Cycle of Violence in Wajir," in *Transforming Violence: Linking Local and Global Peacemaking*, ed. Robert Herr and Judy Zimmerman Herr (Scottdale, Pa.: Herald Press, 1998).

10. Alcinda Honwanda, "Sealing the Past, Facing the Future: Trauma Healing in Rural Mozambique," *Accord* 3 (1998), 75–80.

11. Honwanda, "Sealing the Past, Facing the Future," 78–79.

12. Honwanda, "Sealing the Past, Facing the Future," 79.

13. Honwanda, "Sealing the Past, Facing the Future," 80.

14. Karen Elliot Greisdorf, "The City That Dares to Talk," *For a Change* 15, no. 1 (February/March 2002): 4–9.

CHAPTER 2

Understanding Ritual
and Symbolic Acts

Some people view ritual as boring, useless, and too out-of-touch with today's reality to be meaningful. Many scholars schooled in Western science dismiss emotions, senses, and symbols as ineffective or irrational tools for communicating. They promote scientific inquiry and rational discussion in which people "mean what they say and say what they mean." Some scholars within the field of conflict resolution fall into this camp by virtue of their calls for principled negotiation and effective verbal communication.

Supporters of ritual and other symbolic tools usually are actively pursuing spiritual knowledge or come from "softer" academic fields such as theology, psychology, anthropology, and sociology. Ritual advocates write books to record the theoretical functions of ritual and the practical significance ritual has in people's lives. Theologian Tom Driver's book *The Magic of Ritual* asserts that life's greatest moments happen in ritual places and times in "churches, temples, state ceremonies, weddings, feasts, [and] funerals." Ritual, he claims, links our greatest moments with our most primitive tendencies.[1] Ritual is a fact of life. Human life is drama—ritual adds lights and action to a stage full of actors. Exploring the concept of ritual is a means to study the most fascinating and powerful elements in human life.

People may be for or against ritual, depending on their understanding of the concept. Edmund Leach is correct when he writes that there is the widest possible disagreement as to how the word ritual should be understood.[2] Ritual has come to be defined in so many ways and may include so many different types of behavior that critics such as anthropologist Jack Goody claim the term means almost nothing.[3] The field of ritual studies has had a difficult time bringing together these diverse definitions of ritual into a coherent, unified, perspective. Box 2.1 demonstrates the diversity of ways scholars have defined ritual.

Box 2.1 Diverse Definitions of Ritual

Bobby Alexander (anthropologist), *Ritual as Social Change:* Ritual is a "planned or improvised performance that effects a transition from everyday life to an alternative framework within which the everyday is transformed."

Robert Bocock (sociologist), *Ritual in Industrial Society:* "Ritual is the symbolic use of bodily movement and gesture in a social situation to express and articulate meaning."

Charles Laughlin, Eugene d'Aquili, and John McManus (neurobiologists), *The Spectrum of Ritual: A Biogenetic Structural Analysis:* "Ritual . . . is an evolutionary, ancient channel of communication that operates by virtue of a number of homologous biological functions (i.e., synchronization, integration, tuning, etc.) in man and other vertebrates."

Erik Erikson (psychologist), *The Development of Ritualization:* Ritual is "a special form of everyday behavior."

Clifford Geertz (anthropologist), *The Interpretation of Cultures:* "In a ritual, the world as lived and the world as imagined, fused under the agency of a single set of symbolic forms, turn out to be the same world, producing thus that idiosyncratic transformation in one's sense of reality. . . ."

Theodore Jennings (theologian), *On Ritual Knowledge:* "Ritual action is a means by which its participants discover who they are in the world and "how it is" with the world."

David Kertzer (political scientist), *Ritual, Politics, and Power:* Ritual is "action wrapped in a web of symbolism."

Peter McLaren (educator), *Schooling as a Ritual Performance: Towards a Political Economy of Educational Symbols and Gestures:* "As forms of enacted meaning, rituals enable social actors to frame, negotiate, and articulate their phenomenological existence as social, cultural, and moral beings."

Many ritual theorists attempt to define ritual within smaller and smaller boundaries. Religious studies scholar Catherine Bell's comprehensive book *Ritual* outlines the checkered history of the study of ritual.[4] Bell resists defining ritual at all and claims scholars and writers have made ritual into whatever they wanted or needed it to be. Anthropologist Mary Catherine Bateson claims that ritual is flexible, a "more-or-less" rather than an exact phenomenon.[5] In other words, what counts as ritual falls along a spectrum with some actions being more ritual-like than others. Box 2.2 defines ritual as it will be used in this book.

This definition is briefly reviewed in this chapter. Future chapters then use this definition to examine ritual's various functions.

First, rituals are symbolic acts. Symbolic acts are physical actions that require interpretation. The message in a symbolic act is nonreferential, not directly discussing the people or events at hand, but communicating through

> **Box 2.2 Definition of Ritual**
>
> Ritual uses symbolic actions to communicate a forming or transforming message in a unique social space
>
> **Symbolic actions:** Actions that communicate primarily through symbols, senses, and emotions rather than words or rational thought.
>
> **Forming and transforming:** Some rituals reinforce the status quo by forming people's worldviews, identities, and relationships. Other rituals mark and assist in the process of change. People's worldviews, identities, and relationships may be transformed in a ritual process.
>
> **Social space:** A unique space set aside from normal life.

symbols, myths, and metaphors that allow for multiple interpretations. As Catherine Bell notes in her review of ritual theory, "shaking hands is a ritual, but planting potatoes for food is not . . . there is no intrinsic causal relationship between shaking hands and forming a non-threatening acquaintance with someone."[6] The handshake is a symbolic form of communication that has come to *represent* or symbolize friendship. Rather than using direct forms of communication that immediately relate to and reference the core meaning of the message, symbolic acts give messages through symbols that can convey multiple, ambiguous messages to different people. Symbolic acts that are formal or repeated in a tradition are often referred to as rituals. The handshake as a greeting is a ritual. It is repeated through time. However, many scholars have widened their definition of ritual to include several other distinctive elements.

Second, rituals often take place in unique spaces. They are set off from everyday life in a variety of ways. Thus, one way of identifying ritual is to analyze the context in which the symbolic act takes place. Third, rituals aim to form (build) or transform (change) people's worldviews, identities, and relationships. Two of the stories told in chapter 1 show how this definition of ritual works as an organizing tool to analyze the functions and dynamics of ritual in peacebuilding.

In the South African story, an informal activity, fishing, creates an opportunity for the two negotiators to establish a relationship. Fishing is not always a ritual. Fishing became a ritual because of a number of contextual factors:

- The communication between the negotiators when the fishhook became embedded in one man's thumb was symbolic and nonverbal. The act of prying the hook from his thumb communicated trust. The interaction was a metaphor for building their relationship. The whole experience together at the fishing camp became a shared foundation for communicating about other, more important issues.

- The context was set apart from everyday life. These two adversaries never would have gone fishing together under normal social conditions. Their presence together at the fishing camp made for a unique space.
- The situation was transformational. The relationship between the ANC and the National Party representatives changed through the symbolic experience together at a fishing camp. They gained new perspectives of each other through the experience, and their relationship became central to the design for elections. This story was frequently remembered and referenced throughout the remaining negotiations.

In the Wajir peace prize story from Northern Kenya, the same principles hold true.

- The peace prize was symbolic. It provided a new cultural value (peace gained status). The committee communicated new cultural values that supported peace through the symbolic action of giving the peace prize to a chief.
- The Peace and Development Committee created a unique social space: a peace festival.
- The peace festival helped form and transform people's worldviews, identities, and relationships. It aimed to heighten existing cultural values for peace. Somali chiefs wanted to participate in the peace festival and competed earnestly to win the peace prize. Losing chiefs wanted to know how they could change their behavior to win an award in the future, for winning would bring them increased social status.

These two examples show how two very different activities can be defined broadly as rituals. Yet there are distinctions between these two examples as well. The fishing trip and peace festival are examples of different types of ritual.

Types of Ritual

Refusing to limit the concept of ritual, the field of ritual studies examines a broad array of activities. Rituals may be religious or secular, traditional or improvised, formal or informal, forming or transforming, and destructive or constructive. Box 2.3 lists ten categories or types of ritual, which fall along five spectrums. Any particular ritual can be located on this chart as "more or less" of each of the ten types named at the ends of the spectrum. While other types of ritual exist, the ten types identified here provide a way of talking about ritual for this book.

Box 2.3 Types of Ritual

Religious .... **Secular**
Rituals based on relationship with supernatural powers and religious values versus those reflecting secular values.

Traditional .... **Improvised**
Rituals based on tradition and repetition of past rituals versus those created for new circumstances.

Formal .... **Informal**
Rituals based on a clear awareness of a structured ritual context versus an activity such as eating or dancing that may not be structured in such a way that participants are aware of the activity's ritual qualities.

Socializing .... **Transforming**
Rituals based on support for the status quo or existing cultural values/structures versus rituals that challenge and change existing cultural values/structures.

Constructive .... **Destructive**
Rituals based on satisfying needs of all people versus rituals that sacrifice the needs of one person or group at the expense of others.

Between Religious and Secular

All rituals reflect beliefs and values. Some rituals have more to do with religious beliefs or cosmology, how people understand their place in the order of the universe, and their idea of a higher power. Religious rituals include weddings and funerals held in religious settings, Buddhist meditation, Muslim prayers, Catholic Mass, or Mennonite foot washing. Secular rituals enact some aspect of people's values and beliefs without explicitly referencing religious beliefs. Secular rituals include national holidays such as Independence Day, political inaugurations, and weddings at a state-based justice of the peace.

Early ritual theorists such as Emil Durkheim described ritual in religious terms.[7] Some authors still insist on ritual's religious or cosmological nature. Driver notes the link between ritual and symbol is based on the nature of ritual's message to invisible cosmological or supernatural powers. In invoking, addressing, or even manipulating the unseen powers of the universe, Driver says, it is imperative to construct these powers symbolically. "The agencies with which ritual is concerned, then, are such that they must be represented symbolically if they are to be depicted at all."[8] Ritual theorist Victor Turner also adds that without rituals, religion would die, for religions socialize new and old members to their values, beliefs, and cultural lifestyles through ritual.[9]

While ritual is clearly linked with religious expression, it also takes nonreligious forms. In *Ritual Theory, Ritual Practice*, Bell notes that ritual is now a "more embracing category of social action, with religious activities at one extreme and social etiquette at the other."[10] Secular rituals also include the multitude of informal rituals such as smoking, eating, and drinking that occur at almost every high level negotiation and more formal rituals such as the Somali Peace Prize Festival described in chapter 1.

Between Traditional and Improvised

Ritual is often defined as an action that is traditional in the sense that it represents a set of meanings repeated over time. Anthropologist Margaret Mead noted that ritual relates a current activity with a past event through a repetitive act, for example, some death rituals relate and connect a particular death to all the deaths that came before it.[11] Mary Catherine Bateson also observes that rituals tend to be repetitive.

> Many peoples perform their rituals and ceremonies again and again in the conviction that the sun rises, the tides ebb, seasons come and go, and the game continues plentiful because they are doing their part, in dance and song and prayer, to sustain these rhythms.[12]

While these earth-based, seasonal rituals reflect traditional cultural beliefs, Western examples of repetitive traditional rituals also exist. Catholic Mass will no doubt continue to be held regularly around the world as followers enact their belief in the incarnate body and blood of Christ in the bread and wine of the Eucharist. Likewise, new presidents or prime ministers will be inaugurated in a ritual of initiation with symbols used for this occasion throughout each country's history.

Some traditional rituals are losing popularity and devotees in today's world. Margaret Mead claimed that many Americans are bored with repetition. "We do not know or understand very much about boredom, except that it is one of the most painful sensations a human being can experience."[13] The desire to avoid boredom contributes to a frustration with traditional rituals.

Western cultures are developing new secular rituals to fill the gap left by ritual boredom. While some people see ritual as "the antithesis of creativity," Bateson says that people improvise new meaningful rituals in their lives through "the creation of a shared performance" in many rituals of human interaction.[14] For example, new rites of passage for male and female teenagers are increasingly popular among parents trying to find a way to become a part of their children's maturation process in media-saturated cultures such as North America.

Even new or improvised rituals draw on ritual traditions from the past. There appears to be an element of repetition and an element of newness in every ritual. Margaret Drewal notes in *Yoruba Ritual* that creativity is part of all traditional rituals.

> When Yoruba people say that they perform ritual "just like" their ancestors did it in the past, improvisation is implicit in their re-creation or restoration. Innovations in ritual, then, do not break with tradition but rather are continuations of it in the spirit of improvisation. In practice, improvisation as a mode of operation destabilizes ritual—making it open, fluid, and malleable."[15]

Improvised rituals often blend old or familiar symbols in new ways to create a new ritual with a familiar feel. In *The Re-Enchantment of Everyday Life,* Thomas Moore, for example, speaks of ritualizing human life by eating, walking, and living more of life in ritual spaces where humans connect emotionally, sensually, and symbolically with each other and their environment.[16]

Likewise, Driver asserts that "to ritualize is to make (or utilize) a pathway through what would otherwise be uncharted territory."[17] Rituals are not born out of affluence and leisure, but are instead created out of necessity by those people who hang most desperately to life. It is in times of desperation, such as the death of John F. Kennedy and Princess Diana or the terrorist attacks of September 11 in New York and Washington, DC, that humans develop and use ritual to give meaning to extraordinary events and to act in a symbolic way with others to express their pain. The funerals of President Kennedy and Princess Diana included both traditional elements of state or royal funeral protocol as well as improvised actions that symbolically represented the unique characteristics of these two people. The memorial services for those buried at ground zero of the World Trade Centers also reflect the need to improvise new rituals for unprecedented events.

The Wajir Peace Prize story also reflects the urgent need for the creation of new, improvised rituals. The Wajir Peace and Development Committee assessed the lack of cultural celebrations for the value of peace, and in turn took it upon themselves to ritualize their way into a new cultural value.

While ritual boredom may be contributing to a decline in the level of participation in traditional religions, the fastest growing spiritual movements are encouraging people to develop new rituals. Enthusiasm for ritual among North American women's groups certainly seems to verify this trend. The women's spirituality movement and the feminist rituals that have developed within this movement are examples of improvised rituals to help address conflict.

Traditional rituals have a relatively greater amount of repeated material in the ritual than improvised rituals, which have a relatively greater amount of new material. While taking communion is a ritual with hundreds of years of history, drinking beer in a pub on Friday night mirrors some of the same symbolic intentions Jesus shared with his disciples at the last supper. In some sense, then, any act of eating and drinking is at once traditional and improvised. Ritual attempts to provide unity through time by linking past events with present circumstances. In varying ways, improvised rituals reconstruct and weave familiar or traditional symbols with new symbols that represent new, changed contexts.

Between Formal and Informal

The word ritual is often associated with formality. Mead emphasized the importance of being self-conscious or having "ritual awareness": "An action is not ritual if the participants are not aware that it is ritual."[18] People generally know, for example, that they are participating in a ritual when they take communion, get married, or attend a funeral.

If formality is a requirement of ritual, then informal rituals such as eating or dancing may be better termed symbolic acts. Yet the framework of ritual as a formative or transformative experience makes the term ritual also seem an appropriate descriptor.

Perhaps neither the Turkish nor Greek Cypriots would have called their actions of eating, dancing, and informally talking together a ritual. Yet their actions were certainly symbolic and transforming in the sense that the relationships in the group seemed to be changed through the actions of eating and dancing together. The restaurant turned into a ritual space where symbols and actions communicated a message of transformation. Moreover, the context was distinct from any other location on the island. Greek and Turkish Cypriots normally have no place to interact. The presence of these unlikely customers transformed the restaurant into a ritual space.

Rituals can either be formal, in that the participants are aware that they are participating in a ritual, or informal, in that the participants are less or even not aware that they are participating in a ritual. Improvised rituals, such as a self-constructed ceremony to grieve the loss of a parent, are often formal. Participants consciously create a ritual context and expect it to be transforming and meaningful. Yet other improvised rituals are less formal. Rituals of eating and dancing are traditional in the sense that they follow a set structure based on prior experience. Yet these rituals are typically informal in that there is usually no conscious awareness that the actions are ritual or ritual-like.

Between Forming and Transforming

It is no accident that ritual exists in all cultures. People use ritual to both confirm and create the values and structures that create a sense of community. Rituals assist the socialization process to teach the rules, values, and structures of a society to new members of a community. Children learn about what a community values through its rituals. Ritual also reconfirms the values that adults were taught in their youth. Some rituals help form and perpetuate the status quo in societies.

For example, many countries around the world celebrate "Independence Day" when the state or community freed itself from external or colonial rule. Independence days teach and remind citizens, both young and old, of their triumphant history of struggle and glory. The public rituals that accompany independence days, such as fireworks and public festivals, heighten a sense of patriotism and a commitment to protect the existing state. Informal rituals such as parades maintain, justify, and gather support for the status quo.

Transforming rituals, on the other hand, challenge and change the status quo. When a critical number of people in any community desire change, they may use ritual to act as a rite of passage toward a new vision, a new set of values, or new structures in a community. During the South African transition from apartheid to democracy, a number of public rituals including national moments of silence, nationwide singing of the song of peace, and even the more functional ritual of going to the polls to vote served as rites of passage from apartheid-based values and structures to democratic values and structures.

Both socializing and transforming rituals are needed for peacebuilding. All cultures have existing, traditional rituals for building relationships, limiting violence, and solving problems. While these traditional rituals often are socializing and preserve the status quo, sometimes peacebuilders can help revive or draw on existing rituals within a culture that can help set the stage for transformational peacebuilding activities and processes.

For example, the Fijian kava ceremony described in chapter 1 is used extensively within the indigenous Fijian community to address conflict and rebuild relationships. However, it has not been used between the Fijian and Indo-Fijian communities and their ethnic conflicts. In this case, a traditional ritual could be used in a new, transforming way. At other times, peacebuilders may want to use socializing, status quo–preserving rituals to maintain peace or limit violence within a society. Socializing rituals such as celebrating Martin Luther King Day in the United States reaffirm the constructive values of diversity, nonviolence, and the devotion to racial equality. Peacebuilders supporting the public celebration of Martin Luther King Day may use ritual to keep some aspect of the status quo in place, such as a public commitment to ending racism, however shallow it may be.

Between Constructive and Destructive

Both ritual and conflict are parts of the human experience. They exist in every culture, in every time. Conflict can be constructive, leading to positive social change, or destructive, ending in war and trauma. Like conflict, ritual is a neutral tool and people can use it for either the betterment or destruction of humanity. Ritual abuse and sacrifice deliver oppressive messages and have horrific, destructive outcomes. Yet other types of ritual can have positive, constructive effects on individuals, communities, organizations, and nations.

Ritual is constructive when it is used to better the lives of the people who use it, without causing harm to others. Ritual can play important roles in communicating between groups in conflict, in transforming conflict-defined identities, and in forming and transforming relationships between groups.

Other scholars have detailed the destructive role ritual can play in exacerbating and escalating conflict and violence. Marc Howard Ross describes how conflict is escalated in Northern Ireland through what he calls the "psychocultural dramas" or rituals of marching and Loyalist parades commemorating important dates in history.[19] David Kertzer's book *Ritual, Politics, and Power* argues that ritual is used for both constructive and destructive political purposes precisely because it is powerful enough to achieve either peace or war.[20] Ritual can breath life and hope into a community or bring a deadly, dehumanizing message leading to destruction and even genocide.

Although this book focuses on the constructive roles ritual and other symbolic acts can play in peacebuilding processes, it is important to remember that ritual and symbolic acts are not inherently peaceful. Like other social tools, they can be used for good and bad.

Researching Ritual

To explore how the dynamics of ritual function in conflict and peacebuilding I conducted exploratory research, studying the literature on ritual and symbols outside of or not explicitly connected to the field of peacebuilding. I also engaged in a two-year participant observation process in three different cultural communities that use ritual to address conflict.

All three case studies explore the constructive rituals and symbolic acts within these communities.

1. First Nation communities in Ontario, Canada, and their use of the *formal, traditional,* and *religious* smudging ceremony to address the daily conflicts many Natives experience living in a white society;
2. Women's spirituality groups and their use of *formal, improvised, secular* and *religious* feminist rituals to deal with everyday conflicts experienced in a patriarchal society;
3. The use of *informal, improvised,* and *secular* rituals and symbolic acts by professional peacebuilders in a workshop for Greek and Turkish Cypriot youth.

These case studies provide examples of constructive rituals that are both socializing and transforming. A brief description of each of the main case studies here will provide background for more detailed exploration in the following chapters.[21]

Smudging Ceremony

The first case study looks at a specific Native ritual called the smudging ceremony and examines how Native people use it to address conflict in their communities. For most of the history of the Americas, white people have ignored, trivialized, and dismissed Native culture. While Euro-Americans are still at an awkward and sometimes patronizing stage in their journey toward understanding tribal peoples around the world, there is increasing interest in learning from Native peoples about alternative, sustainable ways of living with other people and the natural environment.

In 1990, I was a full-time advocate for Native land claims and Aboriginal rights in Canada. After several years of frustrating political work, I returned to graduate school to study conflict resolution. I recognized in school that I had overlooked resources for building peace within Native communities while I was busy working the Canadian political system. Coming to the Native community years later for help in thinking about conflict and how ritual might be used to deal with it, I felt a bit like the pilgrims who landed sick and hungry on the East coast shores, or maybe even my own Mennonite ancestors who came to Native peoples for survival tips in their first cold winters in Canada.

Too much Native culture has been appropriated by others, and attempts at cultural exchange may in fact end up following the practice of colonialism where Native goods are stolen by needy outsiders.[22] While I in no way encourage peacebuilders to appropriate rituals from indigenous cultures, this case study may enable peacebuilders to articulate the functions of ritual and include new rituals in their practice. Examples of the smudging ceremony are used throughout the book to show how Native communities use ritual to deal with both interpersonal and structural forms of conflict. The smudging ceremony is an example of a traditional ritual that has been repeated for hundreds if not thousands of years. It is also explicitly religious and formal.

Women's Rituals

The second case study looks at feminist ritual and the ways women's groups are improvising rituals to address conflicts women experience in their personal lives. Consciousness-raising groups or women's groups became the foundation for the women's movement and the growth of feminist ideas in the last four decades. Women around the world continue to meet regularly in unstructured, nonhierarchical groups to share the stories of their everyday lives. These support groups are transformational experiences for many women, including me. New, improvised feminist rituals are a central form of healing and empowerment in these groups.[23]

Feminist liturgist and psychotherapist Diann Neu claims these groups play a number of important roles in women's lives, including providing support and friendship, and giving value and legitimacy to women's experiences, problems, and power.[24] Neu, director of the Women's Alliance for Theology, Ethics, and Ritual (WATER) in Silver Spring, Maryland, describes women's spirituality groups as "springing up like wild flowers" all over North America.[25] Anne Kent Rush notes that the popularity of feminist ritual is based on women's earlier history as the witches, midwives, and healers in Europe's Middle Ages. She sees women's spirituality groups as "birth centers for social change."[26] The emergence of female-centered spirituality reflects the desire for ideological, social, and cultural change away from systems where men have exclusive control over ritual, culture, and religion toward a time when men and women cooperately create and participate in ritual.

Cultural theorist Kay Turner claims feminist ritual gives women power to create and define culture.[27] Turner sees the feminist use of ritual as a way of promoting and sanctioning a "serious turning away from the old to the new" form of human relationships based on partnership rather than domination.[28] She sees women's use of ritual as a powerful symbolic statement of women's equality.

> Asserting the right to ritual means as a source of power, vision, and solidarity is the symbolic corollary of equal pay, choice of abortion, domestic freedom, the establishment of women's businesses, etc. Successful and enduring change in the status of women will come only through the parallel transformation of symbols and realities. Feminist ritual practice is currently the most important model for symbolic and, therefore, psychic and spiritual change in women.[29]

While feminist ritual is an alternative to the rituals that have been passed down through patriarchal religious institutions, it does not seek to simply replace male authority with female authority. Women's spirituality groups offer a vision of alternative human relationships based on coexistence rather than domination. This book includes examples of women's rituals to show how formal, improvised, secular, and religious rituals are created to deal with both interpersonal and structural forms of conflict experienced by women.

Greek and Turkish Cypriot Peace Workshop

The third case study examines a conflict resolution workshop to analyze the variety of rituals included in the process and the ways ritual impacted the participants. I gathered this information as a participant observer in a two-week workshop for forty Greek and Turkish Cypriot youth ages fourteen to sixteen at a camp in Pennsylvania as part of the Cyprus Consortium Peacebuilding Project in July 1997.[30] The Cypriot youth camp design was considerably different from the 1994 two-week training discussed in chapter 1. While most of the Cyprus Consortium trainings are for adults and are held on the island of Cyprus, this training was for youth and was held at a camp in the United States. Adult workshops involve long days of role plays, skill development, and conflict analysis with evenings spent at restaurants or in people's homes. The youth sessions had only three to four hours of formal conflict resolution workshop time on most mornings, and a wide array of sports, arts and crafts, social, and recreational activities planned for the afternoon and evenings. The youth lived and ate all of their meals together.

These activities are symbolic and ritual-like because they took place in specially created spaces that transformed the ways the youth could interact with each other. It is not normal for Greek and Turkish Cypriot youth to play together, eat together, or dance together. A generation of Greek and Turkish Cypriot youth has grown up without ever meeting a member of the community on the other side of the island. The youth camp was the first effort to engage Cypriot youth in an intensive peacebuilding project. Eating, dancing, and playing became symbolic ways of communicating about shared humanity and human diversity. These activities have a symbolic subtext that reads "This is what we do with friends" or "This is how we act in this situation." By creating a context full of symbolic images of friendship and fun, the trainers in this peacebuilding workshop employed the transformative powers of ritual to build peace between Greek and Turkish Cypriot youth.

Examples from the improvised and informal rituals in this camp show explicitly how rituals can be and already are included in peacebuilding processes. These examples may help legitimize and give a language to describe the ritual activities that many peacebuilders already include in the processes they design. Funders of peacebuilding processes may be particularly interested in hearing that the meals and "extra" activities are crucial to the desired goals and outcomes.

Nailing Down Ritual

Humans are sensual creatures with a penchant for symbol, action, and the need to create and re-create. Ritual is part of the drama of life itself. As Shakespeare said, life is a stage and all humans are actors in a series of grand and not-so-grand ritual acts. After I describe these three case studies in a graduate class I teach on conflict transformation, students often are awed by the vast nature of ritual. It is not difficult to make a case for ritual

---

Box 2.4 Ritual vs. Not Ritual

Ritual . . . . **Not Ritual**

Ritual	Not Ritual
• a special, unique space	• a normal space, not special in any way
• actions that symbolically do something (lighting incense to create ambience)	• actions that do something directly (washing hands to clean them)
• emotional and sensual communication	• rational, direct communication
• plays socializing and/or transforming roles in community life	• does not play socializing and/or transforming roles in community life

---

occurring in almost every moment of life. It is so vast, so evasive and resistant to word-bound communication it may be difficult to say what is *not* ritual. The enormity of ritual does not, in my opinion, make it irrelevant.

Rather than simply discarding the concept of ritual or searching for some other category to explain the stories in chapter 1, this book instead uses the term ritual very loosely. The book uses the term symbolic actions rather than ritual at points where the activity is less formal or traditional. Some acts are more ritual-like than others. In closing this chapter, I offer yet another spectrum. In some parts of life, space is more unique than normal, and action is more symbolic than functional, more sensual and emotional than rational, and more socializing or transforming than irrelevant to larger social processes. The stories in the book fall closer to the ritual end of the spectrum.

Many peacebuilders fail to fully recognize or articulate why ritual is important in their work and what ritual can do for people in conflict. Half of the problem that prevents people from recognizing the connection between ritual and peacebuilding is a lack of understanding about symbolic actions and ritual. The other half of the problem is a limited understanding of the dynamics of conflict and the breadth of the field of peacebuilding. The next two chapters address these issues.

Notes

1. Tom Faw Driver, *The Magic of Ritual: Our Need for Liberating Rites That Transform Our Lives and Our Communities* (San Francisco: Harper San Francisco, 1991), 14.

2. Edmund Leach, "Ritual," in *International Encyclopedia of Social Sciences*, ed. Claude Levi-Strauss (New York: MacMillan, 1968), 526.

3. Jack Goody, "Against 'Ritual': Loosely Structured Thoughts on a Loosely Defined Topic," in *Secular Ritual*, ed. Sally F. Moore and Barbara G. Myerhoff (The Netherlands: Van Gorcum, 1977), 25.

4. Catherine Bell, *Ritual: Perspectives and Dimensions* (New York: Oxford University Press, 1997).

5. Mary Catherine Bateson, "Ritualization: A Study in Texture and Texture Change," in *Religious Movements in Contemporary America*, ed. Irving I. Zaretsky and Mark P. Leone (Princeton, N.J.: Princeton University Press, 1974), 150.

6. Bell, *Ritual: Perspectives and Dimensions*, 46.

7. Emile Durkheim, *The Elementary Forms of the Religious Life* (Glencoe, Ill: Free Press, 1915).

8. Driver, *The Magic of Ritual*, 97.

9. Victor Turner, *The Anthropology of Performance* (New York: PAJ Publishers, 1988), 48.

10. Bell, *Ritual: Perspectives and Dimensions*, 39.

11. Margaret Mead, "Ritual and Social Crisis," in *The Roots of Ritual*, ed. James D. Shaughnessy (Grand Rapids, Mich., Eerdmans, 1973), 89.

12. Mary Catherine Bateson, *Peripheral Visions: Learning Along the Way* (New York: HarperCollins Publishers, 1994).

13. Mead, "Ritual and Social Crisis," 98.

14. Bateson, *Peripheral Visions: Learning Along the Way*, 16, 18.

15. Margaret Thompson Drewal, *Yoruba Ritual: Performers, Play, Agency* (Bloomington: Indiana University Press, 1992), 23.

16. Thomas Moore, *The Re-Enchantment of Everyday Life* (New York: HarperCollins, 1996).

17. Driver, *The Magic of Ritual*, 16.

18. Mead, "Ritual and Social Crisis," 91.

19. Marc Howard Ross, "Psychocultural Interpretations and Dramas: Identity Dynamics in Ethnic Conflict," *Political Psychology* 22, no. 1 (2001): 157–78.

20. David I. Kertzer, *Ritual, Politics, and Power* (New Haven: Yale University Press, 1988).

21. Much of this research was first written about in my dissertation "Ritual Peacebuilding: Creating Contexts Conducive to Conflict Transformation" for the Ph.D. program in Conflict Analysis and Resolution at George Mason University. For more information about my research process and longer chapters on each case study, see the unpublished dissertation, available from UMI Dissertation Services.

22. Elizabeth Cook-Lynn, "American Indian Intellectualism and the New Indian Story," *American Indian Quarterly* 20, no. 1 (Winter 1996): 57–76.

23. Rosemary Radford Ruether, *In Memory of Her: A Feminist Theological Reconstruction of Christian Origins* (New York: Crossroad, 1985).

24. Diann L. Neu, "Women's Empowerment through Feminist Ritual," *Women and Therapy* 16, no. 2/3 (1995): 185–200.

25. Neu, "Women's Empowerment through Feminist Ritual," 190.

26. Anne Kent Rush, "The Politics of Feminist Spirituality," in *The Politics of Women's Spirituality*, ed. Charlene Spretnak (Toronto: Doubleday, 1982), 384.

27. Kay Turner, "Contemporary Feminist Rituals," in *The Politics of Women's Spirituality*, ed. Charlene Spretnak (Toronto: Doubleday, 1982), 221.

28. Turner, "Contemporary Feminist Rituals," 220.

29. Turner, "Contemporary Feminist Rituals," 222.

30. The Institute for Multi-Track Diplomacy (IMTD), the Conflict Management Group (CMG), and the Cypriot Bicommunal Training Group coordinated the Cyprus Consortium Peacebuilding Project. More than the Cyprus Consortium has offered dozens of conflict resolution training programs on the island. Since 1991, more than 600 Greek and Turkish Cypriots have been trained.

CHAPTER 3

Material, Social, and Symbolic Dimensions of Conflict

T he focus of this chapter is on the nature of conflict itself. Conflict practitioners William Hocker and Joyce Wilmot developed a widely accepted definition of conflict as "an expressed struggle between at least two interdependent parties who perceive incompatible goals, scarce resources, and interference from others in achieving their goals."[1] The key elements of this definition are 1) that people need or desire resources to meet their goals; 2) that conflict is expressed or communicated with others in a struggle; and 3) that perceptions shape how people understand and act in conflict. This definition sets the stage for a three-level analysis of the dimensions of conflict.

Communication theorists John Cragan and Donald Shields propose three general approaches to problems in Western thought: rational, relational, and symbolic.[2] Conflict theorist Jayne Docherty applies these three categories to different understandings of the causes of conflict.[3] She argues that conflict happens in rational, relational, and symbolic "worlds."

Table 3.1 and the following descriptions build on this analysis. They illustrate how people describe the causes of conflict, how the concept of human needs can be expressed legitimately or illegitimately in each dimension, and what type of intervention each dimension prescribes.

The third column of Table 3.1 describes how each dimension of conflict is articulated in the language of human needs and human rights. These central concepts are foundational to the fields of conflict studies and peacebuilding and need a brief explanation here. Conflict scholars such as John Burton pioneered the idea that unmet "human needs," or "inherent drives for survival and development such as identity, security, and recognition" cause conflict.[4] Peacebuilding aims to create societies that affirm human dignity through meeting human needs and protecting

31

human rights. Human needs receive legal backing through human rights documents. They direct all types of decisions about how people can live with the least amount of violence and the greatest amount of common good.

Human needs are met through relationships with others. If communities of people do not meet the needs of their members, or if they obstruct the needs of members in other communities, people will engage in conflict.[5] People have choices about how to satisfy their needs. Everyone needs respect, for example, but people earn and give respect in different ways. We want to satisfy our needs in the same ways other people satisfy their needs. We imitate the desires of others, particularly of those we deem to be powerful, in an effort to belong to their "group."[6] It is important to distinguish need from greed. Some people perceive that they have the right to meet their own needs at the expense of others. Greed is the desire to accumulate excessive amounts of material resources, decision-making power, respect and cultural authority or power. Table 3.1 details the material, social, and symbolic types of human needs and rights; the italics show how these needs can become unhealthy greed.

The three dimensions of conflict form different plot lines in the stories people tell about conflict and peacebuilding. In the material dimensions, conflict arises over land, office space, or other material resources that people need or want. Rational approaches to the material dimension of conflict stress using objective, rational, and logical problem-solving methods. The plot line in this conflict drama is often posed as the realist version—the real world, according to the Hobbsian school, is "man against man" in life's brutish effort to secure food, shelter, and other goods. Everyone struggles to hoard more resources for themselves so they can survive.

The social dimensions of conflict focus on relationships, communication, and interactions between parties. Here the plot line falls in the Robin Hood tradition: Conflict occurs because of hierarchy and prejudice between the elite class and the underdogs when the latter have no say in how decisions get made. Another plot line under this approach is a Greek tragedy like *Oedipus* where lack of communication or miscommunication renders people unable to address problems. Creating new social structures and improving communication are two peacebuilding strategies that fall in this category.

The symbolic dimensions focus on how people's worldview shapes how they understand and make meaning of the world, and in particular, conflict. It brings attention to the perceptual, emotional, sensual, cultural, value-based, and identity-driven aspects of conflict. The plot line here is of two cultures that understand the world in vastly different ways and are unable to see a conflict from the other's point of view. Symbolic approaches to peacebuilding include efforts to shift perceptions through creative strategies to engage people's physical and sensual selves, their emotions, identities, and values. The symbolic dimensions of conflict provide a context for

Table 3.1 Dimensions and Approaches to Conflict

Dimensions of Conflict	Description of Conflict	Human Needs and Human Rights	Approach to Peacebuilding and Conflict Transformation
Material/ Rational	Competing interests over an issue or scarce resource cause conflict.	Material needs include food, shelter, water, healthcare, and resources to meet physical needs. *Material needs become greed when some people take an unfair share of resources.*	• Think analytically and rationally about problem • Engage in problem-solving to develop a creative way of sharing resources
Social	Ineffective communication patterns, competitive social attitudes, an imbalance of power, and/or unequal social structures cause conflict.	Social needs include a sense of belonging and predictability in relationships, security from attack, participation and influence in making decisions that affect one's life, and an ability to earn respect and recognition from others. *Social needs become greed when some people make decisions for others and when they fail to respect the humanity of others.*	• Improve communication skills • Balance power • Switch from a competitive to a cooperative model of relationships • Construct social structures that meet human needs
Symbolic or Cultural	Clashing values, perceptions, or worldviews cause conflict. Conflict is experienced and understood through physical senses, emotions, values, perceptions, and the dynamic of identity.	Symbolic or cultural needs include the ability to make sense of the world, to give it meaning through a worldview. They also include the freedom to portray and practice one's identities, cultures, and religious beliefs without persecution, threats, or intimidation. *Cultural needs become greed when some people promote cultures and religions that discriminate against others.*	• Involve people in processes that allow for physical, sensual, and emotional ways of knowing and communicating • Focus on perceptual change • Use dialogue to discover shared values • Recognize the need for identity • Develop common worldview frames for communicating about the problem through symbolic tools such as myth, metaphor, and ritual

Source: Adapted from Schirch 1998.

understanding the use of ritual and symbolic acts in peacebuilding. It fills in the other half of the problem noted in chapter 2: that many scholars and practitioners have so limited their understanding of conflict that the idea of using ritual is difficult for them to grasp.

There are a few important caveats to this discussion. It is important to recognize the overlap of and connection between all three dimensions. Each dimension is related to the others, yet each deserves special attention. Peacebuilders need to understand and engage all three dimensions of conflict. No single approach is sufficient for all conflicts. The main point of this book is *not* to argue that ritual, a symbolic approach to conflict, is better than rational or relational approaches to conflict. Rather, this chapter explores each dimension and shows how each dimension requires attention by peacebuilders, and noting its strengths and weaknesses. Assuming that this is not the first book in the field of peacebuilding for most readers, this chapter surveys material and social dimensions of conflict more briefly than the symbolic dimensions as readers should recognize these widely-published approaches. A major portion of this chapter examines the theoretical assumptions of the symbolic dimensions of conflict, as these provide a theoretical setting for the next chapter's examination of the role of ritual and symbolic acts in peacebuilding.

The Material Dimension/The Rational Approach

The material dimensions of conflict are usually obvious and are often articulated clearly. People need basic material resources like food, water, and land to live. In today's materialistic world, there is a never-ending scramble to accumulate more resources. Israelis and Palestinians make competing claims to land. Office workers debate who deserves prime office space. Children fight over toys.

Approaches to addressing the material dimensions of conflict are rooted in Western philosophy. The Greek philosophers began the effort within the Western intellectual tradition to understand the world in a reasonable, rational way in order to find the objective truth about the world. This pursuit has dominated thought in the Western hemisphere since the beginning of Europe's Enlightenment period. Rene Descartes popularized the Western notion that human emotions, senses, and beliefs are inaccessible if not irrelevant to study and are therefore unknowable.[7] His understanding of rationality involved suppressing emotions, which hinder objectivity, and categorizing the subject to be studied on its own rather than in its relationship to its context.

Given this theoretical background, it is not surprising that many scholars trained in Western thought have emphasized the material dimensions of conflict, for they are far more tangible than the more elusive social and symbolic dimensions. Rational theories in the social sciences assume humans are capable of communicating through detached, unemotional, objective logic. Rational approaches to conflict push for objectivity in understanding and addressing conflict. Just as a geographer can stand back from a rock and look at its properties, rationalists attempt to approach conflict objectively with a focus on problem-solving skills.

In the early days of conflict studies, many theorists saw disputes as isolated social situations that could be settled or resolved with a variety of rational strategies or formulas to address the "incompatible goals" and "scarce resources" elements defined by Hocker and Wilmot. Roger Fisher and Bill Ury's *Getting to Yes: Negotiating Agreement Without Giving In* is probably the best-known and clearest example of this approach to understanding and managing conflict. Viewing conflict as emotionally messy and confusing, Fisher and Ury propose a "concise, step-by-step, proven strategy" of principled negotiation for addressing conflicts.[8] Their strategy includes the following suggestions:

1. Separate the people from the problem,
2. Focus on interests, not positions,
3. Invent options for mutual gain, and
4. Insist on using objective criteria.

The process of focusing on interests, inventing options for mutual gain, and finding objective criteria contributes to the management of conflicts. Fisher and Ury's book marks an important shift in understanding and approaching conflict and certainly deserves credit for helping people begin to think about how to address conflict, particularly the material dimensions of conflict, within Western-based cultural frameworks that favor rational, linear approaches. However, some people react negatively to the idea of separating the people from the problem when identity is a major factor in the conflict. This approach is not as helpful in addressing the human element in conflict.

Processes that try to order and organize conflicts into neat, rational packages are not sufficient. While politicians or activists may frame a conflict over land or some other material resource, once that specific dispute is settled, other issues will arise. Efforts in the Middle East to address land disputes are necessary. But many aspects of the conflict between Israel and Palestine have to do with relationships between the groups, their identities, values, perceptions of each other, and the symbolic actions such as attacks on important religious sites made by both Israelis and Palestinians.

These factors are not rational in the Western sense, but they are real. The whole idea of approaching conflict with rational, analytical tools is problematic in many cultures. What is rational to the Western-educated mind might be irrational to someone with a different worldview. For some people, it is difficult if not impossible to think about principled negotiation in the way Fisher and Ury and other rationalists have outlined it. Thomas Kochman, for example, notes in *Black and White Styles of Conflict* that African-Americans generally have a cultural approach to conflict that favors the expression of emotion.[9] How rational is it to contain feelings of anger or sadness? Research on cultural models of conflict suggests that the answer to this question is not at all self-evident.[10,11] Problem-solving approaches to conflict also overlook the cultural bias of Western-based conceptions of rationality. While rational approaches to conflict may deal successfully with the resource issues in some contexts, they may be less appropriate for conflicts in non-Western cultural settings or for dealing with the social and symbolic dimensions in any conflict.

The Social Dimension and Approach

The relational dimensions of conflict are also widely acknowledged in peacebuilding. Good relationships are central to addressing conflicts constructively. Ineffective communication patterns, competitive attitudes, hierarchical social structures, and unequal access to power and resources contribute to the intractability of conflict.

The New Testament commandment to "love thy neighbor" is one of the earliest calls for a relational approach to conflict. It is thought that if people can improve their relationships, conflict will be less damaging and that it may even be productive. Many relational approaches to addressing conflict emerge from Western social sciences such as sociology, economics, political science, and anthropology. Practitioners, researchers, and theorists in conflict studies have proposed relational approaches to conflict based on this theoretical tradition. These approaches see conflict as "an expressed struggle" involving a perception of "interference from others" according to Hocker and Wilmot's definition. They focus on relationships, communication, power, and social structures to analyze and resolve conflict.

Fisher and Brown added to the rational approach in *Getting to Yes* with *Getting Together: Building Relationships As We Negotiate*,[12] in which they survey communication skills as a means for improving relationships. The authors' encourage readers that objective, rational discussion of issues needs to be kept separate and "disentangled" from the conflict's relationship issues. Hocker and Wilmot along with many other conflict theorists also focus on improving communication in relationships as a means for handling conflict and have developed a number of skills to improve communication through both listening and speaking with greater care.[13]

Other conflict scholars focus on the power dynamics between people in conflict. Conflict is a likely outcome when some people have more sources of power than others, and when they use that power to dominate others. Peacebuilding strategies for addressing power imbalances include helping people create new sources of power for themselves through a variety of nonviolent tactics (see chapter 4).

The goal of peacebuilding is a world in which everyone has access to power, and people use their power to do constructive tasks with others rather than to dominate them. In other words, peacebuilding encourages people to cooperate rather than compete. It envisions a set of economic, political, cultural, and social structures that support equal relations between people. Social approaches to peacebuilding encourage the creation of participatory methods of democratic decision-making that foster respect and recognition of others.

While relational approaches to conflict contribute to the analysis of conflict and the practice of building peace between adversaries, they too are not sufficient alone. Relational theories of conflict do not always take into account different cultural ways of communicating, defining, and satisfying human needs. Many of the communication techniques taught in peacebuilding seminars around the world are based on Western worldview assumptions about the most effective ways of communicating. These Western techniques are not only biased toward the English language, they often are offensive and "foreign" to other cultures. For example, Western communication specialists recommend using "I" language that describes personal feelings and states the problem directly, such as in the formulaic phrase, "I feel _____ when you _____ because _____." Some cultures are uncomfortable using this direct approach or for that matter beginning any sentence with the word "I." While speaking in "I" language may be appropriate in individualistic cultures such as North America, in community-based cultures some people feel more comfortable using "we" language. Nonverbal communication is equally diverse. Many Westerners prefer direct eye contact and interpret it as a symbol of honesty. Other cultures avoid eye contact to show respect.

Balancing power between groups in conflict is also insufficient in and of itself. Even groups who have roughly equal levels of power find themselves in conflict with each other. Sometimes groups in conflict have equal decision-making power and clear communication with each other. In these cases, such as political conflicts between Democrats and Republicans in US politics, the groups hold different worldviews. Symbolic approaches to peacebuilding help fill in the missing dimension.

The Symbolic Dimension and Approach

The United Nations Educational, Scientific, and Cultural Organization (UNESCO) constitution begins with a simple statement: "Since wars begin in the minds of men, it is in the minds of men that the defenses of peace must be constructed." Some early conflict theorists, such as Kenneth Boulding in *The Image*, described how individuals perceive the world differently and how this affects conflict.[14] A growing number of theorists argue that our "perceptions" and "expressions" of conflict, in Hocker and Wilmot's definition, are incomprehensible without an understanding of the symbolic dimension. This is the messy dimension of conflict often overlooked, neglected, or discarded in the theoretical trashbin. It has been easier to leave these messy and unpredictable elements of conflict on the edge of our map of conflict. Several conflict studies scholars reference and try to grab hold of the symbolic dimension, but rarely dive deeply into its themes or offer clear symbolic tools. Only a handful of scholars are known for their efforts to develop symbolic tools or skills for peacebuilding.[15]

While people may view conflicts as competing claims to scarce resources, people often cannot see how they are symbolically constructing the meaning and value of resources. Environmentalists and indigenous groups may value land because it symbolically represents health, wholeness, and life. Loggers and paper companies look at the trees on that land as a resource, as a farmer looks at a field of crops.[16] Although interest-based negotiations will likely raise a superficial awareness of basic cultural differences, it is unlikely that negotiating over the land itself will lead to resolution.

People symbolically construct conflicts through their worldview, a dynamic lens to understand the world through senses, emotions, complicated perceptual dynamics, culture, values, and identity. It is necessary to uncover and experience the different worldviews to more fully understand the land's symbolic meaning for the parties in conflict. What does the land symbolize for the different groups of people? How do people emotionally and sensually relate to the land? What basic values do people hold about the land? How does the land help define people's identity?

Negotiating rooms are often sterile environments. Can a bridge across worldviews be constructed apart from the central symbol of the dispute, in this case, the land itself? Some of the most creative and successful land claims negotiations in North America have occurred when negotiators from both sides of the conflict ritually walk on the disputed territory and talk about its symbolic significance. The symbolic act of treading earth together becomes a transformational experience.[17]

Building peace requires stretching and transforming worldviews. When in conflict, people's perceptions of their identity, their adversary, and the conflict issues differ. While many people in Western cultures are preoccupied with searching for objectivity or lamenting our subjectivity, other cultures actively embrace the concept of worldviews. Magoroh Maruyama claims the concept of objectivity is virtually untranslatable in many African or Asian cultures. He believes some cultures have "polyocular" vision that allows everyone to see the world differently and allows differences between people to be seen as normal and accepted. Maruyama argues that in some of these cultures, children grow up learning to see a situation from multiple points of view. Other cultures nurture a respect for different worldviews rather than constantly searching for some objective reality. People value being able to describe different points of view in a situation.[18]

"Worldviewing," as coined by Jayne Docherty, is a dynamic process of creating and re-creating the world.[19] People express, confirm, and re-create their worldviews each day to explain why the world is as it appears or what the world could or should be. As individuals live in the world, they perceive it through their own unique worldview lenses, which shape and filter what they see. People assimilate and organize this information in ways that connect it with past experiences of their environment. Worldviews shape how each person thinks about conflict and how they behave in a conflict.

To grasp the possibilities for using ritual as a peacebuilding tool, it is important first to understand worldview dimension. Worldviews are shaped by five interacting elements: perception, emotional and sensual cognition, culture, values, and identity. A deeper exploration of each follows.

Perception

The process of perception forms the core of all worldviewing, for perception is ruled by human's biological structure. In any given day, an individual will experience thousands of ideas, people, and objects. As the human mind seeks to fulfill its need for meaning, it tries to order and make sense out of these experiences in some common processes by categorizing these experiences and creating systems of meaning according to the patterns that are evident to the individual. The psychological processes of perception help do this ordering.

Immanuel Kant is credited for first articulating the centrality of perception in the Western context.[20] William James's *The Principles of Psychology*[21] and Susanne Langer's groundbreaking *Philosophy in a New Key* later described the ways humans symbolize, conceptualize, and seek meaning in experience. Langer claimed the world is always and only understood through symbolism, the new key in philosophy. Langer's philosophy moves away from the belief that humans can make objective observations about the world and toward examining how humans understand and give meaning to the world through perceptual lenses.[22]

While it is essential that humans be able to sort through information, the sorting process often has unfortunate outcomes. Humans seek to perceive the world in ways that are consistent with their past experiences and understandings. Individuals desire "cognitive consistency" or a consistent understanding of the world.[23] The process of perception is a self-corrective system. Gregory Bateson claims when humans perceive something that is inconsistent with their past experiences or beliefs, "their self-corrective mechanisms work to sidetrack it, to hide it, even to the extent of shutting their eyes if necessary, or shutting off various parts of the process of perception."[24] If individuals perceive the world in a way that is incongruent with their worldview, they experience "cognitive dissonance," a term coined by Leonard Festinger to describe the anxiety and discomfort of a new experience or idea that does not fit in with past experiences or understandings of the world.[25] People maintain cognitive consistency and avoid cognitive dissonance in two ways: First, they *filter their experiences* with the world in a way that retains only information consistent with their current way of viewing the world, and second, they *actively create the world* they expect and want to experience.

Figure 3.1 illustrates the perceptual processes for filtering and creating reality. Perception is one element of the worldview lens. A pair of glasses represents how perception filters and creates the world.

Figure 3.1 Perceptual Dynamics

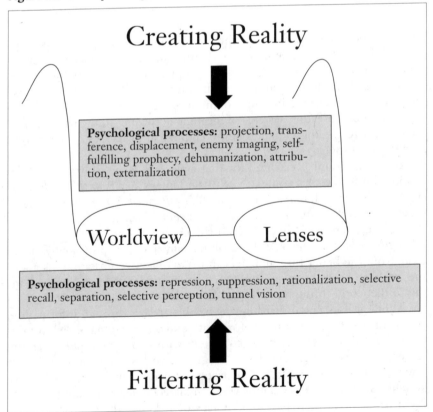

Individuals filter reality by selectively perceiving only that information that is consistent with the current understanding of their environment. Any experience or information that is ambiguous or counter to their worldview is likely to be avoided by either conscious or unconscious removal of the incongruent information. Humans selectively perceive information by either discarding dissonant information, or distorting it to fit current understanding. Tunnel vision describes the processes by which humans perceive only the small part of the world that is consistent with previous experiences. Cognitive defense mechanisms justify existing ways of thinking and protect against change. Freud developed the idea that people rationalize their behavior and their beliefs to maintain a positive self-image.[26] Rationalization describes the process of explaining to oneself why information can be discarded. Information may also be selectively remembered through repression or suppression. Repression is an unconscious process of forgetting and suppression is a conscious process of avoiding dissonant memories.

Psychological processes are particularly important in conflicts. People in conflict often have tunnel vision about how they understand their adversaries' actions. They may see only the bad things their adversaries do and disregard or ignore the good things. They may rationalize any positive actions by their adversaries by believing for example that these actions are exceptions to the rule, or are just the adversaries' superficial attempts to hide their evil nature.

People also cognitively create the world by projecting onto reality their current beliefs and values. In so doing, they may actually create what at first was only in their minds. For example, people in conflict may project untrustworthiness onto their adversaries. The more distrustful people are of others, the less likely an adversary is to actually try to build trust. In conflict, the psychological process of projection may become a self-fulfilling prophecy where people create the world they expect to see. Similarly, transference is a process where the attributes of one thing or person are transferred to another thing or person. A man, for example, who is unhappy with his supervisor at work may come home and transfer his anger onto his wife.

By far the most tragic perceptual process of creating reality is dehumanization. In conflicts, enemies may dehumanize each other so that they may kill freely, without having to experience cognitive dissonance over treating a fellow human cruelly. Ralph White in *Nobody Wanted War* described how enemies often purposely dehumanize each other by creating diabolical or animal enemy images of the other.[27]

Neurobiologists Laughlin, McManus, and d'Aquili have written extensively in *Brain, Symbol & Experience: Toward a Neurophenomenology of Human Consciousness* about how neurological structures in the brain guide human experience in the world. They note the "cognitive imperative" to assimilate all new experiences into the existing ways of understanding the world occurs both biologically and symbolically. Neurological structures maintain current understandings of the world, and the authors suggest that worldviews are reflected in actual physical structures in the brain that become "entrained" or engraved in the brain. These structures influence how we understand new experiences. New experiences and ideas tend to flow through the existing patterned structures in the brain rather than change those structures.[28]

Peacebuilders face a continual challenge to find ways to break through the perceptual defense mechanisms all people use to bring order and meaning to their experiences. It is challenging to help people see each other and their conflict in new ways because the process of perception works against change and seeks to reconfirm old ideas or old ways of seeing and naming the world. If the old ideas or ways of thinking happen to be the dehumanization of some "other," then there will be great resistance to seeing the "other" as human. Later chapters explore how ritual and other symbolic acts afford people the safety to explore new information and new experiences that may penetrate the perceptual defenses resistant to new, more peaceful worldviews.

Emotional and Sensual Cognition

The second element in the worldview lens is the emotional and sensual process of cognition. Humans see, hear, touch, taste, and feel the world around them to make sense of it. Recently there has been an upsurge in theory about how the mind and the body are connected.[29–33] In the West, most people have been trained to think of their mind and their body as separate. Yet all of the body's senses function to *make sense* of the world. Gregory Bateson notes, "the biologists worked hard to un-mind the body; and the philosophers disembodied the mind."[34] Bateson and many others put the pieces back together and emphasize the unity of body and mind, allowing recognition of and value for the importance of all the body's senses.

Experimental psychologists have conducted extensive research verifying that data about the world around us is gathered through all of our bodily senses: seeing, hearing, feeling, tasting, and smelling.[35] Visual and auditory symbols are found everywhere in our lives, from the ring of a telephone that symbolizes an incoming communication, to a wedding ring that symbolizes marriage. The smell of a rose symbolizes a rose, in its clearest form, but also may signify romance, weddings, Valentine's Day, or any other experience an individual connects with a rose. The feeling of sand in our hands represents sand, and also perhaps the beach, vacation, and rest. The sight of snow symbolizes cold temperatures, and maybe Christmas, family times in the home, or the adventure of skiing. The body's senses become the receptors of information, connecting images, sounds, or objects into symbols with unique personal histories.

Maturana and Varela claim humans do not understand their world solely through one sensory vehicle, like a voice over a telephone. Rather, communication depends on multiple paths, both verbal and nonverbal, to transmit a single message.[36] Most educational processes use only two senses, hearing and seeing, in the effort to transfer knowledge to students. More effective teaching engages the entire body and all of its senses in a learning experience. "All knowing is doing" because it is in doing that we know, and in knowing that we do.[37]

Our bodies may, in some cases, learn more quickly than our brains. As Clifford Geertz points out, "A child counts on his fingers before he counts in his head; he feels love on his skin before he feels it in his heart."[38] People learn how to play guitar by playing the guitar, not by thinking about it. Learning to cook comes from practice, not just reading cookbooks.

Emotions, like the five senses, are also crucial to an ability to make sense of the world. Most rationalists discount the value of emotions, suggesting they cloud reasonable thinking. However, research by psychologists and cognitive theorists, such as Carlson and Hatfield's comprehensive *The Psychology of Emotions*, documents the importance of emotions.[39] Harries-Jones echoes Gregory Bateson's writings, stating that "emotions set a context for reason and knowing, and should never be separated from a process of 'self-knowing.'"[40] Humans learn about the world not only through physical or sensual interactions with it. Emotions help people recognize the significance of events, objects, and people in their lives.

Langer argues that emotions help us recognize, understand, and express our depth of connection to an experience. She sees humans as able to process and learn from emotional experiences in a way that is not possible with linear logic. Verbal language is often incapable of expressing the emotions people feel about an experience, whether the emotions are happiness or despair. Words are symbols of the feelings we have about an experience. Emotions and music, which has been called the "language of emotions," express the way an event or experience makes a person feel inside and how they relate it to the feelings they have had in similar experiences.[41]

Emotions help us make sense of experiences first by gaining our attention and making us aware of an experience such as death or marriage. Emotions also indicate the intensity humans feel toward an experience and the importance an event has for our lives.[42] Furthermore, Langer notes that while emotions may at first simply express inner feelings, they come to demonstrate and communicate those feelings for others. Emotions are physiological responses that work interdependently with other cognitive processes. Our bodies express emotions physically through laughter, crying, or physical tension. Langer describes how this can happen.

> Lively demonstration makes an emotion contagious. Shout answers shout, the collective prancing becomes dancing. Even those who are not compelled by inner tension to let off steam just at this moment, fall into step and join the common cry.[43]

The external act of expressing an emotion comes to symbolize the emotion itself and symbolically connects with all past expressions of that emotion. The act of crying, for example, symbolizes and is part of the cognitive process of identifying the intensity of pain or feeling brought about in a particular experience and communicating that pain to others. Ray Rappaport asks and answers the right question: "How may information concerning some state of a transmitter better be signaled than by displaying that state itself? . . . Action speaks louder than words."[44]

Conflict is both a sensual and an emotional experience. People perspire, their heart beats faster, blood rushes to their face, and knees knock. Past emotional and sensual experiences with conflict help shape how people understand current and future conflicts. It also shapes how they choose to respond to new conflict. Palestinian or Israeli children who have never met someone from the other side will still bring a history of emotional and sensual experiences of the conflict between their peoples to a first meeting with their adversary.

Since humans are by nature both sensual and emotional, peacebuilders should engage people in conflict with processes that address the full range of ways humans know and make sense of their world. This means including multiple methods of knowing and learning, through traditional lectures and writing activities, as well as activities such as drama or theater, sports, eating, dancing, and walking outside together that will allow people to use more of their emotional and sensual capacity in the peacebuilding process. Later chapters will examine how peacebuilding rituals can create a safe space in which adversaries can create new emotional and sensual connections with each other and their conflict.

Culture

There is increasing confusion in the way theorists use the terms culture and worldview, and they are often used interchangeably. Individuals have worldviews based on their own unique lenses. Anthropologist Clifford Geertz in his classic *The Interpretation of Cultures* suggests that groups rather than individuals hold culture. Culture is "the fabric of meaning in terms of which human beings interpret their experience and guide their action. . . ."[45] He further notes that culture is "expressed in symbolic forms by means of which people communicate, perpetuate, and develop their knowledge about and attitudes toward life."[46] Culture, simply put, is the way groups of people live and make sense of their collective lives together.

Geertz notes that the need to symbolically understand and give meaning to the world is "evidently as real and as pressing as the more familiar biological needs." Everyone "knows" something of the world, but what each person knows is different since it is symbolically created through unique life experiences and interactions. The world humans experience is a symbolically created world.[47] Cultures are systems of meaning that help people make sense of the world. Existentialist philosophers such as Soren Kierkegaard[48] and Jean-Paul Sartre[49] and psychologists such as Rollo May[50] and Victor Frankl[51] expounded on the human need for meaning in their writings and practice. The existentialists hold that no human can live with the idea that the world is completely unknowable.

Cultural groups share common ways of being, values, social structures, and rules of interaction. Each person belongs to and interacts with many different cultures. People who share time and space develop unique ways of being. Families, organizations, religious groups, sports teams, and other groups within society each hold a unique culture that may share aspects with other cultures but has distinct rules for behavior and interaction among the culture's members. An individual's worldview will reflect the multiple cultures he or she experiences. Each individual has a unique mix of cultural influences. Worldviews reflect multiple cultures rather than mirroring any particular culture. Each cultural group an individual belongs to gives that person one aspect of their identity and shapes one part of their worldview lens. Figure 3.2 shows the variety of different cultural groups one individual can belong to.

Cultural groups develop common ways of seeing and understanding conflict. Cultural groups share ways of thinking and even hold a group memory of important events the group experienced. Vamik Volkan describes how cultural groups create "chosen traumas" and "chosen glories" in their collective memory.[52] These are specific events or moments in a cultural group's history that have taken on enormous symbolic meaning. For example, Pearl Harbor and September 11, 2001 represent chosen traumas in American history while Hiroshima is a chosen trauma in Japan. Cultural groups mobilize for and justify conflict and even war according to their shared chosen traumas.

Cultural groups also develop common ways of addressing conflict. Culture defines the metaphors and language people feel comfortable using to talk about conflict. While culture is often viewed as an obstacle to addressing conflict, particularly by theorists rooted in the material or social dimension of conflict, symbolic approaches use culture as a resource for building peace. Each culture has a tradition of how to handle conflict. Some cultures even have elaborate rituals already in place to help adversaries within their culture address their problems. Using cultural resources for peace gives peacebuilders a wider agenda in peacebuilding processes. Peacebuilders need to both share the conflict skills developed in the wider

Figure 3.2 An Individual's Multiple Cultural Groups

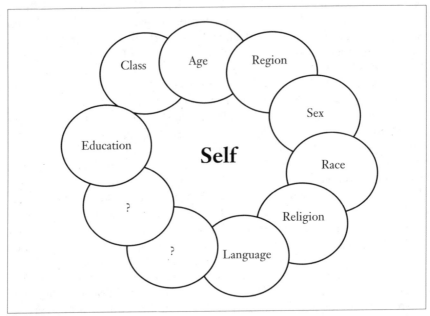

Source: Lisa Schirch, "Ritual Reconciliation: Transforming Identity/Reframing Conflict." In *Reconciliation, Coexistence, and Justice in Interethnic Conflicts: Theory and Practice,* ed. Mohammed Abu-Nimer. New York: Rowman and Littlefield, 2001. Reprinted with permission.

field and elicit, encourage, and build upon local cultural knowledge and capacity for building peace.[53] Peacebuilders can use both existing rituals within a culture and develop new rituals that build on important symbols, metaphors, and myths within a culture.

Values

An individual's values are related, but distinct from one's cultural groups. Cultures try to socialize particular values into their members. Most people today live outside an all-encompassing tribal cultural group. They interact in many different cultures, with different values. Therefore individuals have to decide which values will guide their life.

According to Stanley Jeyaraja Tambiah, cultural values are "those orienting principles and conceptions that are held to be sacrosanct, are constantly used as yardsticks, and are considered worthy of perpetuation relatively unchanged."[54] While cultural values influence individuals, in the end, the basic questions "Who am I?" "Where am I going?" and "Where did I come from?" play an important role in how each individual makes sense of and gives meaning to the world. Values are the most important meanings or principles that guide individual choices in life. They also help shape the core values an individual holds: "What do I hold as most important in my life?" "How do I spend my time?" "How do I spend my money?" "What or who is my god?"

If an individual interacts in a variety of secular cultures that emphasize the accumulation of wealth, this person will likely define his or her life and values around the pursuit of material goods. If a person spends a great deal of time in cultural groups that urge the pursuit of just and peaceful relationships and the mutual satisfaction of human needs, this person will spend time quite differently. If these two people were in conflict, their values would shape every aspect of how they understood and behaved in conflict.

Although peacebuilding lacks an in-depth discussion of the role of values, Docherty's book, subtitled *When People Bring Their Gods to the Table*, addresses the need for and design of peacebuilding processes that clarify values people bring to the negotiation table that may silently steer all of their decision-making.[55] Understanding how each individual's worldview shapes his or her values is an important lesson for people interested in addressing conflict. The rational and relational approaches to conflict overlook underlying value differences between people in conflict. Principled negotiation and cooperative communication techniques may not begin to address or reveal vast differences in values.

Moreover, while most conflict theorists and peacebuilding practitioners operate within a value framework that favors the protection of human life and the satisfaction of human needs, these values are rarely laid out as competing with secular values such as the accumulation of wealth or gain in political power. The values of each peacebuilder also affect the choice of the peacebuilding process that is favored, from more conservative efforts at dialogue to more radical approaches such as nonviolent direct action. A focus on the analysis of conflict and the skills of peacebuilding often eclipse questions of people's underlying motivations.

Ritual symbolically communicates about basic values. Ritual can heighten hatred and rejection of others or can build on and enhance values for peace. For example, the candlelight vigils to remember the victims of September 11, 2001 communicated and strengthened the value in human life. These vigils reflected the worldviews of the people participating in them who portrayed their sorrow at the loss of life.

Identity

Identity is the final element of worldview discussed here. It too is related closely to the other elements of worldview, particularly culture. Humans have a basic need to define themselves, to say to others through their clothing, mannerisms, homes, and lives: "This is who I am."

Each person defines himself or herself in multiple ways based on the social or cultural groups that influence and shape them. Figure 3.2 illustrated how the self is defined by membership in multiple cultural groups. Each person's sense of self will shift according to this cultural context. To understand any identity component, one must look at the interactions between that identity component and the others held by that individual or group. To describe a person as "white" says very little about their identity. To describe someone as a "white, middle-class, well-educated, Protestant, professional, Californian mother" enriches the description of a person, although it still does not define all of that person's characteristics and qualities.

Since individuals usually move between different cultural groups associated with diverse contexts, their behaviors and identities are constantly changing. As identity theorist Kenneth Gergen points out in *The Saturated Self*, individuals will experience a unique sense of themselves in the different contexts in which they interact.[56] For example, I belong to a number of different cultural groups. I am Mennonite, politically active, educated, white, female, married, a teacher, and I live in the Shenandoah Valley on the east coast of the United States. Belonging to each group gives me a particular set of cultural values (some more loosely defined than others) and has exposed me to particular experiences that have shaped my unique worldview. My identities grow out of each of these cultural contexts. Together, my memberships in these groups compose who I am, my "self." Yet each is an identity in and of itself. When I am with other women, I notice my identity as a woman. When I am with other Mennonites, I perceive my Mennonite identity.

The need for a sense of identity influences the dynamics of conflicts in a number of ways. Terrel Northrup argues that many conflicts become "stuck" on identity. Peace settlements that deal with the material dimensions of conflict but do not address identity needs and dynamics are unlikely to succeed.[57] Social psychologists Tajfel and Turner developed a "social identity theory" to explain the ways in which people seek to increase their self-esteem through favoring groups they belong to and discriminating against the "out group" or "other."[58] Coser and Volkan also posit that keeping one's own sense of identity requires an ongoing denigration of an "other."[59] In his classic work *The Functions of Social Conflict*, Lewis Coser described the benefits individuals and groups derive from engaging in conflict. Building on the work of Georg Simmel, Coser claims conflict is an "essential element in group life and formation" and is premised on the identification of an "other."[60] Vamik Volkan (*The Need for Enemies and Allies*) makes a similar argument.[61] Ted Gurr, in *Minorities at Risk*, concludes that the identities of oppressed groups become stronger and the differences between groups become more pronounced in conflict situations.[62]

People gain a sense of self both through their relationships with people who are the same as they are and those who are different. Forms of identity based on sameness use positive comparisons with others: I know who I am because of my positive relationships with others. For example, adopted children may belong to an association of other adopted children to find social support. Identities based on difference use negative comparisons with others: I know who I am by knowing who I am not. People distinguish themselves from others through biological differences (such as sex, height, or age) or socially constructed differences (such as religion, ideology, or class).

Forms of identity based on difference are often a source of conflict. The psychology of ethnocentrism leads people to believe their social group identity is superior to others. People may be willing both to kill and die defending certain identities. For example, some Americans were so certain that capitalism was superior to communism during the cold war that many said they "would rather be dead than red." In other words, Americans were willing to fight and die to preserve their sense of identity as Americans and not Soviet communists.

Forms of identity based on difference may also be a result of conflict. Conflict plays a role in creating "in groups" or allies and "out groups" or enemies. Conflict strengthens perceptions of who is good and who is bad, allowing people to create simplified ways of understanding the world. For example, many early white immigrants who settled in the "New World" peacefully coexisted with First Nations peoples and shared a sense of common humanity and friendship. When struggles for land and resources increased between whites and Native peoples, the group identities of "white" and "Native" took on new importance. In these conflicts, the "new" Americans set out to dehumanize and often do away with the "Native" Americans and in some cases, vice versa.

The way an individual identifies himself or herself seems to differ in conflict and nonconflict situations. In nonconflict situations, people seem to define themselves broadly, as shown in Figure 3.2, according to many different identities. However, during conflict, people may come to see themselves through the lens of conflict. Therefore, people engaged in gender conflicts may perceive being male or female as their primary or sole identity. In conflicts involving race, people may see themselves as primarily white or black. Figure 3.3 shows how one identity can dominate other sources of identity if it is threatened or engaged in conflict.

The way an individual or group defines others also seems to differ in conflict and nonconflict contexts. In nonconflict situations, people are less likely to stereotype others or categorize them according to only one social group. The psychological process of ascribing an identity to another person or group seems to increase in conflicts. People tend to dehumanize each other by stripping each individual of other sources of their identity and humanity. In the US context in which racism is an ongoing macroconflict, many if not all people who have been socialized by a racist social structure

Figure 3.3 Identity Formation in Ethnic Conflict

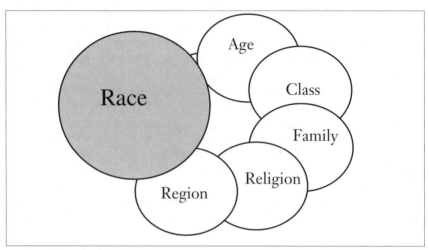

Source: Lisa Schirch, "Ritual Reconciliation: Transforming Identity/Reframing Conflict." In *Reconciliation, Coexistence, and Justice in Interethnic Conflicts: Theory and Practice,* ed. Mohammed Abu-Nimer. New York: Rowman and Littlefield, 2001. Reprinted with permission.

will make immediate judgments about the character of others based solely on the color of their skin. However, white people do not usually spend a great deal of time determining the characteristics of the white people they cross paths with each day because the social conflict of racism is not pertinent to these interactions.

Because of the connection between conflict and identity, perceptions of self and other may need to be transformed in peacebuilding efforts. Threats to identity seem to impact conflict. Refugees fleeing conflict, for example, have often lost their families, communities, religious places, and other important symbols of their identity. Victims of violence and their families also lose important ways of understanding who they are. Rape victims, for example, may carry the identity of victimhood for years after the crime. Rituals that reaffirm or create new identities may actually assist the healing process necessary for reconciliation and peacebuilding.

Rehumanizing requires transforming or increasing the flexibility of how people perceive of themselves and the enemy. As people become aware of their interdependence with many other social groups, including shared identities with their enemy, they gain a fuller sense of their own and their enemy's complex humanity. For example, Palestinian and Israeli women who have met each other and discussed the many shared aspects of their lives as mothers, widows, sisters, wives, and victims of a painful conflict have gone through a process of rehumanizing their sense of self and other. Together, they are in a stronger position to build peace in the region.

Perceptions of identity may change according to physical and relational contexts. When people are in the workplace, they relate to others through their professional identity. But a person in his or her own home interacts with others according to family role, father, mother, daughter, or son.

The typical negotiation room is sterile and encourages people to identify each other as negotiators or members of only one identity group related to the conflict. Peacebuilders can intentionally create contexts that encourage adversaries to see themselves and others through other lenses that allow a fuller definition of both self and other. Since ritual is set apart from other social contexts, it may enable people to transform their perceptions of their own and their adversaries' identity.

Worldviewing and the Symbolic Dimensions of Conflict

The worldview elements of conflict make it clear that peacebuilders need more tools to deal with the symbolic dimensions of conflict. In their important book on the process of how people understand the world, *The Tree of Knowledge*, Maturana and Varela emphasize the importance of recognizing different worldviews in conflict situations. They claim "the world everyone sees is not *the* world but *a* world which we bring forth with others."[63]

> If we know that our world is necessarily the world we bring forth with others, every time we are in conflict with another human being with whom we want to remain in coexistence, we cannot affirm what for us is certain (an absolute truth) because that would negate the other person. If we want to coexist with the other person, we must see that his certainty—however undesirable it may seem to us—is as legitimate and valid as our own because, like our own, that certainty expresses his [worldview] however undesirable it may seem to us. Hence, the only possibility for coexistence is to opt for a broader perspective, a domain of existence in which both parties fit in the bringing forth of a common world.[64]

More recently, even renowned rationalist Karl Popper claims there is great value in interworldview discussions. He notes, "[A]t any moment we are free to break out of the prison [of our worldview] by criticizing our framework and by adopting a wider and truer framework and a richer and less prejudiced language."[65] While "breaking out of the framework" may not be the best metaphor for worldview engagement, conflict may help spur the growth of a framework or the transformation of worldviews.[66] Popper claims that each person must explicitly lay out his or her worldview to be understood by others. Rather than ignore or deny our worldview differences, Popper suggests that humans need to acknowledge being captive to their worldviews. Peacebuilding, then, must include each person in the world sharing through word, symbol, and ritual his or her own unique worldview.

If people learn through their bodies, emotions, and senses, then it is also rational to think that ritual offers another pathway toward peace. If the process of perception shapes how people understand conflict, peacebuilders need tools such as ritual that can help shift people's perceptions. If cultural groups already have ritual resources for peace within their traditions, it makes sense for peacebuilders to help groups further develop these tools within their own community. If people in conflict have basic value differences, peacebuilders need ritual to help people recognize these differences and discover similarities between people. If people's identities are central to their perception of conflict, then it seems logical that peacebuilding processes need to assist in the transformation of identity. The next chapter provides an overview of how ritual functions in peacebuilding.

Notes

1. Joyce L. Hocker and William W. Wilmot, *Interpersonal Conflict* (Dubuque, IA: Wm. C. Brown, 1995), 21.

2. John F. Cragan and Donald C. Shields, *Symbolic Theories in Applied Communication Research: Borman, Burke, and Fisher* (Cresskill, N.J.: Hampton Press, 1995), 20.

3. Jayne Seminare Docherty, *Learning Lessons from Waco: When the Parties Bring Their Gods to the Negotiation Table* (New York: Syracuse University Press, 2001).

4. John W. Burton, *Conflict: Human Needs Theory* (New York: St. Martin's Press, 1990), 29.

5. Mary Clark, "Meaningful Social Bonding as a Universal Human Need," in *Conflict: Human Needs Theory*, ed. John Burton (New York: St. Martin's Press, 1990), 34–59.

6. Vern Neufeld Redekop, *From Violence to Blessing* (Ottawa: Novalis, 2002).

7. Rene Descartes, *The Philosophical Works of Descartes*, trans. E. S. Haldane and G.R.T. Ross (New York: Dover, 1955).

8. Roger Fisher and William Ury, *Getting to Yes: Negotiating Agreement Without Giving In* (Boston: Houghton Mifflin, 1983), back cover.

9. Thomas Kochman, *Black and White Styles in Conflict* (Chicago: University of Chicago Press, 1981).

10. Kevin Avruch, *Culture and Conflict Resolution* (Washington, DC: US Institute of Peace, 1998).

11. Mohammed Abu-Nimer, *Dialogue, Conflict Resolution, and Change: Arab-Jewish Encounters in Israel* (New York: State University of New York Press, 1999).

12. Roger Fisher and Scott Brown, *Getting Together: Building a Relationship That Gets to Yes* (Boston: Houghton Mifflin, 1988).

13. Hocker and Wilmot, *Interpersonal Conflict*.

14. Kenneth Boulding, *The Image: Knowledge in Life and Society* (Ann Arbor, Mich.: University of Michigan Press, 1956).

15. See the following sources for other descriptions of the symbolic dimension of conflict and peacebuilding: Kevin Avruch and Peter Black, *Conflict Resolution: Cross-Cultural Perspectives* (New York: Greenwood Press, 1991); John Paul Lederach,

Preparing for Peace: Conflict Transformation Across Cultures (Syracuse, N.Y.: Syracuse University Press, 1995); Oscar Nudler, "On Conflicts and Metaphors: Toward an Extended Rationality," in *Conflict: Human Needs Theory*, ed. John Burton (New York: St. Martin's Press, 1990), 177–204; Jayne Docherty, *Learning Lessons from Waco: When the Parties Bring Their Gods to the Negotiation Table* (Syracuse, N.Y.: Syracuse University Press, 2001); Sara Cobb, "Empowerment and Mediation: A Narrative Perspective," *Negotiation Journal* 9, no. 3 (1993): 245–59; Michelle LeBaron Duryea, *Conflict and Culture: Research in Five Communities in Vancouver, British Columbia* (Victoria, BC: University of Victoria Institute for Dispute Resolution, 1993); Marc Gopin, *Between Eden and Armageddon: The Future of World Religions, Violence* (New York: Oxford University Press, 2000); Tamra Pearson d'Estree, "The Role of 'Symbolic Gestures' in Intergroup Conflict Resolution: Addressing Group Identity" (Ph.D. diss., Harvard University, 1990); and Marc Howard Ross, "Psychocultural Interpretations and Dramas: Identity Dynamics in Ethnic Conflict," *Political Psychology* 22, no. 1 (2001): 157–78.

16. Frank Blechman et al., Finding Meaning in a Complex Environment Policy Dispute: Research into Worldviews in the Northern Forest Lands Council Dialogue 1990–1994, George Mason University Working Paper Series (no. 14) (Fairfax, Va.: Institute for Conflict Analysis and Resolution, 2000).

17. Judge Barry Stuart, interview by the author. September 17, 1997. Harrisonburg, Va.

18. Magoroh Maruyama, "Most Frequently Found Mindscape Types," in *Mindscapes: The Epistemology of Magoroh Maruyama*, ed. Michael T. Caley and Daiyo Sawada (Langhorne, Pa.: Gordon and Breach, 1994), 49–50.

19. *Docherty, Learning Lessons from Waco.*

20. Immanuel Kant, *Critique of Pure Reason*, trans. N. Kemp Smith (New York: Humanities, 1781).

21. William James, *The Principles of Psychology* (New York: Smith, 1890).

22. Susanne Langer, *Philosophy in a New Key: A Study in the Symbolism of Reason, Rite, and Art* (New York: Penguin Books, 1948).

23. F. Heider, "Attitudes and Cognitive Organization," *Journal of Psychology* 21 (1946): 107–12.

24. Gregory Bateson, *Steps to an Ecology of Mind* (New York: Ballantine Books, 1972), 429.

25. Leonard Festinger, *A Theory of Cognitive Dissonance* (Stanford: Stanford University Press, 1957).

26. Sigmund Freud, *The Complete Psychological Works*, trans. J. Strachey (New York: Norton, 1922).

27. Ralph White, *Nobody Wanted War* (New York: Doubleday, 1968).

28. Charles D. Laughlin, John McManus, and Eugene G. d'Aquili, *Brain, Symbol & Experience: Toward a Neurophenomenology of Human Consciousness* (Boston: Shambhala Publications, 1990).

29. Sergio Moravia, *The Enigma of the Mind: The Mind-Body Problem in Contemporary Thought* (Cambridge: Cambridge University Press, 1995).

30. Bill Moyers, *Healing and The Mind* (New York: Doubleday, 1993).

31. Francisco J. Varela, Evan Thompson, and Eleanor Rosch, *The Embodied Mind: Cognitive Science and Human Experience* (Cambridge, Mass.: MIT Press, 1991).

32. Morris Berman, *Coming to Our Senses: Body and Spirit in the Hidden History of the West* (New York: Simon and Schuster, 1989).

33. Mark Johnson, *The Body in the Mind: The Bodily Basis of Meaning, Imagination, and Reason* (Chicago: University of Chicago Press, 1987).

34. Gregory Bateson, *A Sacred Unity: Further Steps to an Ecology of Mind* (San Francisco: Harper San Francisco, 1991), xvii.

35. M. W. Levine and J. M. Shefner, *Fundamentals of Sensation and Perception* (Pacific Grove, Calif.: Brooks/Cole, 1992).

36. Humberto Maturana and Francisco J. Varela, *The Tree of Knowledge: The Biological Roots of Human Understanding* (Boston: Shambhala, 1987), 163.

37. Humberto Maturana and Francisco J. Varela, *Autopoiesis and Cognition: The Realization of the Living* (Dordrecht, Holland: D. Reidel Publishing Company, 1980).

38. Clifford Geertz, *The Interpretation of Cultures: Selected Essays* (New York: Basic Books, 1973), 81.

39. J. G. Carlson and E. Hatfield, *Psychology of Emotion* (Fort Worth, Tex.: Harcourt Brace Jovanovich, 1992).

40. Peter Harries-Jones, *Ecological Understanding and Gregory Bateson* (Toronto: University of Toronto Press, 1995), 92.

41. Langer, *Philosophy in a New Key*, 100.

42. R. S. Lazarus, *Emotion and Adaptation* (New York: Oxford University Press, 1991).

43. Langer, *Philosophy in a New Key*.

44. Roy A. Rappaport, *Ecology, Meaning, and Ritual* (Richmond, Calif.: North Atlantic Books, 1979), 199.

45. Geertz, *The Interpretation of Cultures*.

46. Geertz, *The Interpretation of Cultures*.

47. Geertz, *The Interpretation of Cultures*.

48. Soren Kierkegaard, *A Kierkegaard Anthology*, trans. Robert Bretall (New York: Modern Library, 1959).

49. Jean-Paul Sartre, *Existentialism and Humanism*, trans. P. Mairet (London: Methuen, 1948).

50. Rollo May, *Existence: A New Dimension in Psychiatry and Psychology* (New York: Basic Books, 1958).

51. Victor Frankl, *Man's Search for Meaning: An Introduction to Logotherapy* (Boston: Beacon Press, 1963).

52. Vamik Volkan, *Blood Lines: From Ethnic Pride to Ethnic Terrorism* (Boulder, Colo.: Westview Press, 1997).

53. Lederach, *Preparing for Peace*.

54. Stanley Jeyaraja Tambiah, *Culture, Thought, and Social Action* (Cambridge, Mass.: Harvard University Press, 1985).

55. Docherty, *Learning Lessons from Waco*.

56. Kenneth J. Gergen, The *Saturated Self: Dilemmas of Identity in Contemporary Life* (New York: Basic Books, 1991).

57. Terrel A. Northrup, "The Dynamic of Identity in Personal and Social Conflict," in *Intractable Conflicts and Their Transformation*, ed. Louis Kriesberg, Terrell A. Northrup, and Stuart J. Thorson (Syracuse, N.Y.: Syracuse University Press, 1989).

58. H. Tajfel and J. C. Turner, "The Social Identity Theory of Intergroup Behavior," in *The Social Psychology of Intergroup Relations*, ed. S. Worchel and W. G. Austin (Chicago: Nelson-Hall, 1986).

59. Lewis A. Coser, *The Functions of Social Conflict* (Glencoe, Ill., Free Press, 1956).

60. Coser, *The Functions of Social Conflict*, 31.

61. Vamik Volkan, *The Need to Have Enemies and Allies: From Clinical Practice to International Relationships* (Northvale, N.J.: J. Aronson, Inc., 1988).

62. Ted Gurr, *Minorities at Risk* (Washington, DC: United States Institute of Peace, 1993).

63. Maturana and Varela, *The Tree of Knowledge*.

64. Maturana and Varela, *The Tree of Knowledge*, 245.

65. Karl Raimund Popper, *Knowledge and the Body-Mind Problem: In Defence of Interaction* (London; New York: Routledge, 1994), 137–38.

66. Popper, *Knowledge and the Body-Mind Problem*, 137–38.

CHAPTER **4**

Finding Ritual on a
Map of Peacebuilding

Concern about social change dates back thousands of years. Pacifists in each of the world's major religions were concerned about the use of violence long before activist movements in this century articulated nonviolence as a strategy for social change. Academic researchers in the mid-1900s began their own study of violence, peace, and conflict in many disciplines, such as anthropology, psychology, behavioral science, and political science. More recently, pragmatic community workers, policymakers, and government branches began addressing conflicts with a variety of Alternative Dispute Resolution (ADR) approaches, including community mediation centers, Victim Offender Reconciliation Programs (VORP), labor conciliation, and peer mediation in schools. The interdisciplinary academic field of conflict studies, based on these processes, began in the 1980s.

Today the term peacebuilding is increasingly used to refer to the tasks of preventing, reducing, transforming, and helping people to recover from violence, even structural violence that has not yet led to massive civil unrest. At the same time peacebuilding empowers people to foster relationships within families, communities, organizations, businesses, governments, and cultural, religious, economic, and political institutions that aim to meet human needs and protect human rights. Peacebuilding includes a wide range of activities such as human rights activism, relief aid, peacekeeping, dialogue, negotiation, mediation, restorative justice, transitional justice, development, military conversion and transformation, education, and research activities.[1]

There are four main approaches to peacebuilding, ranging from short-term, crisis-oriented processes to long-term strategies. The four approaches (Figure 4.1) are: Waging Conflict Nonviolently; Reducing Direct Violence; Transforming Relationships; and Building Capacity.

The first category of peacebuilding includes processes to wage conflict nonviolently. This circle seeks to balance power between groups in conflict,

Figure 4.1 Peacebuilding Map

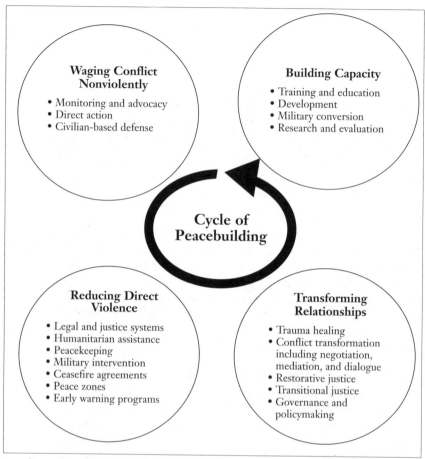

Source: Lisa Schirch, *The Little Book of Strategic Peacebuilding.* Intercourse, Pa.: Good Books, 2004. Reprinted with permission.

increase awareness of the conflict issues, and create a sense of readiness for change, negotiation, and problem solving among reluctant groups. In the short term, waging conflict nonviolently escalates conflict. The methods, tactics, and strategies of nonviolent direct action—practiced and articulated by Gandhi, Martin Luther King, Jr. and countless other peace activists around the world—form the core of this circle. Ritual is used widely among nonviolent activists and forms an important tool in the activist's kit. From Gandhi's symbolic march to the Indian Sea to make salt and African-Americans' dramatic lunch counter sit-ins, to the antiwar "Not in Our Name" vigils held by New Yorkers after September 11, peace activists create a unique space, communicate a symbolic message, and seek the transformation of worldviews, identities, relationships, and social structures through peacebuilding rituals.

The second category of peacebuilding includes crisis-oriented processes and programs to address the victims and offenders or perpetrators of direct violence. At the community level, community policing, offender programs, homeless and women's shelters, and charity programs offer support to the victims of violence while seeking to contain offenders and prevent future violence. At the macro level, reducing violence requires peacekeeping, relief and refugee programs, and work toward ceasefires and peace settlements in countries ravaged by war.

Traditional or improvised rituals can nurture the social commitment to values of peace in times of crisis, creating a space in which people can release pent-up emotions and trauma. In the days and weeks after September 11, 2001, many Americans felt the need to "do something" to help the victims and their families. Giving blood became a national ritual, and people waited in lines for many hours in order "to do their part for their country." In times of crisis, some people need help and other people want to help. Leaders can organize actions such as blood donations that play both a functional and a symbolic role in helping people heal from trauma. The goal is to reduce the violence felt by the entire community.

Ritual also has broad application in the third category of peacebuilding, the intermediate stage that includes a broad array of processes to transform relationships and address the roots of conflict. In this circle, high-level official negotiation and mediation ideally connect with mid-level initiatives by religious leaders and organizations, the academic community, and grassroots community leaders. Trauma healing programs build relationships among survivors. Restorative and transitional justice programs hold offenders accountable to victims' needs. As a complement to the verbally-based methods of courtrooms, negotiation, mediation, dialogue, problem-solving workshops, and trauma healing seminars, ritual offers an alternative way of communicating the difficult, complex, and dissonant emotions and ideas so prevalent in people experiencing conflict. Ritual's ability to make meaning, create relationships, transform and heal identities in a unique, safe space are invaluable to peacebuilders seeking to transform conflict. In many peacebuilding workshops, informal rituals like smoking cigarettes in the hallway or eating meals together are significant events in changing the ways people in conflict relate to each other.

Building capacity is the final circle of peacebuilding. It includes long-term strategies such as education, development, military conversion and transformation, and the creation of new social structures to meet human needs. Ritual again complements the verbal, direct forms of communication that are needed in education and development in particular. Creating and performing rituals are key tools for communities of people to empower themselves to engage with oppressive social structures that need

transforming. Long-term peacebuilding visions need the constant sustenance that traditional rituals can provide, for change is usually slow and
requires tremendous work.

The use of ritual is not new to peacebuilding. Traditional societies and
some symbol-savvy trainers and workshop leaders have a sophisticated
sense of when to use ritual. As a peacebuilding practitioner, I am still
learning to balance the need for more straightforward, verbal methods of
training and facilitating peacebuilding workshops with ritual and other
symbolic approaches. As someone trained within the Western, rationalist
tradition, I often find myself forgetting about the power of ritual in my
own practice. One of my personal goals in writing this book was to help
myself articulate the need for and functions of ritual, so that I can more
intentionally employ it in my own practice.

In each of the four approaches to peacebuilding reviewed above, ritual
complements other peacebuilding tools and processes. Ritual is needed
and useful both in times of crisis and the long-term work of capacity building. The dynamic of ritual seems to be useful in conflicts in a variety of
ways. It fools the dragons of hatred and violence by offering tools that
stimulate the mind, body, and senses of humans engaged in conflict. Table
4.1 summarizes the functions of ritual under each category that will be
explored in future chapters. The rest of the book consists of examples and
further explanation of each of these functions.

Limitations of Ritual Peacebuilding

Some weaknesses exist within the symbolic dimension of conflict. Ritual
may not adequately address issues of injustice in the distribution of material resources or imbalances in power between groups in conflict, and it
may gloss over negative emotions and thoughts. While ritual may be very
useful in addressing the symbolic dimensions of conflict, it may be less
helpful in addressing resource issues. Peacebuilders need to use tools that
address each dimension of conflict. Verbal processes such as problem-
solving workshops, dialogue, and mediation will always play an important
role in peacebuilding.

As detailed in chapter 2, rituals can be constructive or destructive.
Negative perceptions of ritual's usefulness in peacebuilding may build on
real-life experiences with destructive or ineffective rituals. Peacebuilders
need to use great care with ritual and symbolic tools, for they can create
great harm or great good.

The third limitation of ritual peacebuilding comes from ignorance.
The lack of understanding about the ways people learn through their emotions and senses, the psychological dynamics of perceptions, and discomfort with discussion of values, for example, lead many people to feel

Table 4.1 Functions of Ritual in Peacebuilding

Space	Communicates Symbolic Message	Forming	Transforming
Creates a safe space for people in conflict away from the site of their adversarial relationships	Communicates complex, difficult, ambiguous, and dissonant messages through symbols, senses, physical actions, and emotions	Helps participants understand and make sense of the world through cultivating values and shaping memory	Reframes problems so that people in conflict are more able to find a mutually satisfying way of addressing their human needs
Provides a "focusing frame" to bring attention to common ground between people	Communicates across cultures through symbols and symbolic actions that allow for multiple interpretations	Assists transitions in worldview, identity, and relationships that support a community's values and structures	Assists transitions in worldview, identity, relationships, and social structures that challenge and transform the status quo values and structures
Allows for a liminal or in-between place where transformation can take place	Expresses and channels emotions in a safe way, often through rhythm, repetition, and patterned actions	Builds, affirms, and heals identities that may be at risk or damaged in conflicts	Creates and/or strengthens joint identities for groups in conflict that create a bridge across their shared humanity
Creates an atmosphere where people can relax, feel fully human, and see others as fully human	Allows people to enact their full humanity and share it with others	Improves self-esteem of participants, allowing them to see and feel their ability to act in the world.	Rehumanizes people who have been dehumanized through perceptual processes fueled by conflict
	Allows people to learn through improvised ways of acting and behaving with others	Builds bridges and boundaries around relationships, giving people a structured way of interacting with each other	Provides a pathway for transformation, a rite of passage from one state to the next

uncomfortable with ritual, calling it "new age-ish" or "touchy feely." Using ritual goes against Western logic. I have heard it said many times that ritual may make a person feel good, but it does not change the real world. Using ritual in conflict may present problems for people who see it as strange or irrational. Ritual is commonly thought of as exotic, demonic, or an experiential commodity for tourists visiting indigenous cultures. Westerners often see the formal traditional rituals of other cultures as quaint while ignoring the ritualistic roles that modern pop culture plays in their own societies.

In my research on feminist ritual, many of the women interviewed expressed an inner struggle to validate the use of ritual. One woman said she thought a lot of the feminist rituals were "kooky" at first, even though she was really moved by participating in them. Another said that "part of me knows that ritual is really powerful for me . . . but part of me dismisses it because it doesn't make logical sense. . . ." Another woman noted that while she often plans to do ritual, and she is convinced it makes a difference in her life, "there is a sense in which I resist it and I don't do it . . . it is so powerful and so simple, but until I'm in it, it seems meaningless." Asked to explain her hesitation, one woman said, "I think it is our society. We just don't value it and so somewhere in my core I don't value it." Western society's disdain for ritual clearly has made an impact even on the women who support and use feminist ritual.

As a peacebuilder, I am hesitant to engage groups in ritual activities that may feel strange or irrational. The Western antiritual influence may repel people from wanting to participate in traditional rituals or developing new types of ritual. Peacebuilding is already thought of as too touchy feely by some critics. I have chosen to use the word ritual in this book to capture a wide range of practices and to speak of ritual functions identified by a variety of academic disciplines. In practice, the word ritual may turn people off if it is associated with boredom, formality, or religion. The terms activities, recreation, free time, events, symbolic acts, or even ceremony can be substituted for the word ritual. Rituals need not feel boring, touchy feely, or hokey. Paying attention to the language and culture of people in conflict can help prevent using terms or developing rituals that will feel uncomfortable to the group.

Peacebuilders can experiment by developing secular, improvised, informal rituals based on symbols and stories that reflect important transitions in the conflict. Depending on the group, a variety of informal, unstructured, and improvised rituals can engage people in activities that play many of the same functions as more formal and traditional rituals. A wide variety of rituals can be used in peacebuilding. The more people understand the dynamics of ritual, the more "logical" it will seem to them to use ritual in peacebuilding.

The Ritual Paradox

Reviving ritual in today's technological world offers a paradox to peace-builders. Using ritual may seem counterintuitive. Conflict is already confusing and messy. Methods that sort out and analyze conflict and deal with it piece by piece have more appeal to many Westerners. For many intellectuals in particular, it is difficult to digest the idea that a ritual context can speak symbolically and influence people's emotions and thoughts; that humans communicate in ritual primarily through their bodies, senses, and emotions rather than in words; and that people's perceptions of themselves, their enemies, and the conflict itself can be transformed through ritual. These ideas seem like remnants of an earlier time, and indeed they are. Our ancestors used ritual without hesitation or justification to mark and represent the most significant moments and changes in human experience.

The use of seemingly contradictory, surprising, or indirect methods to address problems rather than directly resisting and dealing with problems has a long history. The Eastern art of Aikido reflects a value in paradoxical interventions into conflict. The Aikido artist never opposes or clashes with their opponent. Instead, they move with the challenger in the same direction. As the challenger prepares to attack, the Aikidoist opens with arms and palms "welcoming" the attacker, which further serves to surprise and disarm the opponent.[2]

Nonviolent activism often uses paradox by doing the opposite of what is expected; by receiving violence without resisting. The idea of nonresistance or "loving the enemy" is grounded in a belief that people's perceptions change through creating a situation of cognitive dissonance. Nonviolent activists make the opponent fully aware of the brutality of their actions by allowing their enemy to continue beating and killing people who are not resisting. Nonviolent activists hope to shake the cognitive frameworks of their enemies by refusing to either submit or fight back.[3]

While some forms of Western psychological therapy treat symptoms and address the problem directly, paradoxical forms of therapy use the back door approach. Paradoxical therapists aim to help their patients ignore the problem or come to see it in such a different light that the problem disappears on its own. Seltzer claims, "Anything predictable is therapeutically inefficient . . . people are most influenced when they expect a certain message and receive instead a message at a totally different level."[4] If a child is wetting the bed at night, rather than addressing the problem by scolding or talking to the child about the bedwetting, a paradoxical therapist will give the child permission or even orders to wet the bed. In relieving the anxiety about the problem, paradoxical therapeutic interventions effectively render the problem powerless to define and capture the attention of the patient.

More recently, the development of the field of appreciative inquiry as a model for organizational change brings the paradoxical approach to other types of problems. The normal, expected approach to organizational change involves identifying problems, diagnosing and analyzing them, and then searching for solutions. Practitioners of appreciative inquiry believe that organizations grow in the direction of their inquiry. If organizations put energy into solving problems, the result is likely to be more numerous and complex problems. On the other hand, if an organization identifies what is working best and uses that as the basis of forming a powerful, positive image of the future, it is possible to transcend problems in moving toward that guiding vision.[5]

Positive Approaches to Peacebuilding documents how peacebuilders can reframe problems and conflicts by focusing on expanding common ground and peace between people. This shift in focus from "conflicts" to "opportunities for peace" creates a significant new way of approaching peacebuilding.[6]

The process of peacebuilding through ritual is paradoxical. For many, it will require a stretch in imagination. For others, ritual peacebuilding will seem as natural and intuitive as shaking hands. Rediscovering the potential uses and functions of ritual particularly calls Westerners and those influenced by Western thought to stretch our imaginations and to question the concept of rationality. The next few chapters lay out a language for talking about what ritual can do for peacebuilders and provide case studies that flesh out the theory.

Notes

1. Lisa Schirch, *The Little Book of Strategic Peacebuilding* (Intercourse, Pa.: Good Books, 2004).

2. Thomas Crum, *The Magic of Conflict* (New York: Simon and Schuster, 1987).

3. Walter Wink, *The Powers That Be: Theology for a New Millennium* (New York: Doubleday, 1999).

4. L. F. Seltzer, *Paradoxical Strategies in Psychotherapy: A Comprehensive Overview and Guide* (New York: Wiley, 1986), 151.

5. Sue Annis Hammond, *The Thin Book of Appreciative Inquiry* (Bend, Ore.: Thin Book Publishing Company, 1998).

6. *Positive Approaches to Peacebuilding*, ed. Cynthia Sampson et al. (Washington, DC: Pact Publications, 2003).

CHAPTER 5

Designing the Stage: Peacebuilding Spaces

I arrived at York University late on my first day of research. I followed the smell of sage and sweetgrass across the hallways of two large building until I found the "Native Elders Conference on Traditional Teachings." The smoked-filled room reminded me of my first smudging ceremony at the Chippewas of Nawash Reserve in a sunrise ceremony in October 1990. That was just months after the Oka conflict in Quebec, when Canadian tanks rolled onto a Native burial ground that was to be turned into a golf course. As people around the world watched a group of armed Mohawks attempting to stop the development, many non-Native people like myself woke up to the harsh reality of Native Canada and the struggle for Aboriginal rights and land claims.[1] I felt clumsy and self-conscious the first time I lifted the sage and sweetgrass smoke over my head and down my body. In the months and years after that, I participated in the ceremony many times as a full-time land claims advocate. On this day, though, my thoughts were not on land claims, but on the significance of ritual in urban Native life.

Native people in North America are surrounded by a largely hostile white culture. They live daily in the midst of this conflict. The smudging ceremony is performed before almost every Native gathering and plays an important role in the struggle to maintain Native culture. The smudging ceremony is a peacebuilding ritual.

A Native Elder led the opening prayer and smudge ceremony. She began by lighting a mixture of cedar, sweetgrass, tobacco, and sage. These four sacred plants are used for purifying and protecting people from evil spirits. The Elder told me she also added fungus from the birch tree as a purifier, and a mixture of other plants that she found along the way in the bush. She lit the mixture in a copper bowl set inside a larger stone bowl and fanned the burning herbs with an eagle feather. Eagle feathers are used as fans to help the herbs burn and to direct the smoke towards the circle's participants. The Elder leading the ceremony noted that the straight quill in the feather marked the straight path people needed to follow.

After the herbs were burning well, the Elder offered a prayer thanking the Creator for more parts of the world than I am used to appreciating. It takes a keen awareness to notice and give thanks for the song of the birds, the greenness of the growing grass, the warmth of the sun, the freshness of the winds, and the many other gifts of the Creator cited in Native prayers. The Elder instructed the circle of people as to how the smoke carried thoughts and prayers to the Creator.

She then walked sun-wise, inviting each person to smudge by fanning the smoke toward themselves. Native and non-Native people around me participated in the smudging. Individuals in the circle received the smoke in different ways. Some gently brought it toward themselves with their hands. Others were more careful to "wash" their hands in the smoke first. Then they scooped it over their hair and heads and then down toward their ears, eyes, mouth, heart, and down each leg. They ended by taking a deep breath of the smoke. Some treated the smoke with such care that it was clear it held sacred properties. The smoke's sweet, rich smell quickly filled the whole room.

In this Elder's conference, the smudging ceremony was used to start each morning session. After each person in the circle smudged, people introduced themselves and shared why they came to the conference, what events were happening in their lives, their struggles, and their joys. This sharing circle helped build community during the weekend conference. It created a sacred space for the Elder's teachings, lending tone and quality to the atmosphere. The lingering smell of sage and sweetgrass lasted throughout the day, reminding all participants of the way we started the meeting.

Space Matters

The smudging ceremony provides an example of how ritual space is formally created and set apart from everyday life. Smudging creates a unique space through a variety of smells, actions, and visual symbols that indicate to participants that something important and unusual is going to happen. Participants in ritual become aware that they are participating in ritual in part because the physical space is different. Interpreting ritual as symbolic space requires an understanding of ecological thinking, otherwise known as systems theory.

In the mid-1900s, an interdisciplinary group of theorists developed a new theoretical framework variously called systems theory, cybernetics, complexity theory, or synergetics. Many of the original principles of systems theory are based on indigenous values and beliefs. Thinking systemically provides a metatheory, an overarching framework for analyzing the world and the patterns of relationships that occur within it. Systems theory is holistic in that it focuses on the whole, rather than on parts. Systems theorists believe that a part of a system can only be understood by examining its relationship to other parts. Everything—including conflict, humans, ideas, and language—exists in an ecological relationship.

Gregory Bateson gives the example of cybernetic relationships in language. A word has meaning in a sentence, and the sentence has meaning only within its larger linguistic context: "without context, there is no communication."[2] Parts of a system do not function or have meaning according to their nature in isolation from other parts but according to their position in the systems network and how they are related to other parts.

Bateson popularized the idea that any given situation or context holds symbolic meanings. Each particular environment, whether a bathroom, a kitchen, a ballroom, or a soccer field has symbolic meanings that define (frame) all interactions that take place in it. In their books *The Tree of Knowledge* and *Autopoiesis and Cognition,* cognitive theorists Maturana and Varela describe their concept of autopoiesis: knowledge gained by an organism interacting with its environment. Both the organism and the environment are changed by their relationship with each other. Maturana and Varela use the term autopoiesis to describe systems' ability to generate and define themselves.[3] The recursive nature of systems means that relationships between parts of the system are dialectical. Each part of a system defines the other parts.

In *Frame Analysis* Erving Goffman examines how individuals make sense of and create symbolic frames for certain social situations.[4] Humans make sense of a situation and, at least in part, know how to act according to their physical context. Systems theory provides a new lens for interpreting the importance of context. Meaning is determined by relationships, particularly how humans relate to their physical context and other people. In ritual, it is impossible to separate *what* happens from *where* it happens. Context is tied to meaning. Ritual space informs participants what is going on within its borders of time and space through the interaction of symbols. This chapter discusses the role of context or space to show how ritual creates an "oasis for peace."

Set Design

Peacebuilders need to set the stage for peace. Theater directors understand that each play they direct will need a specially-designed set with special lighting to set the emotional tone, symbols to conjure up a time and place for the play, and other forms on the stage to give the actors a context for their words and actions. In the same way, peacebuilders need to become set directors, thinking about the very space where people in conflict will come together and how it can symbolically support the work of building peace.

Physical contexts help shape how people think and feel about themselves, others, and conflict. The typical negotiation room is filled with adversarial images and symbols. Sitting across from an adversary at a paper-filled table signifies a competitive, win/lose situation. Other contexts, such as eating together, hold more cooperative images and connotations. As discussed in chapter 1, many successful mediation efforts have had major breakthroughs when the people in conflict were eating dinner, smoking, dancing, or were in some location other than a negotiating room. Yet there is relatively little documented information on the importance of physical context in peacebuilding processes.

The idea of creating a safe space for addressing conflict is noted throughout the peacebuilding literature, although it is not connected to the concept of ritual. Yarbrough and Wilmot's *Artful Mediation: Constructive Conflict at Work* lists ways mediators can create safe space conducive to engaging conflict constructively. They give the following advice on establishing and creating a context for mediation.

1. Find a setting that neutralizes hostility, away from the physical space where the conflict itself normally takes place.
2. Create a setting that provides psychological support, such as seating people physically beside each other rather than across from each other.
3. Find a setting where the people involved have equal power, one that is not owned or considered home turf by any of the people.
4. Create time limits and ground rules that will determine and shape the kinds of interactions people will have in the mediation.[5]

These practices are fairly well known in peacebuilding. Many practitioners are highly skilled in making sure chairs are arranged in a circle or that round tables are used, as these both indicate and create equality and cooperation.

While the peacebuilding literature acknowledges the concept that space is symbolic and helps define the interactions that happen inside of it, the current literature does not acknowledge the power of designing the peacebuilding set for the drama of transformation and construction. A deeper understanding of how space is symbolic and communicates messages about what can and should take place within it may allow peacebuilders to take full advantage of the power of ritual.

Liminal Space

In ritual, humans create an idealized world. Victor Turner speaks of ritual contexts as liminal spaces. Liminal spaces or frames are in-between, set-aside contexts where the rules for acting and interpreting meaning are different from the rest of life.[6] These liminal spaces are thresholds or places in limbo that are symbolically separated from other social settings. Often, what happens in ritual is allowed to happen only because the space has been separated from the everyday, regular spaces where people interact. Joseph Campbell describes ritual space as

> a room or a certain hour or so a day, where you don't know what was in the newspapers that morning, you don't know who your friends are, you don't know what you owe anybody, you don't know what anybody owes you. This is a place where you can simply experience and bring forth what you are and what you might be. This is the place of creative incubation.[7]

Campbell concludes that something special always happens in ritual space.

Several of the Native people interviewed for this book noted that the smudging ceremony created a special frame or set the scenario for the kind of special social interactions that followed. The smudging ceremony helps people understand and give meaning to a space that is separate from and more sacred than everyday life. The smudging ceremony takes people out of the everyday frame and creates a special place where transformation will occur.

One Native woman claims, "Smudging is basically about focusing; it helps you leave everything you were doing and just focus in on why you are there. It puts you in a new frame of mind; at the beginning of a new day we start with new selves, clearing out what happened the day before."[8] Another Native person who works in a social service agency agreed that smudging creates a fresh way of looking at the world. He uses the smudging ceremony at the start of working with his Native clients. He notes that "smudging loosens people up; makes them more relaxed and clear . . . I do it seven or eight times a day; each time I see a client I do it; we do it together if they are tense. . . ."[9]

People create rituals around special places and times. Acts become ritualized when they are repeated. Mary Catherine Bateson describes how a couple who decides to marry over a romantic dinner may return to the same restaurant each year to celebrate their anniversary. This couple has created a ritual frame. The restaurant becomes the "space set apart" where they perform a yearly ritual to remember their love.[10]

On the other hand, people may create a special frame in hopes of performing a ritual within it. Women's spirituality groups create a symbolic space first, and then let the ritual develop on its own once the context is constructed.

The development of ritual space in both cases shares similar characteristics. There is an art to creating a place that can facilitate ritual's transforming power. In theater, this art is known as set design. Ritual space is set off from normal space in a number of different ways including time, location, architecture, symbols, smells, tastes, sounds, and people.

Time

Rituals may be set apart from the rest of life by special times when they occur. The smudging ceremony is often performed at sunrise or sunset, at the transforming times of the day. Traditional rituals often take place according to the seasons, the cycle of the moons, or anniversaries of special events. Christmas, Rosh Hashanah, and Ramadan are examples of specific times that help separate religious ritual from normal life.

People often use ritual to mark particularly significant and symbolic moments in history such as the "chosen traumas" and "chosen glories" described in chapter 3.[11] For example, April 19 has become a significant day in US history, as the attack on the federal building in Oklahoma City, and the FBI attacks at Waco and Ruby Ridge all occurred on this day. Given this horrific history, each year in Oklahoma City relatives of the bombing victims gather on the anniversary to remember, mourn, and continue to heal themselves. Victims of the Waco and Ruby Ridge attacks as well as supporters in a variety of militia movements also recognize April 19 as a special day for memorial rituals.

Chosen traumas or glories may lock people into a view of history that discourages transformation for the future. Ritual can help connect the past with the present by using a symbolic time to communicate the transformation toward a new future. Will September 11 ever be a day of celebration? One can only hope that someday there will be a global conference celebrating the dawn of a new era of relationships between Muslim and Christian people held on September 11 and we will remember the date as a moment of chosen glory in global history.

Location and Architecture

Spatial location is also important in creating ritual. Doors, arches, gates, or other physical markers such as stone circles or grand cathedrals and mosques usually separate ritual space.[12] Indigenous rituals often take place in special geographic locations such as beside rivers, on mountains, or near geological rock formations.

Physical space is created for the smudging ceremony by placing chairs in a circle. Participants who arrived at the Elders' conference walked into the room and into a physical circle that served as a type of doorway into the ritual space.

At the closing of some peacebuilding workshops, participants walk through an archway to symbolize their new relationships and identities as peacebuilders. Nonviolent protests have always taken place at symbolic locations such as Seattle's downtown during the G8 economic meetings, the steps of the US Congress, in the racially-segregated stores of downtown

Nashville, or in front of a public building where important decisions are made. In the effort to heal the city of Richmond, Virginia, from the trauma of slavery and centuries of racism, peacebuilders organized a symbolic walk through the city to stop at the historically-significant locations where enslaved peoples stepped off the boats from Africa, were jailed, and were then sold to white farmers.

Symbolic Objects

Ritual spaces often contain numerous symbolic objects. People use elements such as fire, earth, water, flowers, and foods as symbols in ritual to give meaning and order to a setting. Candles were originally used in sacred shrines to give light. Today, candles are used to recreate a spiritual atmosphere even though electricity may be available. Candles help separate ritual space from nonritual space.[13]

Ritual participants in the smudging ceremony interact with symbols, making physical and sensual connections with their environment. The bowl, the eagle feather used to fan the smoldering herbs, and each of the herbs hold special meanings in the ceremony. These symbols help identify the smudging circle as ritual space.

In judicial courts, judges have a gavel on their desks, which they use to bring order to the court. The gavel symbolizes their authority to control what happens in the courtroom. The courtroom becomes a ritual space that aims to do justice and prevent violence in the community. UN peacekeepers mark zones of peace with special colors. They monitor these zones wearing their blue helmets, which serve to symbolize the peaceful space set apart from neighboring war zones. In some conflict regions, such as the Green Line between Greek and Turkish Cyprus, these zones of peace become transformative, symbolic spaces for people to meet and negotiate.

Smells, Tastes, Sounds

People mark or create ritual space with specific smells, sounds, or tastes. Many cultures use incense to provide a powerful, physical cloud of pungent air to set ritual space apart from normal life. In Buddhist rituals, a bell is often rung to mark the onset of ritual. In more secular rituals, a visit to the pool hall on a Saturday night will start off with the consumption of one or more pints of beer. All of these sensual markers make ritual space unique.

The smudging ceremony's ambience is created by the sweet-pungent smell of sweetgrass, sage, tobacco, and cedar. This smell helps communicate that, for a portion of time, humans will retreat from regular time and space to focus on a different set of values and relationships.

A variety of trauma therapy programs use aromatherapy, specific smells mostly from herbs and flowers, to help people heal and relax. In some cultures, the smell and taste of chicken soup or homemade bread conjures up a feeling of calm and health. In other places, a glass of red wine, a good cigar, or a sip of kava creates an atmosphere in which people who are adversaries can relate to each other with more ease.

People

Bringing together unique combinations of people who would not normally relate to each other under normal social structure also helps create a ritual context. Ritual space develops in part when a unique combination of people joins in some unique action.

Greek and Turkish Cypriots who eat, drink, and dance together create ritual space by the very act of being together. Eating is not necessarily a ritual act. Normal, everyday meals eaten by Greek or Turkish Cypriots are not done in the company of members of the other ethnic group. However, when two groups of people from an ethnically divided island come together to eat, the context is unique and set apart from normal rules and patterns of interaction. Eating together takes on heightened symbolic meaning and becomes ritual.

A Place for Peace

Time, location, symbols, smells, tastes, sounds, and unique combinations of people jointly define and set ritual space apart from the rest of life. Creating a separate space is especially useful in conflicts, when normal space may be emotionally or physically dangerous or painful. Ritual can create a special oasis for peace where people in conflict can find respite from conflict's destruction. For people in conflict, ritual offers the unique opportunity to move beyond the conflict into a place where the conflict itself seems to have no currency.

Ritual's liminal or transformative space allows new ideas and relationships to form. Ritual forces recognition of two competing realities. In the midst of everyday social structures and values that define and limit human relationships, idealized ritual space allows new values and relationships to form.

Ritual space alters the surroundings, bringing important symbols or creating a sense of beauty in a context that will announce the unique relationships about to take place. For people in conflict, ritual space is a "jumping ahead to the end of the book" experience in which they can imagine living in a peaceful future.

The First Nation's smudging ceremony described in the introduction to this chapter creates an idealized world in which humans respect each other and are connected with their Creator. Native people use the powerful smell of burning herbs, the shape of a circle, the symbols of bowls and eagle feathers, and prayers to the Creator to help separate the smudging circle from the often oppressive non-Native world around them. The smudging circle becomes a free space where people find peace within themselves and in their relationships with others. The smudging ceremony frames the space where people gather. The burning herbs drench every part of the circle in the same smell. Smudging connects people to each other by its circular form that allows everyone to be equal and see each other clearly. In addition to raising awareness of the physical and social context, smudging unearths explicit values and religious beliefs that engage each participant in the symbolic meaning of participating in the gathering. The smoke takes prayers to the Creator and purifies the participants in preparation for their interactions.

The smudging ceremony preempts conflict by creating a sacred space where people are reminded of their relationships, and people have intentionally washed their eyes, ears, mouth, mind, and heart of any bad intentions. The smudging ceremony provides a powerful statement of "we want to get along with each other."

Examples from feminist groups and the Cypriot peacebuilding workshop show how ritual space can be created in secular, informal, and improvised ways.

Patriarchy-Free Zones

Many women view their everyday life as full of conflict. Feminists identify billboards and television commercials that exploit women's bodies to sell products as attacks on their identity. Their sense of living in conflict with their society is bolstered by seeing that men overwhelmingly dominate politics, business, higher education, and many other sectors of society. Like Native people, many women feel that everyday life assaults their very sense of humanity. In the midst of patriarchal societies, women's ritual is a patriarchy-free zone for experiencing gender equality and empowerment.

Women's groups use a variety of ways to help create a space that feels separate from the outside world. Women often bring candles and scarves to transform someone's living room into a place for women's empowerment. Some women use the term "casting a circle" to signify the creation of a ritual space. Sometimes casting the circle is a formal ritual in and of itself. Women may verbally declare a ritual space, create a physical mark of a circle on the ground, or simply sit in the form of a circle that envelops the ritual space.

The efforts to physically mark ritual space enable women to psycho-logically experience a place free from patriarchy. Feminist ritual scholar Starhawk notes, "Ritual can become a free space, a hole torn in the fabric of domination."[14] In feminist ritual, women find a place to value the stories, experiences, and changes in their lives. To do this, women need to feel empowered to go against everyday social structure. "In ritual, we create a symbolic space of protection and safety, in which we break the Censor's dominion and express freely whatever comes."[15]

Ritual becomes a place for women's empowerment, a place where women create "a 'little universe' within which women try out what they want the macrocosm, the 'big universe,' or the real world to be."[16] Creating a women-oriented environment allows women to share stories and break the solitude of living in a world where their voices are often not heard. One interviewee noted that her women's group provided "an opportunity to share things that I didn't think I'd ever share with anybody. It was such a safe environment. It gave me confidence to be more open."

Diann Neu claims women join groups to empower themselves, voice their concerns, heal from violence, and reconnect their psychological/social/spiritual selves.[17] Neu argues that feminist rituals "provide a collective place where women's ways of knowing—thinking, feeling, reacting and living—become normative."[18]

Camp Space

The workshop for Greek and Turkish Cypriot youth became a ritual space by virtue of the neutral camp space where the workshop was held, and by the unique activities performed by two groups of people who usually do not interact. The Cypriot youth camp acted out an imaginary peaceful conclusion to the conflict in the ritual spaces of a remote camp. It brought together the children of parents who had fought each other in a place where they could play, sing, and live together for two weeks.

At the rural camp in Pennsylvania, four cabins nestled into a wooded area provided shelter for the forty Cypriot youth. Cabins were divided into groups of the same sex and mixed ethnicity. The cabins were very rustic. Bare wood frames displayed hundreds of spider webs. There were two toilet stalls and two showers in each cabin. Participants ate their meals in a separate dining hall with cement floors and old wooden tables and chairs.

"Camp" holds a number of symbolic meanings. It is an outdoor place for recreation, fun, and relaxation. People go to camp to enjoy themselves with friends. Camp is a liminal space, set aside from the rest of society and the world. Camps are usually found in remote, natural places. People expect to be changed at camp. Outdoor survival camps offer people an opportunity to learn how to survive on their own, to become self-sufficient animals in an ecological world. Religious camps create opportunities for people to be spiritually renewed and transformed. Sports camps are training grounds for athletes to improve their skills.

The idea of a conflict resolution camp for Greek and Turkish Cypriot youth builds on these symbolic meanings. In her letter to the parents of the Cypriot teenagers selected to come to the camp, project director Louise Diamond described the types of activities planned for the youth. Diamond creates the setting or the frame for understanding and giving meaning to what camp will mean to the youth who participate.

> The program will combine training in the skills of conflict resolution (mornings) with traditional summer camp activities (afternoons and evenings). These activities include sports (tennis, soccer, volleyball, swimming, boating, hiking, martial arts and rocketry); crafts (tie-dyeing, jewelry making, wood working and silk painting), and arts (music, drama, dance and photography). In the evenings, there will be campfires, cookouts, a talent show, folk dancing, cross-cultural sharing with the teenage camp located nearby, a carnival night, a fireworks celebration on American Independence Day, a skit night, and other such events.[19]

Diamond set the expectation for a fun and friendly experience. The trainers and staff also set this tone, and it continued throughout the two weeks. The camp space symbolically spoke a message of normality. Enemies do not usually go to camp together. The gathering of a group of youths from a divided island with a history of violence and hatred was unusual. However, the context read "relaxation," not stress. There was considerable tension at some points during the two-week experience, particularly during the first few days. However, the daily creation of spaces for social and recreational activities delivered a symbolic message that said, "We are friends here, we can trust each other, we can work together."

Many campers reported in their evaluations that simple things such as sleeping in the cabins and the joint camp cleaning time had a significant impact in building bicommunal relationships.[20] One young camper stated, "The nights at the cabin were very wonderful, because all people in the room shared their problems, secrets, and other things. I think this is the cause of close friendship. . . ." Others noted that sleeping in the cabins "helped us to feel that we are a family" and claimed that "our trust in each other was mostly built in the cabins." Some noted that this familial experience was thrilling. "It is a great experience to share the same cabin, the showers, the toilets . . . we passed wonderful time together." Others felt the experience was more of a challenge. "We had to share many things in order to survive!" Another wrote that she had "learned to share two toilets with ten people . . . in one room where we share everything and sleep with spiders. . . ." One camper felt that the structure of the camp, sleeping in the cabins, and the daily cleaning time when the whole camp worked together to clean the cabins and the dining hall was "the most important experience" because the group was "doing something together." It appeared as if the routines of everyday life took on new meaning. Regular activities—sleeping and cleaning—took on the characteristics of ritual. Sleeping and cleaning together occurred in a unique social space, created by the presence of two adversaries living and working together in a remote woods. The campers interacted with each other in progressively closer ways throughout the two weeks. There was more talking and laughing each night in the cabin. At the end of the two weeks, there was generally less tension between the two ethnic groups than when they had first arrived.

Oasis for Peace

Ritual removes people in conflict from the site of their problematic relationships. It takes people out of everyday social structures that often fuel the flames of conflict. Just as an oasis is welcome relief to a desert traveler, ritual can provide refreshing relief from the pain and anxiety of conflict. Peacebuilders who bring people in conflict together are glorified hosts and hostesses, leading people out of the desert of conflict toward an oasis of peace. Hospitality is high on the peacebuilding agenda.

In my experience the process of mediation is a ritual in the sense that mediation provides a special, safe space for addressing conflict with a ritualized, patterned process. Mediation takes place outside of normal, everyday social rules. In the mediation room, new behaviors and attitudes are encouraged. Mediation allows discussion between parties in conflict outside of everyday pressures and sometimes outside the fear of punishment.[21] The starkness of the mediation room, the equal seating positions around a round table and the absence of symbolic references to power allow mediation to function as a ritual. A number of authors detail the role of symbol and ritual in the mediation process.[22] Although the structured process of mediation already contains some elements that make it ritual-like, this chapter poses a challenge to all peacebuilders to search for more significant ways to create a ritual space for mediation.

It also compels those working in trauma healing, development, education, nonviolent activism, restorative justice, and other approaches to peacebuilding to consider how they create a ritual space for their work. Peacebuilders should ask themselves a series of questions as they prepare to work with people in conflict, whether they are in a familiar or unfamiliar cultural context.

1. What kinds of space will help people set apart their meeting space from everyday life where the conflict is experienced?

2. How will timing of the meeting, the size and shape of rooms, the geographic location, symbolic objects, smells, tastes, sounds, and combinations of people shape the kinds of discussions or activities that will occur?

3. What is the best way to set the stage for good communication and construct a context conducive to emphasizing peaceful values of shared humanity among the participants?

People from within the cultural context must be involved in answering each of these questions, but it is the peacebuilder's responsibility to ask the questions and to be aware of his or her role as set director.

Notes

1. I deeply appreciate the guidance of the Native people involved in this project. Proceeds from the sale of this book will be divided equally among the groups that helped me conduct the research. I hope that I have captured some of the meanings and functions that the smudging ceremony plays in their lives. I also hope more universities will provide scholarships and encouragement to Native scholars to continue writing about their own cultures.

2. Gregory Bateson, *Steps to an Ecology of Mind* (New York: Ballantine Books, 1972), 402.

3. Humberto Maturana and Francisco J. Varela, *Autopoiesis and Cognition: The Realization of the Living* (Dordrecht, Holland: D. Reidel Publishing Company, 1980).

4. Erving Goffman, *Frame Analysis: An Essay on the Organization of Experience* (New York: Harper & Row, 1974).

5. Elaine Yarbrough and William Wilmot, *Artful Mediation: Constructive Conflict at Work* (Boulder, Colo.: Cairns Publishing, 1995), 113.

6. Victor Turner, *The Anthropology of Performance* (New York: PAJ Publishers, 1988), 34.

7. *Joseph Campbell: The Power of Myth with Bill Moyers*, ed. Betty Sue Flowers (New York: Doubleday, 1988), 92.

8. Carleen Elliot, interview by the author, February 22, 1995, Toronto, ON.

9. Mike McTague, interview by the author, February 28, 1995, Toronto, ON.

10. Catherine Bateson, "Ordinary Creativity," in *Social Creativity* (Cresskill, N.J.: Hampton Press, 1999).

11. Vamik Volkan, *Blood Lines: From Ethnic Pride to Ethnic Terrorism* (Boulder, Colo.: Westview Press, 1997).

12. Van Gennep, *The Rites of Passage* (Chicago: University of Chicago Press, 1960).

13. Bateson, "Ordinary Creativity."

14. Starhawk, *Truth or Dare: Encounters with Power, Authority, and Mystery* (San Francisco: Harper & Row, 1987), 98.

15. Starhawk, *Truth or Dare*, 99.

16. Diane Stein, "Introduction," in *The Goddess Celebrates: An Anthology of Women's Rituals*, ed. Diane Stein (Freedom, Calif.: The Crossing Press, 1991), 2.

17. Diann L. Neu, "Women's Empowerment through Feminist Ritual," *Women and Therapy* 16, no. 2/3 (1995): 186.

18. Neu, "Women's Empowerment through Feminist Ritual," 191.

19. Excerpted from Cyprus Consortium letter, written by Louise Diamond, to parents of the Greek and Turkish Cypriot youth who attended the workshop.

20. All of the following quotes are taken from the anonymous final evaluations of the Greek and Turkish Cypriot participants.

21. Court-based mediation programs do not allow discussions or information revealed in the mediation to be used in a court trial.

22. Jennifer Fisher, "Symbol in Mediation," *Mediation Quarterly* 18, no. 1 (Fall 2000): 87–107.

CHAPTER **6**

Peacebuilding Pantomime: Negotiating without Words

Just outside of Washington, DC, an organization called the Women's Alliance for Theology, Ethics, and Ritual (WATER) seeks to rekindle and fulfill the human desire for meaningful ritual in a world where many women and men feel disenfranchised from traditional religious ritual. As part of my research on ritual, I wanted to learn how groups go about developing new rituals. At my request to learn about her work, Director Diann Neu invited me to help her plan a women's ritual for Father's Day for the WATER community. We worked together to design an evening for a group of women to share with each other about their relationships with their fathers. Recognizing the wide variety of father-daughter relationships, we developed symbols to represent and hold together the multiplicity of these important, yet often ambiguous and conflictual relationships.

The ritual space was created by a circle of chairs around a central altar, which included a bowl of salt water and watermelon pieces surrounded by a wreath of colorful scarves. The ritual began with a lineage naming, an opportunity for women to name and tell stories of their male ancestors. After several songs and readings, women took a scarf from the middle of the circle and made a knot in it while talking about how they have experienced living in a patriarchal culture. The knots represented the frustration, shame, lack of self-esteem, sexual abuse, and violence that so many women have experienced in their interactions with their fathers. Next, the women dipped watermelon in salt water as they shared "sweet" times with their fathers. The salt water represented the tears and pain, while the watermelon stood for the happy times and good interactions women have had with their fathers. We designed this ritual to be meaningful to women who had both good and bad relationships with their male ancestors and to represent the ambiguity so many women feel about these important relationships.

The Logic of Words

In workshops, when I tell the story of the salt water–dipped watermelon, I usually get a variety of perplexed or embarrassed responses. Western rationalists emphasize the abilities of the human brain for logical problem solving while dismissing any useful cognitive role for the human body and its senses. Western models favor referential forms of communication in which people use words rather than symbols to communicate directly about an object, feeling, or activity. The field of conflict studies is a prime example. Communication techniques for managing conflict encourage people to speak clearly and directly about conflict. Many scholars over-value the "logic of words."

Communication researchers estimate that between sixty and ninety percent of communicated meaning comes from nonverbal cues.[1] Given the research on the value of nonverbal communication, why do Westerners favor a mode of communication that only gives ten to forty percent of the meaning of a message? Why not become equally savvy on how to communicate nonverbally? Words are limiting. When humans feel strong emotions, it is often difficult to express the depth of feeling verbally. When life's events are confusing, complex, and ambiguous, it is challenging to articulate events and relationships through verbal language.

Ritual is primarily a form of nonverbal communication. Some ritual theorists suggest that ritual action is to rational thought as the body is to the mind. Bell describes the history of this errant dichotomy in *Ritual Theory, Ritual Practice*. She proposes that dichotomies such as "thought and action" were the instigators of the idea of ritual as action. However, as theorists continued, they endowed ritual with the properties of thought as well, leaving the paradox of ritual as both thought and action. Bell is critical of ritual theorists who do not acknowledge this paradox by first citing ritual as action and then proceeding to show how ritual bridges thought and action.[2]

Using a systems perspective, this dilemma becomes moot. Rituals are not anti-intellectual or antirational. In ritual, people gather information using all the body's senses and communicate both verbally and nonverbally. Ritual actions are not to be dichotomized with thought. Ritual is simply a different form of thought, a different form of communication.

Ritual can be a powerful tool for communicating about conflict. Conflict is often a highly emotional, difficult to articulate, complex, and ambiguous experience. As opposed to the stark formality of many negotiating rooms, where talking heads banish emotions and only the most basic senses are employed, peacebuilding rituals allow people to eat, drink, smell, dance, laugh, cry, and express the full range of human activity as they communicate their humanity, learn to rehumanize their adversary, and develop new and creative ways of understanding their conflict. While communicating with words is an essential element in effective peacebuilding, ritual's ability to communicate without words in a "peacebuilding pantomime" is also necessary.

Ritual communication is unique in three ways: it can be interpreted in multiple ways, it is delivered through the body and its senses, and it relies on feeling and emotion to interpret the significance of a message. This chapter gives words to ritual's nonverbal gifts. Examples from the three case studies demonstrate how ritual communicates.

The Role of Symbols in the Process of Cognition

On any given day, an individual will experience thousands of ideas, people, and objects. As discussed in chapter 3, the human mind seeks to make sense of this multitude of interactions by categorizing and creating systems of meaning according to the patterns that are evident to the individual.

Symbols assist humans in creating, coding, and decoding their meaning systems. Early theorists such as Charles Peirce and Kenneth Burke established the role of symbols as significant elements in the meaning-making process.[3,4] Individuals perceive and understand their environment through symbols that attach meaning to experiences. Symbols are basic to thought: humans transform all of their experiences in the physical world into symbols. Through what Susanne Langer calls the "symbolic transformation of experience," the mind processes information and creates symbolic forms to capture experiential information that is stored for later "recognition" of another environment.[5]

Kertzer and others claim that symbolic forms act in three ways: through condensation, multivocality, and ambiguity.[6] Symbols condense information about the world into a single unified form. For example, the American flag is one object, yet the stars and stripes and colors on the flag are symbolic in that they convey a great deal of information to those who know what the symbols mean. Multivocality refers to symbols' ability to communicate different meanings to different people. The American flag is a symbol to people around the world for the government and goals of the United States. Yet this symbol can be interpreted in different ways, as a symbol of either freedom or tyranny, depending on the worldview of the observer.

Symbols are ambiguous precisely because they allow for multiple interpretations. Clifford Geertz claims symbols "account for, and even celebrate, the perceived ambiguities, puzzles, and paradoxes in human experience."[7] For example, the American flag can be seen as a symbol of freedom and democracy to one person and a symbol of the responsibility to defend the United States to another person. While the flag in this case has two different, although related, sets of meanings, both individuals can use the flag and see it as a positive symbol of the United States even though they may disagree about its meaning.

As discussed in the previous chapter, any object, person, idea, word, place, or action is understood symbolically through its relationships or connection with other things. When asked to list words associated with the word "land," one person might list resource, wood, or paper products. A second person might list mother earth, sacred, or ancestral. While scientific researchers may attempt to look simply at one set of quantitative properties of the land (i.e., how many and what type of plants and trees are on the land), a worldview theorist may look at how ideas about land are symbolically constructed.[8]

Symbols hold together paradoxes by representing one set of meanings for one person and a different set of meanings for another. Their ambiguity makes them flexible enough to adapt to many different worldviews. Ritual's symbols speak in ways that allow participants to understand them differently. In fact, Humphrey and Laidlaw claim, "A custom does not become 'a ritual' until people can disagree about its meaning. . . ."[9] Durkheim claimed ritual permits people to join in some symbolic activity even though this same group of people might fundamentally disagree with each other over why and how their activity is meaningful.[10] As such, he claimed it was ritual's symbolic nature that allowed individuals to come together, delicately dance around their differences, and participate in an action that was meaningful to all. Using ritual in situations of conflict becomes an obvious strategy to help people who are different come together in a shared experience that allows them both to be together and to find different meanings in the symbols of the ritual.

Moreover, ritual has the potential to communicate in culturally pluralistic communities in which differing worldviews or cultural values and beliefs may contribute to conflict. Theater scholar Richard Schechner claims ritual and theater are particularly effective means of communicating across cultures.

> . . . [W]hen one group wants to communicate to another across various boundaries (linguistic, political, cultural, and geographical) the main initial signal is an exchange of performances, a mutual display of rituals. There is something about dance, music, theatre and ritual that needs no translating—even as there is very much that is so culturally specific that it takes a lifetime of study to understand the performances of a culture not one's own.[11]

Schechner claims that governments use extensive political rituals because they can be easily understood and recognized across cultures. He also argues that rituals arise exactly when these delicate "conflict dances" are most needed.

In both animals and humans, rituals arise or are devised around disruptive, turbulent, and ambivalent interactions where faulty communication can lead to violent or even fatal encounters . . . 'You get the message, don't you!?!' says that what a ritual communicates is very important yet problematic. The interactions that rituals surround, contain, and mediate almost always concern hierarchy, territory, and sexuality/mating. . . . If these interactions are the 'real events' rituals enfold, then what are the rituals themselves? They are ambivalent symbolic actions pointing at the real transactions even as they help people avoid too direct a confrontation with these events.[12]

Ritual offers peacebuilders an opportunity to address conflict in ways that are less confrontational, frightening, and threatening. Ritual is a dance around or through conflict.

Sensing and Feeling the World

Messages are communicated in ritual by the form and structure of the ritual process, the symbols included in the ritual, the form the human body takes in each particular ritual, and information that is recognized by the body's senses. Chapter 3 detailed how senses and emotions help people understand and give meaning to the world. Ritual is a powerful form of communication precisely because it involves people's bodies, senses, and emotions. Ritual communicates through smells such as burning incense, body postures such as kneeling, noises such as bells or music, tastes such as the wine and bread of communion, and facial expressions that reference emotions. The medium of ritual *is* the message in the fullest sense of Marshall McLuhan's influential concept.[13]

In ritual, humans learn from and about our emotional responses to an experience as well. "Ritual controls emotion while releasing it, and guides it while letting it run."[14] The ritual of a funeral can allow people to express emotion jointly in a symbolic, transforming space. Ritual helps people find ways of expressing what they feel together with other people.

Theologian Theodore Jennings coined the term ritual knowledge to explain what humans learn and communicate through ritual. Ritual knowledge comes through the use of symbols, senses such as seeing, hearing, smelling, and tasting, and the bodily expression of emotions, such as crying, anger, and joy. Jennings notes, "Ritual knowledge is gained by and through the body . . . not by detached observation or contemplation but through action."[15] In his article "On Ritual Knowledge," he claims the body undergoes changes during ritual:

It is not so much that the mind 'embodies' itself in ritual action, but rather that the body 'minds' itself or attends through itself in ritual action.

> . . . It is in and through the action that ritual knowledge is gained, not in advance of it, nor after it. . . . Ritual knowledge is gained not through detachment but through engagement—an engagement that does not leave things as they are but which alters and transforms them.[16]

All learning can be transformative. Learning that takes place in ritual is especially transformative, and is described in more detail in later chapters. The point Jennings makes here is that there are some topics, some issues, some feelings, for example, that can be learned and expressed only through ritual. People go to ritual or create ritual for themselves when they need to express something physically or emotionally.

People may be especially attracted to ritual when no other path for addressing an issue or feeling exists. In *Peripheral Visions: Learning Along the Way*, Mary Catherine Bateson explores the way humans learn through doing. She notes, "Living and learning are everywhere founded on an improvisational base. . . . [People] make do with partial understandings, invent themselves as they go along, and combine in complex undertakings without full agreement about what they are doing."[17]

Humans act to learn how to act. Actions in ritual become a way of trying out new behaviors to use outside of ritual. A formal handshake between enemies at a peace accord ceremony is a way of improvising a new relationship in which friendly touching is allowed. There may be no other way of expressing the new relationship.

Ritual knowledge communicates both outwardly and inwardly. Catholic worshippers who kneel by a pew communicate submission and reverence to both their God and themselves. The message is not simply sent outward toward a watching God. The prayer is also sent inward, a message to oneself describing the quality of the relationship a person has to God.

People use ritual to convince themselves of something not fully known. In ritual's liminal space, people can try out new behaviors and new ideas.

> Human beings are by nature actors, who cannot become something until first they have pretended to be it. They are therefore to be divided, not into the hypocritical and the sincere, but into the sane, who know they are acting, and the mad who do not.[18]

Through ritual, humans try out new ways of being. Humans act their way into new behavior. When white and black leaders in the city of Richmond, Virginia, stayed in a retreat center for a weekend dialogue on race, economics, and politics, they shared meals and rooms together in a symbolic space. Leaders interacted in a way that was different than their normal, mostly segregated lives. Engaging in honest conversations on race while practicing a new way of being together created a new path forward.

Similarly, when African-Americans began to sit at the counters of restaurants that only served white people, their actions paved a way forward.

Lunch-counter sit-ins during the civil rights movement were symbolic acts that silently communicated to people both Black and White that African-Americans had the right to be treated equally, that segregation was not a permanent structure, and that people could in fact shape the future of their lives together.

Speaking as Doing

Words spoken during ritual also work in this way. The idea that doing or saying something *as if* it were true can actually make it true has been explored by a number of authors, most notably J. L. Austin and Roy Rappaport. Austin writes that sometimes to say something is to do something. These "performatives" or "ritual phrases" are carried out in rituals. What makes them true is not simply the saying of the words or the performing of an act. Truth is tied to context.[19] In the ritual context of a Catholic Mass, participants believe in the transformation of bread and wine to the body and blood of Christ. The priest announces the ritual change of the symbolic objects, and the receivers are assured that the transformation has indeed occurred. Performatives are words or acts that are made true by their contexts. The space where a ritual takes place sends a symbolic message about the authenticity or appropriateness of what happens within the context. To be considered true and meaningful, the words or acts have to be said in a ritual context that transforms them.

Rappaport argues that explicit and formal rituals communicate more effectively because some people associate authenticity with the more formal structures and spaces of these types of rituals. "The formal characteristics of ritual enhance the chances of success of the performatives they include."[20] Where participation in a ritual is by choice, formally performing a ritual act is a sign that what the ritual participant is communicating is both accepted and believed by the participant.

Moore and Myerhoff note that the formality of ritual is especially effective in communicating messages where there is doubt.

> Since ritual is a good form for conveying a message as if it were unquestionable, it often is used to communicate those very things that are most in doubt. Thus where there is conflict, or danger, or political opposition, where there is made-upness and cultural invention, ritual may carry the opposite message in form as well as in content.[21]

While some may be skeptical that bread and wine are actually transformed into Christ's blood and body in the Catholic Mass, the formality of the context and the serious nature with which the priest announces the transformation may assure any doubters of the ritual reality. Announcing a peace settlement reflects the same dilemma. While the peace may be tenuous, it must be announced in a confident and formal way if it is to have any chance of success. Soon after the 2003 US war on Iraq began, President George W. Bush declared the war a success with a banner overhead that stated MISSION ACCOMPLISHED! At the time, this performative speech act convinced a large number of Americans. Over time, however, these statements were questioned and ridiculed. In this case, while the declaration of peace was temporarily successful, in the end, it was hard to deny that the war did not bring about a quick establishment of peace and democracy in Iraq.

Words used in ritual are a powerful means of creating a new reality, even news of a cure. In *Brain, Symbol & Experience* authors d'Aquili, Laughlin, and McManus note that ritual can be so potent and rich in its symbolism that some cultures use symbolic means such as ritual as healing agents that can "penetrate disorder and affect a cure."[22] The symbols in a healing ritual mark a reflexive form of communication. A shaman or a preacher may pronounce someone healed, and the message itself appears to heal. The use of symbols to penetrate the human mind and its worldview seems essential to the magic of performatives.

The paradox that rituals can and often are used to proclaim a message that is in fact questionable, if not untrue, may be part of the reason why some people have lost interest in ritual in Westernized countries. If ritual is seen as communicating something false, something that is made up, then ritual is for the foolish who want to believe in something that is not true or real. The idea that people make things true by acting as if they were true is essential to understanding ritual communication. In ritual, the impossible and unlikely can come true as people create a unique context where, if only temporarily, symbols, sensory cues, and the expression of emotion communicate what words alone cannot.

Ritual's wordless capacity to communicate has remarkable implications for peacebuilders. If individuals learn by doing, peacebuilding should begin with, or at least include, ritual action rather than rational discussion. Peacebuilding rituals may begin by enacting the desired transformed state of coexistence. It may be helpful for individuals in conflict to enact physically what they cannot consciously acknowledge at first. A handshake, sitting down to a meal together, or sharing a cigarette outside the formal negotiating room might physically symbolize a transformation of a conflict that may not be able to occur on a purely intellectual level. Several examples from my experiences with ritual illustrate this point.

Breathing Smoke

The smudging ceremony is an example of symbolic communication. Communication occurs both verbally and nonverbally in the smudging ceremony. The ceremony opens with a verbal prayer reminding humans of their place within the web of life and remembering the sacred relationships humans have with each other, their Creator, birds, animals, and other parts of the environment. While the leader speaks the prayer, the participants are invited to engage with a number of symbols, including the smoke from the burning herbs and the circle of people around them.

People in the smudging ceremony bring the smoke to their bodies and drench themselves in the distinct herbal odor. The smudging ceremony is a cleansing ritual. The smoke-washing invokes participants to be physically present with clean and clear intentions. An Ojibway man described his understanding of smudging this way.

> Smudging sounds like such a dirty word: but it's a purification ceremony.
> . . . We start each meeting and gathering with a smudge; [it's a] purification of your eyes, it clears your mind out, it clears your ears so you only hear good things, your mouth so you only say good things, and your heart too.[23]

Another researcher documents, "[Y]ou smudge your head to purify your thoughts, heart for spirit, mouth because that's what gets you in trouble the most."[24] People communicate their desire to connect with the Creator, open their ears to hear other people's stories, open their eyes to see other people anew, to speak with only good intentions, and to have a clean heart throughout their interactions with others. The smooth, graceful smoke-washing says more without words than any tongue could.

Words are not sufficient to communicate the lessons of the smudging ceremony. The smell of sweetgrass, sage, tobacco, and cedar serves as a pungent symbolic reminder throughout any meeting, circle, or gathering begun with the smudging ceremony. One Native person said the smudging ceremony was like "aromatherapy," where particular smells are used to invoke and create particular moods and emotions in people. The herbs continue to burn in their bowl throughout the meeting, and each participant wears a reminder of his or her smoky bath.

Emotions play a central role in the smudging ceremony as well. In the Native Elder's conference described in chapter 5, Elders told stories of accompanying community members in their struggle to walk the Native path. One Elder spoke of the importance of Native healing circles that begin with the smudge to cleanse and purify. In the healing circle, people shed tears and shared their struggles with alcohol, drugs, depression, sexual abuse, and unemployment. Crying is seen as the first step in the healing process, and the smudge provides the setting for moving toward wholeness.[25] Elders noted that crying was a way for the body to rid itself of the toxins of interacting with an oppressive world.

The smudging ceremony is authoritative. Inviting the smoke to cleanse has the effect of purifying people of their anger, frustration, or other emotions that might obstruct the gathering. Sam Gill notes that the "performative power" of Native ritual is a creative voice that establishes a new reality. As opposed to the view that associates ritual with boredom and a lack of creativity, Gill proposes that "from the Native American view, their ritual acts are creative acts of the highest order, since the object of their creation is the world itself."[26]

The power of the smudge works through the medicinal herbs that cleanse, purify, and bring focus to the participants. Inviting the smoke to enter into them and move through them seems to bring about the transformation. The smudging ceremony creates a desired world using symbols, senses, and a safe pathway for emotions. The smudging ceremony communicates a number of mostly nonverbal messages to people in conflict. The smudging ceremony is a peacebuilding pantomime.

Awakening the Slothwoman

In feminist rituals, communicating also happens through words, symbols, the use of the five senses, expression of emotion, and physical action. Women engage in acts of cleansing, burning, eating, drinking, and singing to empower themselves and address their conflict with patriarchal structures. Feminist ritual offers a unique perspective on the importance of using emotions, senses, and our physical selves when dealing with a problem. Many of the women interviewed attested to the significance of going beyond verbal communication, particularly around conflictual issues. Feminist ritual seeks to legitimize ritual ways of learning and knowing, validating the human capacity to feel, to be spiritual, and to learn in the process of acting rather than physically passive ways of thinking.

Much of the literature on women's ritual seeks to explain why involving the senses and emotional expression is important to ritual forms of communication. Writer and women's ritualist Z. Budapest vividly describes the appeal of ritual to the remaining "animal" part in modern humans.

> Imagine that inside of you there is an ancient being, I call her the Sloth-woman, the Cro-Magnon, hairy, tall, ungainly, lumbering creature, who is preverbal. . . . The key to our magic is how we can arouse her interest in our work . . . to wake up this ancient being within us. . . . In order to own our magic we must reclaim our own animal nature, because we are part of nature even though we type on computers and think of ourselves as "higher beings." This part of ourselves is older than the modern brain, it is the middle of the brain, without which we cannot survive and certainly cannot do magic. . . . You need to incorporate elements in the ritual that make her stay with you—candlelight, food on the altar, pleasant smelling incense, women humming, dancing around the altar, chanting, singing. . . .[27]

Budapest suggests that ritual, or "magic" in her words, is in essence a means to engage the human mind in ways that stimulate it emotionally and sensually. Smells, sounds, movements, candles, and other objects that are pleasing to the eye and touch arouse humans in ways that words alone cannot.

For Kay Turner, ritual's sensual nature makes it transformative. Turner claims ritual moves people because they *feel* its message physically, emotionally, and sensually.[28] When the body is engaged in giving and receiving messages, the information transmitted has a transforming effect on the receiver.

Interviews with women who have used ritual in women's spirituality groups confirm that it is precisely the lack of words and rational thought that makes ritual most attractive. One woman expressed a clear desire to move away from words and the conflicts that inevitably arise as people verbally communicate what they believe. Ritual for her is an opportunity to "be" together with people, to experience life and relationships with others emotionally and physically without demanding that each person think exactly the same way. Another woman communicated a desire to include her body and emotions in her understanding of spirituality. Another noted a desire to "move into my body instead of my head."

Examples of feminist ritual attest to the power of ritual means of communication. Ritual participants perform an action that creates the intended effect. In the Father's Day ritual, scarves used for knotting and watermelon and bowls of salt water used in the ritual were placed in the center as an altar. These symbols provided a focus to the circle and separated it from everyday time and space. Participants ate watermelon dipped in salt water. This ritual attempts to make sense of and heighten the awareness of relationships between fathers and daughters. The watermelon, salt, and water each symbolically engaged the women in a sensual relationship with memories and thoughts about their fathers. Words alone would have less meaning than the words done with an action that illustrates and carries out the message's intention. Dipping watermelon into salt water and knotting scarves serves to communicate and teach participants through physical actions and sensations such as the taste of salty water. The goal of the ritual is to reframe the ways women view their relationships with their fathers in a form that allows for ambiguity and embracing both the good and the difficult aspects. This feminist ritual illustrates the functions of symbols, senses, and emotions in communicating and dealing with a potentially conflictual relationship.

Performing a Cypriot Peace

Verbal discussions about the causes and solutions to conflict are one way of addressing the ethnic tensions between Greek and Turkish Cypriots.

Playing soccer and paddling a boat in mixed ethnic groups are other ways of communicating about the nature of humanity and conflict. While the formal parts of the Cypriot conflict resolution workshop engaged the campers' minds, the informal camp rituals provided a different way of learning and communicating through symbols, senses, and emotions. During an evening pool party where bicommunal couples held each other in a romantic slow dance, little if anything was said. The clinging bodies of teenage girls and boys attracted to each other across the lines of ethnic conflict spoke volumes about the humanity of each.

The camp activities became a way of enacting a peaceful Cypriot future. Only in this ritualized, set-aside space could a Greek and Turkish Cypriot hold each other romantically. On the island of Cyprus, there would be no place for these types of interactions. Clifford Geertz defines ritual as a place where "the world as lived and the world as imagined, fused under the agency of a single set of symbolic forms, turn out to be the same world. . . ."[29] This definition seems to appropriately describe the significance of this bicommunal camp. The world as imagined, as detailed in the hopes and goals articulated by the Greek and Turkish Cypriot youth on the first day at the camp, became a reality while they were engaging each other in physical actions that symbolically spoke of their relationship with each other. The camp rituals of eating, cleaning, sleeping, singing, and playing together actively engaged the bodies, senses, and emotions of these teenagers.

The conflict resolution training itself also involved nonverbal, physical, and symbolic activities. The trainers in the Cypriot Consortium used a "Three Step" process as the primary framework to structure the conflict resolution workshop. Each of the steps had a verbal component and a physically active component.

The first step is "Know Where You Stand." Trainers James Notter and Doug Stone described the importance of knowing where you come from and knowing who you are as essential elements in building peace. Stone told the youth, "There is a great benefit to spending time with yourself to understand your own expectations, your own desires, your own needs." Activities used to learn this first step included listing goals that each participant brought to the camp and learning about centering through Aikido techniques.

The trainers incorporated the martial art of Aikido to demonstrate the principles of conflict resolution in a physical, nonverbal way. A Japanese fighter who had a spiritual revelation that he should no longer hurt people developed the art of Aikido.[30] While most martial arts focus on neutralizing the attacker with force, Aikido seeks to neutralize the attack without hurting the attacker. The word Aikido is made up of three smaller words. "Do" means the way or the path. "Ki" means steam or energy. "Ai" means harmony or peace. Thus, Aikido means the way of harmonizing energy.[31]

Richard Moon and Carol Yamasaki, two black belt Aikido masters, were part of the Cyprus Consortium training team and guided the participants through lessons in the art of Aikido.

Aikido has many of the characteristics of ritual. It is symbolic in that it nonverbally represents the lessons of conflict resolution. It is transformative in the sense that it harmonizes energy: two people meet on a mat, approach each other, and use physical moves to redirect aggressive energy into a new joint movement. Aikido raises awareness of the physical self and creates new ways of thinking about conflict.

The first Aikido lesson corresponded with Step 1: know yourself. Participants learned the difference between being physically centered and uncentered. Centering includes putting weight on the ball of the foot and "sinking" into the ground or "being grounded." Participants shared the different sensations in their body when they were grounded as opposed to when they were ungrounded, uncentered, and unaware of their bodies. Moon described the empowering sensation of feeling centered when Yamasaki attacked him.

> When we have an understanding of our own power, when we are centered, then I am not so frightened by her, and I don't have to fight with her. I feel like I can protect myself. So I don't need to operate out of fear, and then I can start thinking about how we can do something different. How we can get together and work something out. . . . By working on my integrity, my body, mind, and spirit, my physical body, my thoughts, and my emotions, and the energy of life itself . . . there is power that makes me less frightened, makes me feel like I can take care of myself more safely. . . .[32]

Moon and Yamasaki invited each of the Greek and Turkish Cypriot youth to physically experience being centered and uncentered through a variety of physical exercises.

The second step in the three-step process is called "Meet the Other." Diamond described this stage as a time when "we'll get close enough to the other to see what life looks like to them." Basic communication skills such as active listening, paraphrasing, acknowledging, and the skill of inquiry to learn about the other were shared to help participants talk to and learn from each other. Then in small groups, participants examined intergroup perceptions.

The Aikido concept of blending energy with another person coincided with Step Two. According to Moon:

> The most important thing in Aikido is that we never oppose someone else's force. The way that it is applied in conflict resolution is that we never oppose someone else's beliefs, or someone else's ideas . . . we want to learn more about what they are thinking, we want to learn more about their energy, their spirit, and when we do that, we can get playful and move with it and it can change the situation.[33]

Aikido is a unique way of fighting that engages another person in an exchange of energy. Rather than meeting someone's anger or aggression with resistance, Aikido teaches participants to move in the same direction as the opponent's energy and to redirect it into a mutually safe ending. Moon claims by not opposing force, people are actually stronger because they do not hurt themselves. The goal, according to Moon, is to "understand the force, and redirect it and lead it to a more peaceful resolution."

One particularly effective exercise Diamond introduced was called a "Walk Through History." Greek and Turkish Cypriots worked within their own community to come up with a time line of their history. The groups were asked to write down historically significant events and a few comments and descriptions of the event. The two time lines were then lined up physically on the floor and participants walked the length of the building to silently observe the similarities and differences in the two communities' experiences on Cyprus. The participants were encouraged to be curious about what they discovered on the time line. After the walk through history, the two communities asked each other questions about what they observed. This exercise itself was a symbolic, ritualized act. The space of the dining hall was transformed into a time line. The youth walked the line through history in total silence, shocked and sometimes horrified at how the histories were so different in terms of actual events, yet so similar in terms of the perceptions of victimhood, self-defense, and justification for actions taken by their own side.

The third step, called "See What We Can Do Together," involved engaging with the other in problem solving and teamwork in some joint action. Analytical tools designed to help distinguish positions, interests, and needs in a conflict were shared with participants. In small groups, participants engaged in problem solving and brainstorming sessions to imagine ways that Greek and Turkish Cypriots could satisfy the interests and needs of the other and implement future options for the island.

The trainers created an outdoor problem-solving exercise for the group. Groups of ten were assigned to build a twenty-foot tower out of a variety of plastic pipes. In addition, the groups needed to create a mechanism that could drop an egg from the top of the tower to the ground without having it break. Building the egg tower was rated one of the most important activities during the week.

This problem-solving activity created a number of significant learning moments about teamwork, group process, and decision making. It gave the participants an opportunity to see visibly what they could do together. Several of the youth noted that building the egg tower gave them the opportunity to practice everything they had learned in the conflict resolution workshop. "It was time to use our listening skills," according to one camper. Others said building the egg tower "made us depend on each other" and increased "trust between the two communities" because they were in mixed teams and they had to work together to solve this problem. Correlating "seeing what we can do together" with Aikido, Moon noted:

> If we are at war all the time, all we do is hurt each other. We ruin each other's gardens and we don't eat very well . . . but if we learn some way to understand and support each other . . . we could grow a garden, we could make peace.

Aikido became a powerful physical way for the participants to understand the lessons and skills needed to engage each other in relationship. In practicing Aikido, participants physically learned how to engage with others in a nonadversarial manner.

This simplified framework for understanding the skills and process of conflict resolution formed a base for all the other camp activities. Other portions of the training reinforced and supported these three steps. In their final evaluations, many of the participants noted the importance of the Aikido workshops.[34] One participant noted, "It gave a reasonable explanation of the concepts in an easily understood way." Another participant stated, "It is a way to express a theory so it is more understandable." Yet another said, "We learned how to control, balance, and share our energies." The Aikido lessons were rated one of the most important activities during the camp.

Given the research presented in this chapter, it is not surprising that these Cypriot youth felt that physical activities were extremely important in building peace between their ethnic communities. The Cypriot youth learned about each other and built relationships through playing soccer, dancing, and singing together.

On the final evening of the two-week camp, the campers went through a formal graduation ceremony. At the end of the graduation ceremony for this new generation of peacebuilders, one participant asked the entire group to shout, "WE WANT PEACE." The message rang out from the bottom of their lungs, enacting the urgency and passion so many of the youth felt in their longing for a different Cyprus. The campers cheered and hooted at the end, applauding themselves and perhaps even the universe for the accomplishment of calling peace into being. The campers *performed peace* at that moment. They engaged in a symbolic action that created a world.

Negotiating without Words

The formality of many negotiating rooms favors a "talking heads" approach to conflict that banishes emotions and employs only the most basic senses. In contrast, peacebuilding rituals allow people to eat, drink, smell, dance, laugh, cry, and express the full range of human activity as they communicate their humanity, learn to rehumanize their adversary, and develop new and creative ways of understanding their conflict. Involving people's bodies, senses, and emotions is integral. Peacebuilding is an educational process. It requires people to learn new ways of seeing the world. For centuries, people have used ritual communication when words alone were not sufficient. Peacebuilding needs to include pedagogies that engage people through multiple ways of learning and knowing.

Ritual has the potential to communicate in culturally pluralistic communities where differing worldviews or group cultural values and beliefs may contribute to conflict. To communicate through ritual, especially across cultural divides, the creation of ritual must include symbols that provide meaning to many people. Some rituals reflect basic symbols of humanity. Food is eaten in social groups to provide both sustenance and community. Dancing allows individual expression and encourages a sense of the collective. Soccer, dancing, and singing, for example, highlighted the common cultural interests of both Greek and Turkish Cypriot youth during the workshop.

Symbols allow humans to communicate about situations that defy verbal descriptions. Symbol's multiple meanings hold together competing definitions and perceptions, as in the women's ritual for their relationships to their fathers. The ambiguity of many conflictual situations may benefit from finding symbols to use in myths, metaphors, and rituals that make room for clashing viewpoints.

If individuals learn by doing, peacebuilding may begin by enacting the desired transformed state of coexistence. It may be helpful for individuals in conflict to enact physically what they cannot consciously acknowledge at first. The smudging ceremony acts out a desire to have respectful relationships with others in the circle. Feminist ritual acts out a world in which women are empowered and respected. The informal rituals in the Cypriot youth camp acted out the ways Greek and Turkish Cypriots might be able to live in the future.

Conflict stirs an emotional response. Anger, sadness, guilt, frustration, pain, and anxiety naturally accompany and indicate conflict. Ritual can create a safe pathway for the expression of emotions in a place where they are accepted, channeled, and valued as an important part of human experience. In the smudging ceremony, tears are encouraged as a means for cleansing. Women described the safe expression of joy, anger, and sadness in feminist rituals. Peacebuilders may be able to use ritual as a way of channeling emotions and using them to help people identify what is important to them, as opposed to the common tendency among peacebuilders to suppress the emotions of people in conflict.

This chapter poses challenges to all peacebuilders to create nonverbal ways to communicate.

1. What symbolic actions can be used with a group to help them embrace their commonality?
2. What symbolic actions will help communicate the ambiguity and confusion of conflict?
3. How will peacebuilding processes engage people's sense of smell, taste, sight, and touch?
4. How can symbolic acts make room for the safe expression of emotion in peacebuilding processes?
5. Can performative statements or actions be used to effectively create a desired reality?

Again, these questions must be answered from within a cultural context. Lighting candles and incense may be sacred in one context and inappropriate in another. These generic questions have no absolute answers. People in conflict, when given the opportunity and space, can and will develop symbolic actions for rituals that make sense for their cultures.

Notes

1. Julia Wood, *Spinning the Symbolic Web: Human Communication as Symbolic Interaction* (Norwood, N.J.: Ablex Publishing Corporation, 1992).

2. Catherine M. Bell, *Ritual Theory, Ritual Practice* (New York: Oxford University Press, 1992).

3. Charles Peirce, *The Philosophy of Peirce: Selected Writings.* Edited by J. Buchler (New York: AMS Press, 1978).

4. Kenneth Burke, "The Symbol as Formative," in *Kenneth Burke: On Symbols and Society*, ed. Joseph R. Gusfield (Chicago: University of Chicago Press, 1989), 107–13.

5. Susanne Langer, *Philosophy in a New Key: A Study in the Symbolism of Reason, Rite, and Art* (New York: Penguin Books, 1948).

6. David I. Kertzer, *Ritual, Politics, and Power* (New Haven: Yale University Press, 1988).

7. Clifford Geertz, *The Interpretation of Cultures: Selected Essays* (New York: Basic Books, 1973).

8. Frank Blechman, Jarle Crocker, Jayne Docherty, and Steve Garon, "Finding Meaning in a Complex Environment Policy Dispute: Research Into Worldviews in the Northern Forest Lands Council Dialogue 1990–1994," George Mason University Working Paper Series (no. 14) (Fairfax, Va.: Institute for Conflict Analysis and Resolution, 2000).

9. Caroline Humphrey and James Laidlaw, *The Archetypal Actions of Ritual: A Theory of Ritual* (Oxford: Clarendon Press, 1994).

10. Emile Durkheim, *The Elementary Forms of the Religious Life* (Glencoe, Ill.: Free Press, 1915).

11. Richard Schechner, *The Future of Ritual: Writings on Culture and Performance* (New York: Routledge, 1993).

12. Schechner, *The Future of Ritual.*

13. Marshall McLuhan, *Understanding Media* (Cambridge, Mass.: MIT Press, 1994).

14. Tom Faw Driver, *The Magic of Ritual: Our Need for Liberating Rites That Transform Our Lives and Our Communities* (San Francisco: Harper San Francisco, 1991).

15. Theodore W. Jennings, Jr., "On Ritual Knowledge," in *Readings in Ritual Studies*, ed. Ronald L. Grimes (Upper Saddle River, N.J.: Prentice Hall, 1996), 324–34.

16. Jennings, "On Ritual Knowledge."

17. Mary Catherine Bateson, *Peripheral Visions: Learning Along the Way* (New York: HarperCollins, 1994).

18. Driver, *The Magic of Ritual.*

19. J. L. Austin, *How To Do Things With Words* (Cambridge, Mass.: Harvard University Press, 1962).

20. Roy A. Rappaport, *Ecology, Meaning, and Ritual* (Richmond, Calif.: North Atlantic Books, 1979).

21. Sally F. Moore and Barbara Myerhoff, "Introduction: Secular Ritual: Forms and Meanings," in *Secular Ritual*, ed. Sally F. Moore and Barbara Myerhoff (Amsterdam: Van Gorcum, 1977), 3–24.

22. Charles D. Laughlin, John McManus, and Eugene G. d'Aquili, *Brain, Symbol & Experience: Toward a Neurophenomenology of Human Consciousness* (Boston: Shambhala Publications, 1990).

23. Interview, February 9, 1995. Toronto, ON.

24. Lorne Todd Holyoak, "The Good Red Road: Relations between Native Elders and Non-Native Seekers," (unpublished Ph.D. diss., University of Calgary, 1993).

25. Interview by author, February 16, 1995, Toronto, ON.

26. Sam Gill, "It's Where You Put Your Eyes," in *I Become Part of It: Sacred Dimensions in Native American Life*, ed. D. M. Dooling and Paul Jordan-Smith (New York: HarperCollins, 1989).

27. Z. Budapest, "Teaching Women's Spirituality Rituals," in *The Goddess Celebrates: An Anthology of Women's Rituals*, ed. Diane Stein (Freedom, Calif.: The Crossing Press, 1991).

28. Kay Turner, "Contemporary Feminist Rituals," in *The Politics of Women's Spirituality*, ed. Charlene Spretnak (Toronto: Doubleday, 1982).

29. Geertz, *The Interpretation of Cultures.*

30. Thomas Crum, *The Magic of Conflict* (New York: Simon and Schuster, 1987).

31. Crum, *The Magic of Conflict.*

32. Richard Moon, Interview by author, July 27, 1997, Maryland.

33. Moon, July 27.

34. All of the following quotes are taken from the anonymous final evaluations of Greek and Turkish Cypriot participants.

CHAPTER 7

Forming and
Transforming Worldviews

A group of university students planned a feminist ritual to mark Women's History Month. The students first showed an audience of men and women a film that described how women are portrayed in music videos. The film used clips of music videos that showed a destructive and one-dimensional type of female sexuality: women sexually available to all men at any time and women fighting other women for the privilege of being with men. Mostly naked women writhed with painful eroticism, degrading themselves in front of men, and begging for male sexual attention. The film was painful and disturbing to watch.

The ritual began as the audience changed into ritual participants. The organizers stated that the activity was planned "so that hopefully you can leave with some closure on the experience." In an interview after the ritual, one of the organizers told me they were afraid people would leave depressed and overwhelmed if they just watched the film. The ritual was designed to empower people to move to action on the issues of conflict and justice raised in the film.

As the ritual began, the facilitators explained the three parts of the ritual activity. They encouraged people to first write down their emotional responses to the video, then to burn the papers with their responses and announce how they wanted to transform those negative feelings, and finally people washed their hands and drank water as a way of symbolizing that they were purified of the film's damaging images. A transcript of the three parts of the ritual follows (organizers' directions in italics and my commentary as a participant observer in regular print).

This first part is called Naming and we're going to transform this space into a place for naming the sickness, the disease, the hurt, whatever else this caused you to feel as men and women. So take a few minutes to think about it and write it down.

Here the ritual facilitators set the tone for the ritual and announced the ritual space. About forty people each took a piece of paper and wrote down their negative thoughts and reactions. After a few minutes, the facilitators invited the participants to go outside, where a fire burned in a trash can in a small garden. Again, the facilitators had created a separate, secluded space for the ritual.

> This is a space for ridding ourselves of these negative thoughts and images. This is also a place for transforming. Fire has a lot of transformative properties. We want to take whatever those negative things are and put them in the fire and we want to transform it into something that is positive, something that we can grow from. So we invite you to do that now. If you feel comfortable and if you feel so led, you can speak those out loud, but if you want to do that in silence, that is fine also.

People in the circle brought their papers to the fire. Most participants did so silently. About ten people spoke their message aloud. Messages people read included:

> "One of the messages I've internalized from this culture's image of me as a woman is that femininity means being forever a hopeless victim and I want to transform that into a femininity of power, wisdom, and strength."
>
> "I want to rid myself of the belief that I personally am not big enough to change it."
>
> "I want to burn the idea that beauty is judged by what I wear and what I look like rather than who I am inside."

In this part of the ritual, the facilitators created a space for communicating about the social conflict of how women are portrayed in the media through the symbol of fire and the physical action of burning. They instructed people to transform their negative emotional reactions into positive thoughts and feelings. They allowed people to come forward toward the fire in any way they wanted, to say whatever was on their minds. Many of these messages hinted at performative statements that would announce a resolution to the conflict. "I am not a victim" and "I am big enough to change this." After all the participants had burned their papers, the facilitator invited the group back inside for the cleansing part of the ritual.

> The last part of our activity is to cleanse. There are pitchers of water for drinking, there are basins to wash your hands. You can do one or both—it is up to you.

The ritual ended as each participant came forward to drink and wash his or her hands. Altar tables at the center held flowers, candles, cups, and bowls of water. Several participants improvised a way to help the ritual along by pouring multiple cups of water and passing them around the circle. Participants left one by one as the ritual ended. Small groups of people continued to talk about the film and the experience outside of the "cleansing space."

The facilitators verbally announced that the place where people stood became a special area, set apart from the video watching. In each of the three stages of the ritual, symbols marked the space as separate. In the Naming space, there were candles. In the Transforming space, there was a larger fire in the center of the circle. In the Cleansing space, there were altars with water, flowers, and candles. The ritual allowed people to feel united with others who had experienced the video images. Participants communicated through their bodies, senses, and emotions.

The leaders invited participants to transform the ways they perceived the problem of violence against women. There was also an invitation to imagine and perform a social transformation of the damaging male-female dynamics so often portrayed on television. This ritual transformed a view of the world that sees women as sexually available victims. It replaced this oppressive view with the very voices of men and women who testified, to themselves and others, that they could and would shift lenses to see and be better women and men. The organizers used ritual to raise public consciousness and to transform responses to the media's harmful portrayals of women.

Ritual and Transformation

Rituals have the power to transform. In the peacebuilding process, worldviews, perceptions of identity, relationships, and social structures often need to shift. Ritual's role in assisting the process of transformation of worldview, identity, and relationship during conflicts helps lubricate the change process. The next three chapters explore the ways that ritual transformation aids the peacebuilding process.

Theatrical dramas are made up of different scenes. Each scene or act gives the audience new insights into the overall story. Ritual is a scene in the drama of conflict. It helps people in conflict to see and make sense of the larger conflict.

Ritual's transformative powers work in two ways in relation to worldview. First, ritual helps people make sense of the world around them to create and affirm a shared view of the world. In sociological terms, ritual is a socializing activity that nurtures common social values and behaviors. Ritual can form, build, and protect worldviews. Second, when worldviews clash and conflicts erupt, ritual can give birth to new worldviews and new ways of living and solving difficult problems. It transforms a vision of the world. This chapter details these two ways that rituals shape and shift worldviews and then provides more case study examples of how ritual functions to socialize and transform perspectives in times of conflict.

Socializing for Peace

Ritual connects people to the shared cultural values and beliefs that help them understand the world. In his foundational book, *The Elementary Forms of Religion*, sociologist Emile Durkheim proposed that collective beliefs and ideals are created, understood, and affirmed through ritual. He saw rituals as the means for social conditioning.[1] Similarly, an anthropological pioneer, Mircea Eliade, saw ritual as a way of acting out the primary myths and symbols that cultures used to understand the world.[2] Each cultural group socializes its members in different ways that reflect the shared cultural norms of its members.

In the never-ending human quest for meaning, ritual is a tool that combines, shapes, and acts out the myths, metaphors, and symbols that help us order and understand the world. Barbara Myerhoff describes the grand function of ritual's socializing functions: "The guiding metaphor in ritual serves to remind all concerned who they are, where they are, and what they are doing there."[3] Ritual serves symbolically to weave humans to the world they find themselves in by providing ways of understanding that world. Valerie DeMarinis discusses the culturally specific construction of meaning through ritual. She claims:

> [c]ulture, community, experience, and rituals of meaning-making work together in shaping a person's memory, in the naming and cultivating of values, and in the shaping of strategies for meaning-making in the present and future.[4]

Ritual gives physical form to an individual's lived experience, cultures, values, and identities. Humans experience ritual as a relief from the anxiety of everyday life where contradictions and dissonant information crowd into their worldview at every turn. In ritual, the world makes sense.

Ritual's role in passing on cultural values, beliefs, and ways of being also has implications for peacebuilding. Peacebuilders can use ritual to build worldviews supportive of peace and justice, particularly for children and youth whose process of worldviewing changes rapidly.

There are a number of public peace projects around the world that aim to influence people through creating a ritual space that supports the values of peace. In Sri Lanka, the Butterfly Garden is a public space designed to encourage psychological healing for war-affected children and youth while promoting peaceful and tolerant cultural values in a multicultural society.[5] The Somali Peace Prize and Festival described in chapter 1 is another example of a socializing ritual. Somali communities support and celebrate a culture of peace through the symbolic acts of deciding which leader has contributed most to peace in the last year and creating a festive space to celebrate the work of peacebuilding.

The Changing World

Since rituals help to lay the foundation for cultural values, it is not surprising that ritual is also important when worldviews begin to crumble. The world is constantly changing. As the world shifts, people encounter new ideas, meet new people, and have new experiences. Humans actively seek to create the world they expect and want to experience at the same time that they actively resist new information by filtering experiences that contradict their worldviews. While the dynamic of perception is constantly working to filter reality and create an image of the world that is consistent with what is already known and believed, cognitive dissonance sometimes becomes so great that an individual's worldview becomes overwhelmed by new ideas, relationships, and situations. In times where worldviews are severely tested or crumbling, ritual can actually create new ways of thinking that dramatically alter the ways humans envision the world.

Worldview transformation is often a painful process. Rituals assist in the lens-shifting process, helping people make sense of their world during the ambiguities and paradoxes that often accompany transitions. Ritual has the capacity to break through the filters and structures designed to preserve existing worldview frameworks.

Many authors claim that the symbolic nature of ritual makes it suitable for transforming worldviews and communicating conflict. As Jonathan Smith notes, "Social change is preeminently symbol or symbolic change. . . ."[6] He continues, "When the symbols for the current world no longer express its unity, when chaos and complexity become overwhelming, ritual and its symbols change and create a new reality."[7]

A story from Israel illustrates how a symbol can change someone's perspective and instigate social change. In May 2004, Israeli forces destroyed the homes of many Palestinians living in the town of Rafah in an effort to destroy underground tunnels they believe are used to transport weapons from Egypt. A senior Israeli cabinet minister who watched the demolitions on television later denounced the Israeli actions. "I saw on television an old woman picking through the rubble of her house in Rafah, looking for her medicine, and she reminded me of my grandmother who was expelled from her home during the Holocaust."[8] The cabinet minister defied his government and his party in denouncing the demolitions. By invoking his own memories of the Holocaust, he tapped into a symbolic bank of memories shared by many in Israel. By comparing the woman on television with his own grandmother in Nazi Germany, he compared the brutality of housing demolitions and the lack of respect for humanity. His perception of Israeli actions changed, and in turn, he used his powerful position to influence other people's perceptions.

Another example took place in my home, Harrisonburg, Virginia. While new reports of casualties in Iraq filled American newspapers and televisions in spring and summer 2004, a group of citizens decided to symbolically bring the suffering and death taking place in Iraq home to American soil. Some of the activists wore black to show their mourning while they kneeled next to and placed red carnations on other activists who pretended to be dead bodies covered with sheets. This dramatic act of public mourning took place in front of a sign that read "Mourning All Deaths in Iraq." Others in the group passed out flyers to cars driving by listing the numbers of people who had died in the US-led war on Iraq—both the 800-plus US soldiers and the 10,000 Iraqi civilians.[9] The ritual of mourning aimed to transform the perception that the war in Iraq was far away and removed from this small town in rural Virginia. The group received widespread support from people passing by. Some joined in the act of mourning or broke down in tears at the sight of the bodies; others shifted nervously in their cars, or looked closely at the bodies, then looked away in discomfort; some honked their horns in support of the demonstration. This example again shows the power of a symbolic act to prompt a shift in perception, in at least some of the people who experienced the ritual.

Symbols used in ritual play important roles in finding new ways of understanding and giving meaning to the world during and after conflict. Driver confirms that

> Rational political methods alone cannot bring about transformation of society from a less to a more just condition, because they cannot fuse the visionary with the actual as rituals do. . . . Nor can ideas alone do this, for in order to bear fruit ideas require flesh-and-blood performance.[10]

Ritual allows people not just to talk about peace but also to *be* peace, to *act out* peace. In the fishing story from South Africa described in chapter 1, the negotiators from two sides of the conflict change their perceptions of each other in the midst of removing an embedded fishing hook from a finger. This flesh-and-blood performance of trust and the basic humanity we each have in our own fragile body fused this actual moment in time with the visionary ideal of a post-Apartheid South Africa.

Leach sees ritual as a form of talking to oneself or transmitting messages to ourselves about the world.[11] In translating the world, humans both reflect on it and create meaning for it. Ritual becomes a translating tool used both to create worldview and to continually maintain it in a changing world.

Ritual's liminal space is by definition a place where transformation occurs, for it is in-between one state and another. Ritual is, as Bill Moyers noted in an interview with Joseph Campbell, the "center of transformation . . . where the temporal walls may dissolve to reveal a wonder."[12] Here Moyers describes ritual as a revealing place where people discover some sort of wonderful truth.

Using a different metaphor, Victor Turner likens rituals to magical mirrors that "exaggerate, invert, re-form, magnify, minimize, dis-color, re-color, even deliberately falsify" a person's view of the world.[13] Turner suggests that meaning is circulated in rituals, like a room full of magical mirrors. This creates a potent mixture of present and past, a remembrance of what is known, while gaining new knowledge, communicating with oneself while at the same time communicating to others.[14]

Ethnographic descriptions of rituals practiced in traditional cultures also describe the functions of rituals in transforming worldviews metaphorically. According to Margaret Drewal, the West African Yoruba tribe sees their traditional rituals as journeys that carry them in a personal and communal experience, allowing them to examine themselves and transform their consciousness.[15]

Scholars also use healing metaphors to describe ritual's role in changing perceptions about conflict. In times of severe conflict or "social illness" between people, ritual soothes and suppresses the infection brought about by disrupted relationships. Eva Hunt claims that ritual tends to appear in situations where there is opposition, structured social antagonism, or potential conflict between structurally defined segments of society.[16] Likewise, Moore and Myerhoff assert that ritual appears precisely when there appears to be the most conflict. "[Ritual] action itself may be soothing. . . . Ceremony can make it appear that there is no conflict, only harmony, no disorder, only order, that if danger threatens, safe solutions are at hand. . . ."[17]

After the war in Mozambique, for example, communities had to find some meaningful way of reintegrating former soldiers back into the very communities they terrorized. These trauma healing rituals (see chapter 1), were a way of healing the social illness by purifying the soldiers so that they could be acceptable community members. These healing and cleansing rituals sought to re-create stable, peaceful communities at the end of a very bloody war.

Reframing the World

While it might be tempting to create a cause-effect relationship for ritual's ability to address issues of conflict by shifting worldviews, other scholars warn against this simplistic equation. They argue that ritual does not work in a cause-effect, consequential pattern. Ranjini Obeyesekere says the relationship between ritual and social life is "semiotic" rather than consequential. Obeyesekere notes that if ritual performances solve problems linearly, "then at some point the problem would cease to exist and the ritual becomes unnecessary."[18] Quoting Hanson, Obeyesekere sees ritual solutions to problems rooted in differing worldviews "not [as] a cause before which the problem retreats as a consequence, but a message which declares *that in some contexts at least, the problem is not a problem at all*" (emphasis added).[19] Likewise, Catherine Bell claims that people "do not take a social problem to ritual for a solution." Rather, they create a "ritualized environment" that transforms, rather than resolves, the problem into some new social scheme.[20]

Ritual does not solve problems by negotiating the best solution, but by creating a new frame for interpreting the problem. As David Cheal notes, "In ritual acts, familiar experiences are reframed, and the meanings of things are redefined. Rituals can therefore be used to evoke cultural meanings that are not universally available in everyday life."[21] In the tradition of the systems theorists described in chapter 4, any message can only be understood in its context. Ritual can give a symbolic message that may be interpreted in new ways precisely because of the unique physical context that sets ritual apart from everyday life.

> Unlike linguistic consensus, the way in which rituals create solidarity is not by collective assent to the better argument. Rather, ritualized solidarity takes the form of a subjective experience of *being in the same lifeworld*, due to observing and practicing the same gestures (emphasis added).[22]

By being together physically and performing some social act in a lifeworld—a unique, liminal space—ritual can make conflict irrelevant or at least less destructive by reframing the issues at stake. By creating new symbolic frames for thinking and holding together complex, dissonant, and ambiguous realities, ritual allows for flexibility in thought and acceptance of dissonant or new information. Seeing a problem through a ritual prism enables humans to address problems differently.

For example, a group of students decided to create a ritualized context for declaring a safe space for gay students, staff, and faculty at the university where I teach. In recent years, gay, lesbian, bisexual, and transgendered students at universities across North America have experienced degrading name-calling and humiliation from fellow students. Often university administrations are unresponsive to this verbal and physical intimidation. In some Christian universities, there is also a policy of discrimination against faculty and staff who live with a same-sex partner. The students decided to declare a safe space on campus by unfurling a one-hundred-foot gay pride flag in the center of campus. Their symbolic act created a transforming space that held together the dissonant message that the space had to be declared safe because, in fact, the quiet, peaceful Christian campus was not perceived as safe by gay students, faculty, and staff. This ritual of displaying the pride flag did not negotiate a solution to the problem of safety for gay students. It did, however, create a new frame for interpreting the problem by symbolically declaring—ironically—that the university was a safe space, or at least that there were people in the community who wanted it to be safe.

Ritual and the Brain

Neurobiologists claim there is a biological dimension to ritual's ability to transform worldviews. Ritual may actually change the physical structure of the brain, prompting the brain to process information differently and allowing it to solve complex problems or paradoxes. To understand how ritual transforms neurological cognitive structures, we first need to understand the basic structure of the brain.

The brain is composed of three evolutionary levels and two hemispheres. Paul MacLean developed the concept of the triune brain composed of three evolutionary levels: the reptilian, the limbic, and the neocortex systems. This concept allows theorists to tie specific behaviors to particular parts of the brain and its historical development. The reptilian core of the brain is the relatively unchanging base of the human nervous system that controls essential human functions such as breathing, digestion, and perspiration. It is the place of instinctual responses to conflict such as the impulse to freeze, to fight, or to flee a specific situation. The limbic system is the emotional core of the brain and seems to have been added to the reptilian core roughly a million years ago. The more recent addition, the neocortex, offers humans increased motor and sensory functions and control over the older parts of the brain. It is the place of rational or logical thought and reflection. Ideally, it controls some of the older two brain areas.[23]

In addition to its three evolutionary-based segments, the brain is also divided into two lobes. The two sides of the brain function differently and interdependently. The left, conceptual hemisphere recognizes words better, while the right, imaginal hemisphere recognizes faces better and is attuned to visual-spatial perceptions. This brain division affects how people learn. Each person has a unique, physical set of grooves engraved in their brain that channel communication between different parts of the brain. These grooves both guide and limit thought.[24]

In the midst of conflict or some sort of traumatic experience, the rational brain is often overwhelmed and the other two parts take over with emotional or instinctual reactions. Each individual develops particular "buttons" that, when pushed, lead to reactions that often flow along deeply engraved, biological patterns of response. For example, when a person sees someone he or she considers an enemy or someone who may attack him or her, that person may have a physical and emotional response, including increased heartbeat, clenched fists, and a feeling of fear or anxiety.

Piaget defined learning as a process of integrating what is already known with new ideas and experiences.[25] The brain seeks integration between its two lobes and three evolutionary segments, in addition to the integration of body and brain discussed earlier. Existing grooves or pathways between parts of the brain may limit the range of associations and information that can be connected to a new experience. Integration requires new physical pathways between sections of the brain, allowing for increased memory and ability to make associations in and predictions about the world. Integrating the brain helps ensure that humans are able to adapt to new circumstances and solve complex problems.

Understanding the brain's structure and drive to integrate is essential to identifying ritual's role in transforming worldviews. Scientists claim symbols and symbolic forms of communication such as ritual have the ability to penetrate, integrate, and communicate between different parts of the body and brain. In *The Spectrum of Ritual: A Biogenetic Structuralist Approach*, neurobiologists Laughlin, McManus, and d'Aquili state that the rhythm, repetition, and pattern in certain rituals affect the brain in ways that change its physical structure. Ritual triggers an altered state of consciousness, or simply a shiver up one's back, that signals a neurological reorganizing and transforming of the brain's cognitive system.[26]

In their second book, *Brain, Symbol & Experience*, d'Aquili, Laughlin, and McManus advocate using ritual and other symbols to help integrate these phases of consciousness into a "community of cells."[27] Experiences of dual consciousness are often achieved during meditation, spiritual exercises, and rituals. When the brain shifts focus between different sections, humans experience shifts in consciousness or "dual consciousness." The practice of meditation, for example, is an effort to be aware of the "continuity of consciousness" that is tied to combining memories of past events, anticipation of future events, and an awareness of what is current in the breathing body of the meditator.[28] The authors describe ritual as a "theater of the mind" that controls and induces phases of consciousness, allowing for integration of new information into the cognitive system in both the body and different parts of the brain. "The realm of ritual is one of fluid transformation in which the participant experiences an unencumbered consciousness, which is neither one thing nor another."[29] Ritual helps the brain communicate among its parts, allowing new ways of thinking.

D'Aquili and Laughlin report that ritual stimulates both brain hemispheres and all three evolutionary levels. This simultaneous stimulation holds together the polar opposites of the analytic, emotional, creative, and sensing parts of the brain. This explains the often-reported experience of

individuals solving paradoxical problems during certain states of meditation or during states induced by some ritual behavior.

> It appears that, during certain meditation and ritual states, logical para-
> doxes or the awareness of polar opposites as presented in myth appear
> simultaneously . . . as unified wholes. This experience is coupled with the
> intensely affective "oceanic" experience that has been described during
> various meditation states, as well as during certain stages of ritual. Dur-
> ing [some rituals], the experience of the union of opposites . . . is
> expanded to the experience of the total union of self and other or, as it
> is expressed in the Christian tradition, the union of the self with God.[30]

D'Aquili and Laughlin also note that ritual may be used to solve paradoxical problems that involve dualisms such as good and evil. Usually, these
types of problems are dealt with in the analytical mode. However, "the
slow rhythm of a religious procession or the fast beat of drums or rattles"
may drive the ergotropic system, that part of the brain that is not associated with logic, to reframe and redefine a dualistic problem.[31]

Using a biochemical rather than a neurological model, Schechner
argues that some forms of ritual relieve anxiety through the use of "repetition, rhythmicity, exaggeration, condensation, and simplification." Each
of these qualities "stimulate the brain into releasing endorphins directly
into the bloodstream yielding ritual's second benefit, a relief from pain, a
surfeit of pleasure."[32] From a biochemical perspective, Schechner concludes, Marx may have been correct in noting that both religion and
opium "pacify." Ritual, which is used in all religions, may offer a way of
relieving anxiety about complex problems or paradoxes through chemical
and neurological changes to the brain that allow for new ways of thinking.

The breathing meditations of Buddhists, the repetitive chants of
Catholic monks, the rubbing of rosary beads, the tribal dancing to beating drums, the five daily prayers to Mecca, or the liturgical prayers in
Christian and Judaic traditions may all serve the same purpose: to create a
sense of peace and relieve the anxieties of this world so that people can
better connect with each other and their God. These rituals may help integrate the brain, creating new pathways and biological connections between
the various parts of the brain.

How can peacebuilders use these or other rituals as a means to help
people in the midst of conflict? While a great deal has been written about
the role of religion in promoting violence or building peace,[33] few texts
address how religious rituals may prepare people to reduce their anxiety or
transform their perceptions of a conflict. Conflict theorists rarely delve
into the biological obstacles to finding peaceful solutions to problems.
Since human thinking is bound by physically entrenched ways of thinking,
it may be helpful to conceive of worldview transformation, both metaphorically and biologically, as creating new grooves between sections of

the brain. By integrating parts of our brain and body, ritual can help us discover new ways of thinking about old problems. While neurobiologists may go about the study of the ritual transformation of brains and world-views by taking pictures of people's brains before and after experiencing ritual, social scientists look for social examples. The smudging ceremony, women's rituals, and the Cypriot youth workshop offer such illustration.

Healing and Worldview Transformation on the Red Road

Ritual is an essential element on the Red Road, the Native path toward healing and wholeness. In the last 500 years of contact, Europeans imposed every kind of illness imaginable on Native people as they brought new physical illnesses, destroyed communities, forced Native communities across a Trail of Tears, declared Native culture and spirituality illegal, kidnapped Native children and placed them in residential schools where they were taught, in the words of Native folk singer Buffy St. Marie, "to despise their traditions." The list is endless. Today, golf courses are built on sacred burial grounds, dams flood traditional hunting grounds, and toxic wastes are buried on Native lands. Violence wrought on Native communities from the outside is reproduced on the inside with rampant domestic and sexual violence and self-destructive addictions to alcohol and drugs. It is no surprise that the survivors of hundreds of years of violence need physical, emotional, mental, and spiritual healing.

The themes of healing, cleansing, and purifying are indicative of both cosmology and history in Native North America for those who follow "the good red road."[34] Cosmological and cultural understandings of health differ vastly between Native and non-Native North Americans. Many European Americans go to a doctor or take drugs when they are physically sick. Native cultures have a more complex understanding of health based on the wholeness of the body, mind, spirit, and emotions. Individual health is nested within and dependent upon the health of the community and the surrounding environment. Sickness is not just some germ or bacteria that one catches. Instead, illness is a symptom of imbalance. Wholeness and health are not permanent states but dynamic processes that need regular tunings. Healing is an ongoing process. Native historian Olive Dickason reports that Native spirituality requires "keeping the cosmos in tune and staying in tune with the cosmos" through ceremonies.[35]

Conflict or tragedy in the family or community indicates an offended spirit. Shamans, medicine persons, or elders help Native communities identify their problems and regain balance through healing.[36] Noted Native scholar Paula Gunn Allen claims rituals change people from being in an "isolated (diseased) state to one of incorporation (health). . . ."[37] The smudging ceremony and many other Native rituals take place in a circle and are aimed at bringing healing, order, balance, relationship, and respect. The circle is a powerful symbol in North American indigenous cultures and embodies the desired state of health and wholeness. The Medicine Wheel, a circle divided by four points marking mental, spiritual, emotional, and physical growth, is often used as a guide to how each person can work toward healing and wholeness.

In *The Sacred Hoop*, Allen defines Native ritual as "transforming something from one state or condition to another."[38] She says the Native attraction to repetition in ritual is not a childish psychological need or a desire for control. Rather, Native people who practice cultural rituals recognize the need to transcend the delusion that humans are isolated individuals. Native ritual affirms community; union with each other and the Creator.[39] Allen further asserts that while Westerners associate different states of consciousness with the exotic, strange, and powerful ways of shamans, Native literature attests to it as common among "ordinary" Native peoples who perceive things "not as inert but as viable and alive."[40]

> The distractions of ordinary life must be put to rest and emotions redirected and integrated into a ceremonial context so that the greater awareness can come into full consciousness and functioning. In this way the participants become literally one with the universe, for they lose consciousness of mere individuality and share the consciousness that characterizes most orders of being. . . . Soon breath, heartbeat, thought, emotion, and word are one.[41]

According to Allen, ritual's repetitive sounds and actions in Native rituals have an "entrancing effect" on people, bringing them to an "oceanic" hypnotic state of consciousness where their perceptions of the world begin to change. Allen also notes that the power of ritual within the Native community could "bear deeper study in our troubled, conflict-ridden time."[42] The transforming ability of the smudging ceremony to bring about clarity of mind and perception, for example, is particularly useful in situations of conflict. The role of ritual in dealing with conflict has deep historic roots in Native cultures.

While the smudging ceremony is not used by all Native nations in North America, most nations do have rituals that involve burning herbs and using the smoke symbolically. Basil Johnston describes the origins of the use of tobacco smoke as a symbol of reconciliation, good will, and harmony. The ritual of the sacred pipe, also known as the peace pipe, originated when the spirit Nanabush and his father Epingishmook smoked the pipe as a symbol of the end of their conflict and the beginning of peace between them. Johnston claims, "Thereafter, the ritual of the smoking of the pipe was an essential part of every conference, performed before deliberations began in order to induce temperance in speech and wisdom in decision."[43] The smudging ceremony is thought to be related to the peace pipe ceremony.

A report of the Canadian Royal Commission on Aboriginal Peoples concluded that traditional healing methods and therapies, including the smudging ceremony, make noted contributions to Native health through their ability to bring about healing, wholeness, and help in solving difficult problems. Native people "spoke of applying old practices to new problems, of combining them with western therapies in a spirit of experimentation and learning."[44] My own interviews with Native Elders and Native organizations in Ontario, Canada, confirmed this finding.

The Toronto-based organization Spirit of the People uses the smudging ceremony in healing circles for ex-offenders. Spirit of the People provides a number of social services to Native people released from prison to help them break the cycle of criminal activity and incarceration. They seek to recognize ex-offenders' value, dignity, and potential contribution and to reintegrate them into society. Based on an understanding that health and wholeness include spiritual, emotional, physical, and mental dimensions, the smudging ceremony is part of the healing process. Mike McTague, a counselor at Spirit of the People, describes the role of the smudging ceremony as part of his work in healing circles.

> If a person is having a hard time in the circle, is tense or emotional, we bring the smudge to them; as the bowl goes around, people will give an offering into the smudge bowl. It is like washing, we wash ourselves, our ears, eyes, and mouths, and then our heads, and then to your heart at the end. . . . It is a cleansing of the spirits, it cleanses your body and allows the group to be as one.[45]

The connection between healing and cleansing is profound. McTague believes that the smudging ceremony makes a big difference in how ex-offenders respond during group programs.

> I use the smudging in an anger management group that I run here; no one has ever gotten angry in the group; no one is hotheaded; it puts me a lot more at ease. . . . We speak through the feather, we pass it around the circle, it makes you strong; it is sacred, it is like passing around the Bible for you to speak. Often in the healing circles, people won't speak the first time around, but we keep passing the feather around again and again; sometimes we pass around a small grandfather—a round stone, or the talking stick.[46]

Echoing Allen's theoretical analysis of Native ritual, McTague claims the smudging ceremony "allows the group to be as one," reweaving the web of community that prevents an individual from engaging in criminal behavior. The patterned and repetitive washing in the smudging ceremony takes participants through a conscious re-membering of community with each other and their world. In the process of transforming from being an offender who has both hurt and been hurt into an important, contributing member of society, the smudging ceremony allows a spiritual, emotional, mental, and physical cleansing that allows an offender to develop meaningful relationships with the world.

Many Native people who are not facing extreme circumstances also find regular smudging to be an important part of their lives. One Native person explained how smudging helps her deal with everyday problems and stresses. "It is cleansing. It brings people together. You wash yourself there and it takes you out of what you've been doing all day; it takes it off you . . . that is what smudging does. . . ."[47] Another Native person reports an even more extensive, regular use of the smudging ceremony.

> I do the smudging everyday, every morning as I get ready for the day; I say prayers; I also use it at the end of the day if there is a lot of tension built up; if someone shouted at me; I pray to understand what I am to learn; what the Creator sees, what he teaches me; maybe if someone shouts, I learn how to be assertive; everything that happens to us is to teach us something.[48]

Everyday interactions in the non-Native world can leave Native people feeling tense, anxious, and isolated. According to the interviewees, the smudging ceremony reweaves the web that holds humans together with each other, their Creator, and the environment around them. It is a purifying and cleansing act to purge negative, harmful, and selfish thoughts while strengthening relationships. The smudging ceremony helps Native people regain a sense of health and wholeness in a world that daily attacks their mental and physical integrity. The smudging ceremony is not a simple, one-time, fix-all recipe for problems. It is a repeated process necessary for staying on the Red Road and keeping Native people healthy.

Smudging changes the lens or frame used to view the world. This new frame "puts things in perspective" according to one Ojibway woman. Several interviewees described the way they washed their minds in the smoke. "We do [the smudging ceremony] all the time to help open our minds, to clean us." Allen's description of the physiological changes in participants in Native rituals described above is consistent with the descriptions interviewees gave of the role the smudging ceremony played in changing their perceptions of the world.

In Native ceremonies, the world is constructed, created, and affirmed through a Native cultural lens that establishes values and ways of being. Native cultures value "peacefulness, harmony, cooperation, health, and general prosperity" and have found ways of enacting these values in everyday life through ritual.[49] Smudging provides a metamessage, an overall assertion, that people are one with their environment, each other, their Creator, and that these relationships have meaning. Those Native lives broken by direct and indirect violence and substance abuse may find healing through traditional processes such as the smudging ceremony that allow for and encourage spiritual, mental, physical, and emotional healing.

The smudging ceremony is also a resource for transforming world-views in groups where there is a more specific conflict. Other Native people interviewed in this project cited instances when Canadian officials and Native people began their negotiations over fishing rights or land with a smudging ceremony.

> I use to meet with the fish and game council over Indian fishing and hunting rights. When we met with the white men, we all did a smudge ceremony at the beginning, like we always do before our Native meetings. The white men had a hard time, cause they had to tell the truth after the ceremony and try to see it from our perspective.[50]

In this example, the smudging ceremony sets the tone for an important and potentially conflictual meeting. Smudging changes the way people in the meeting see each other, and influences what they say to each other.

In her study of the role of Native Elders in Toronto Native organizations and social services, Steigelbauer notes the importance of Elders in conflict resolution. "Resident Elders" serve in a variety of urban organizations with Native clients to provide traditional wisdom and rituals in the modern context. Stiegelbauer notes a number of stories in which Elders intervened in conflict in ways that helped bring about a transformation of the problem: " . . . [T]he process of smudging and prayers prior to the discussion as well as the support and discussion of the issue with the Elders helped with [conflict] resolution."[51]

These examples show the smudging ceremony's capacity for cleansing and healing as essential to the challenging work of maintaining dignity, wholeness, and community in a fragmented world that challenges Native people's sense of health and peace. They also show the Native healing and worldview transformation that occur through the smudging ceremony can directly deal with conflict between individuals and groups.

Changing Lenses "Inside the Circle"

Just as Canadian Native people express anger and frustration at living in a largely hostile society, many women hold a continuing sense of outrage at living in societies where their voices are not equally heard and oppressive messages about their gender identity pervade every form of media. Feminist ritual, like the one shared at the beginning of this chapter, aims to change women's worldview. Women's groups allow women the physical space to articulate and share their own experiences of living in a world that often does not value women. Inside this space, commonly known as the sacred circle, feminist ritual serves as a vehicle for sharing personal stories and for learning about and remembering women's history. Women's spirituality groups often study and reflect upon women's history and theology since these top-ics are usually left out of most mainstream education. The information and ideas shared often create a significant change in worldviews among the women who read this literature.[52,53]

The mix of women sharing personal stories of their lives and learning about powerful women in history is potent. Batya Podos argues that women's ritual is a "cathartic experience," an "emotional purge that leads to self-revelation and transformation" where women gain "new knowledge of themselves, their power, and the history and prehistory of women.[54] Podos notes, "By telling the truth about our ancient past, by discovering our own lost history, we are neutralizing over 2,000 years of lies about the nature of women."[55] Neutralizing patriarchy has a profound effect on women. Rather than seeing themselves as insignificant historical actors who have never held important and powerful positions in the world, women's groups learn about the history of women in Europe as healers and leaders in their community before the "witch hunts" singled out and murdered millions of these women, as well as the overwhelming archeo-logical evidence of global goddess religions that revered a feminine image of the Divine. This history inspires new images of womanhood. It shifts women's worldviews.

Theater director and feminist ritualist Barbara Graber notes that the safe space created in women's rituals heightens an awareness of the conflict between women and patriarchal values. "Women's spirituality rituals are a lot about transforming the inner conflicts of women's soul and spiritual health and society's determination to stomp it out. . . ."[56] Graber sees women's spirituality groups as a training ground for all women to "claim their own voice." Feminist ritual helps women begin the process of chang-ing both themselves and the world around them.

One woman I interviewed noted that her women's spirituality group was a highlight of her week, a place to leave behind the stress of hearing men call out derogatory names when she walked down the street and enter into a place where she knew she would be valued and accepted. While each woman may come into the group feeling alone and overwhelmed by her experience in a patriarchal world, reading feminist perspectives on history and participating in feminist ritual seems to provide new ways for each woman to reinterpret their own life experience in the context of other women's lives.

Many feminist rituals focus on healing specific memories of being a victim. One woman noted that feminist ritual played a big part in her own journey of moving from victim to survivor of sexual abuse:

> It seemed like a big part of [our women's group] was creating meaningful ceremonies for ourselves because before [ritual] had always been created by other people . . . we knew we needed ceremony . . . and it worked

when we did it. We found it to have a profound effect on us—our sense
of selves as powerful. And so much healing came through [ritual.][57]

Several women credited their group's rituals for giving them the "strength
to face the abuse." They describe their group's rituals as transformative
experiences. These women struggled with the pain of abuse, which represented both broken relationships and a sense of confusion over why and
how the abuse had taken place within the safety of their families and communities. Ritual was a way of healing the scars from the abuse by creating
a world that made sense. The women came to understand themselves as
strong and capable women through the act of creating their own rituals
and bonding with other women who had experienced similar trauma.

While patriarchal values prevail outside the circle, women's ways of
knowing, feeling, communicating, and being are given preference inside
the circle, making it safe for women to re-vision the world.[58] Changes in
perception are followed by changes in women's identity, how they see
themselves. Social transformation, the change that spins outward from the
transformation in women's rituals, is a natural product of the inner change.
Worldview change within a woman or a group of women inevitably leads
to shifts in their identity and their relationships with others in the world.
These ideas will be discussed in the next two chapters.

Spiders: The Enemy of My Enemy Is My Friend

Earlier in this century, while ethnicities were important sources of identity,
a variety of other identities were also important and allowed Greek and
Turkish Cypriots to live side by side and even intermarry in Cypriot communities. Today, along the Green Line that divides the island, billboards
on both sides recount the horrible atrocities of the other ethnic group.
The similarity between the two billboards is striking. Before tourists and
visitors leave each side of the island, billboards warn them of the evils of
the other side.

The Cypriot youth camp provides a third way of understanding ritual's
ability to transform worldviews. The ritual of living together transformed
worldviews in surprising ways. The rustic nature of the camp itself disap-
pointed both Greek and Turkish Cypriots. They had come with expectations of a cleaner, more modern camp. In the first days of their arrival,
there was considerable joint complaining about the facilities. The identity
of a community of campers seemed to be reinforced by the rugged conditions. One camper noted in his evaluation that "we managed to survive
under disgusting conditions." Soon the spiders that crawled over sleeping
bags, sat on toilet paper, covered the showers, and hung from the ceilings
became the common enemy of all the campers.

Many cultures share the proverb "an enemy of my enemy is my friend." In this case, the unplanned profusion of spiders became the binding glue that united Greek and Turkish Cypriot campers. Sleeping in spider-filled cabins became a transformative, symbolic experience. My observations of living in the cabin with a group of very squeamish teenage girls, along with the campers' evaluations, led me to believe this was a powerful ritual experience. The space was definitely unique and set apart from the conflict zone. The spider-killing became a symbolic and transforming act. European mythology is full of heroic journeys in which princes and knights fight ferocious dragons. This type of imagery filled my imagination as I lay in bed at night hearing Greek and Turkish Cypriot girls scream and giggle as they killed spiders.

In their final evaluations, I asked the campers to discuss the importance of meeting the spiders. The question was meant as a humorous addition to a long list of other activities I asked the group to evaluate. I was surprised, however, at the clarity of their responses. Campers noted that the spiders "provided us with something to talk about instead of staring at each other" and that the spiders were the "first thing we talked about when we entered the cabin." Others noted "It was a common problem that we faced, and it brought us together more easily and more quickly" and "killing them brought us together." Yet another said that facing the spiders together was "the best experience" because it brought the group together.

The imagery of spiders began to pervade the camp and became the primary symbol for the experience. The campers were asked to develop names for their cabins. One cabin chose the name "Spider Girls." Eventually, the whole group came to call themselves "Spider Camp" and the trainers distributed hats with this name to all the campers. Louise Diamond, the training director, began to weave stories of a mythological "Grandmother Spider" into the camper's experience. One day she shared the story of her own struggle with breast cancer. She related her cancer to the pervasive use of chemical bug sprays and other pesticides like the kinds the campers were using to kill the spiders in their cabins. Her message encouraged the campers to put down their defenses against the spiders and to realize that humans are related to everything living, even spiders.

On the last day of the camp, Diamond led the group in a web-weaving ritual. Using a ball of yarn, the group formed a large circle and then wove a web between individuals in the circle with a ball of yarn. In this ritual, each person was asked to share a final thought about the camp experience while holding the ball of yarn. Then they tossed the ball of yarn to someone else across the circle. When everyone had finished talking, a web of green yarn connected everyone in the group.

Both the stories and the web-weaving ritual highlighted Diamond's grounding in a systems approach. She prompted the campers to see the spiders not as their enemies, but as part of the "web of life." She then used the web metaphor to highlight the relationships they had formed with each other. The spider symbols became important meaning-makers for the camp experience and assisted in the worldview transformation needed for these youth to see the conflict and each other in new ways.

The final evaluations revealed some striking parallels between becoming friends with spiders and becoming friends with members of the other ethnic group.[59] One camper wrote, "Before this camp I had been frightened of spiders, but now they are my best friends." Others stated "We learned not to kill spiders," and "I learned to love insects and live with them." These same kinds of statements also described how their relationships with the other ethnic group had changed. At least some of the participants saw life in a new light and recognized that spiders, Greek Cypriots, and Turkish Cypriots all belonged in this valuable category.

In interviews and in written comments, many campers attested to their change in perspective on the conflict. One camper wrote the following testimony of his worldview transformation: "Before the camp, I was sure that there wasn't any solution to the Cyprus problem and that the two communities should live separately. Now, I am positive that there is a better solution and I am sure that the two communities can live together." This testimony voices the efficacy of both the conflict resolution workshop and the ritual context of living in a camp together. The camper describes the intellectual realization that "there is a better solution." The affirmation "Now . . . I am sure that the two communities can live together" likely developed as a result of both the conflict resolution training and dialogue and the informal camp rituals that provided contexts conducive to relationship building.

Numerous other campers noted on their final evaluations that they had experienced a change in worldview as well:

> I see the other side with a more positive perspective and with more understanding.

> There were many things I learned about the other community and I was amazed. . . . I had a wrong opinion about the other community's beliefs, ideas, goals, etc. Now I can say that I look at the Turkish Cypriots much more differently than I used to before coming here.

> I have now seen that the two communities can live together and I know that if our leaders try hard they can find a solution that will be good for both sides.

> Before coming together and meeting with the Greeks and living with them, I thought we could never find a future without fighting . . . but now I see the new generation managed it well. . . .

These sampling of testimonies describe a worldview change in which the youth came to see both the Cyprus problem and their enemies through a new lens.

While my research for this book was qualitative, I collected quantitative data in a single group pre- and post-camp survey to begin to test the idea that ritual is transformative. In the post-camp survey, I asked the group if their perspectives on the situation in Cyprus had changed during the past two weeks. On a Likert scale of 1 to 5 (5 being "yes, definitely" and 1 being "definitely not"), the group average was 3.6.[60] Some explained further that while they did change (learned about the other side during the camp) they also did not change (they were hopeful that a solution could be found before they arrived at the camp, and they left reconfirmed in this belief). The group average attests to a general feeling that their worldview changed over the two-week period.

The Ritual Prism

Conflict sometimes brings on a spiritual crisis of hopelessness and meaninglessness. Problems seem insurmountable and all-encompassing. Discomfort with conflict often stems from either the painful awareness of or refusal to see that there are multiple truths and that right/wrong and good/bad are not clear categories. Rather than solving problems by negotiating the best solution, ritual offers a new frame for interpreting the problem and the world around it. Ritual acts like a prism that allows people to view the world through a new lens that emphasizes relationships and a wider, more complete understanding of the nature of conflict. Ritual prisms can make problems seem irrelevant and bring a sense of order back to people in conflict by providing new symbols, myths, metaphors, stories, actions, or objects that help individuals and groups make sense out of their experience.

Each of the three main case studies highlights the role ritual can play in helping people shift their worldviews. The smudging ceremony and feminist rituals are examples of the way two cultural groups that experience oppression from and conflict in their larger societies use ritual. These two groups use ritual primarily to heal themselves from the daily wounds inflicted by an antagonistic society. In the smudging ceremony, people cleanse themselves of impure thoughts and intentions and transform their relationships with others so that they may have respectful interactions. Feminist rituals reframe a patriarchal world, allowing women to name their oppression and transform themselves into empowered women. The smudging ceremony and feminist rituals bring healing and wholeness to two historically oppressed groups.

The Cyprus case study is different. Here, peacebuilding practitioners use ritual to assist in the process of worldview transformation between two conflicting groups. Rituals help the group see each other and their problem in new ways. The informal rituals in the Cypriot youth camp transformed youth into young peacebuilders who interacted as trusted friends.

Ritual's capacity to penetrate into the symbolic core of frozen, fearful people by engaging their emotions, bodies, and senses is essential to peacebuilding. Ritual's power to transform worldviews can be used by masses of people hoping to symbolically end a conflict, between small groups of people in peacebuilding workshop settings, or within a group in a small meeting to increase empowerment and bolster resistance to a larger conflict.

Rabbi Marc Gopin tells a story of a friend who compares two demonstrations in Israel, one advocating for peace with Palestinians and one advocating for the rights of settlers. The former demonstration was highly intellectual and composed of speeches about justice. The latter included "dancing, singing, and passion. . . ."[61] Gopin ponders the heavy reliance on words within the peace community. Can peacebuilders find a way to supplement their calls for justice with rituals that inspire, involve, and create passion?

The few references to ritual within the conflict studies literature attest to yet another way ritual may be used in worldview transformation for the cause of peacebuilding. Louis Kriesberg has noted that the most stable conflict settlements and resolutions are transformative and allow for a shift in perspective or a redefinition of a conflict. Instead of having peace settlements signed in private ceremonies for government representatives, Kriesberg advocates proclaiming peace agreements in major public rituals because public rituals ensure the "social commitment and pressure for compliance."[62] Psychiatrist and conflict theorist Vamik Volkan also notes that public rituals and mourning processes are necessary for the many personal and relational changes required in high-level peace processes.[63] Today, intrastate conflicts and civil wars are the main forms of direct violence. Official attempts to create a problem-solving end to violence though peace settlements usually rely heavily on verbal and written agreements. Kriesberg and Volkan suggest that grassroots- and community-level rituals may be essential in helping peace settlements last. The postwar healing rituals in Mozambique, described in chapter 1, are examples of the ways rituals may be used to transform people's perspectives on conflict and their traumatic memories of war.

This chapter leaves peacebuilders with another set of questions to add to their toolbox. When planning any peacebuilding process, or when simply analyzing a conflict, these questions provide a guide to some of the worldview dimensions and the possibility of ritual-inspired worldview transformation.

1. What aspect of worldview needs to be transformed? Is it a perception of victimhood? Or a lack of hope about addressing a conflict?
2. Do existing socializing rituals contribute to or hinder the peaceful resolution of conflict?

3. What new rituals could be developed to address perceived problems within groups in conflict or between groups in conflict?

4. How could peacebuilders construct a ritual prism to help people see the conflict or even their immediate environment in new ways?

The next two chapters build on the idea of ritual transformation by examining how ritual shifts perceptions of identity and relationships, especially in times of conflict.

Notes

1. Emile Durkheim, *The Elementary Forms of the Religious Life* (Glencoe, Ill: Free Press, 1915).

2. Mircea Eliade, *Patterns in Comparative Religion*, trans. Rosemary Sheed (New York: New American Library, 1963).

3. Barbara Myerhoff, "We Don't Wrap Herring in a Printed Page: Fusion, Fictions and Continuity in Secular Ritual," in *Secular Ritual*, ed. Sally F. Moore and Barbara G. Myerhoff (Amsterdam: Van Gorcum, 1977), 202.

4. Valerie DeMarinis, "A Psychotherapeutic Exploration of Religious Ritual as Mediator of Memory and Meaning," in *Religious and Social Ritual: Interdisciplinary Explorations*, ed. Michael B. Aune and Valerie DeMarinis (New York: State University of New York Press, 1996), 242.

5. Rob Chase, "Healing and Reconciliation for War-Affected Children and Communities," *International Development Research Center, Canada*, 2000, June 22, 2002, http://www.hri.ca/children/conflict/srilanka2000paper.htm.

6. Jonathan Z. Smith, "The Influence of Symbols Upon Social Change: A Place on Which to Stand," in *The Roots of Ritual*, ed. James D. Shaughnessy (Grand Rapids, Mich.: Eerdmans, 1973), 140.

7. Smith, "The Influence of Symbols Upon Social Change," 143.

8. Jeffrey Heller, "Israeli Cabinet Minister/Holocaust Survivor Condemns Rafah Demolitions," *Reuters* (Jerusalem), May 23, 2004.

9. Sources for the number of dead came from two Web sites: Iraq Body Count at http://www.iraqbodycount.net/ and Coalition Body Count at http://icasualties.org/oif/, June 25, 2004.

10. Tom Faw Driver, *The Magic of Ritual: Our Need for Liberating Rites That Transform Our Lives and Our Communities* (San Francisco: Harper San Francisco, 1991), 184.

11. Edmund Leach, *Culture and Communication: The Logic by Which Symbols Are Connected* (New York: Cambridge University Press, 1976), 45.

12. *Joseph Campbell: The Power of Myth with Bill Moyers*, ed. Betty Sue Flowers (New York: Doubleday, 1988), 92.

13. Victor Turner, *The Anthropology of Performance* (New York: PAJ Publishers, 1988), 42.

14. Turner, *The Anthropology of Performance*.

15. Margaret Thompson Drewal, *Yoruba Ritual: Performers, Play, Agency* (Bloomington: Indiana University Press, 1992), 23.

16. Eva Hunt, "Ceremonies of Confrontation and Submission: The Symbolic Dimension of Indian-Mexican Political Interaction," in *Secular Ritual*, ed. Sally F. Moore and Barbara G. Myerhoff (Amsterdam: Van Gorcum, 1977), 144.

17. Sally F. Moore and Barbara Myerhoff, "Introduction: Secular Ritual: Forms and Meanings," in *Secular Ritual*, ed. Sally F. Moore and Barbara Myerhoff (Amsterdam: Van Gorcum, 1977), 24.

18. Ranjini Obeyesekere, "The Significance of Performance for Its Audience: An Analysis of Three Sri Lankan Rituals," in *By Means of Performance*, ed. Richard Schechner and Willa Appel (New York: Cambridge University Press, 1993), 123.

19. Obeyesekere, "The Significance of Performance for Its Audience," 124.

20. Catherine M. Bell, *Ritual Theory, Ritual Practice* (New York: Oxford University Press, 1992), 106.

21. David Cheal, "Ritual: Communication in Action," *Sociological Analysis* 53, no. 4 (1992): 367.

22. Cheal, "Ritual: Communication in Action," 369.

23. Paul D. MacLean, *A Triune Concept of the Brain and Behaviour* (Toronto: University of Toronto, 1972).

24. Charles D. Laughlin, John McManus, and Eugene G. d'Aquili, *Brain, Symbol & Experience: Toward a Neurophenomenology of Human Consciousness* (Boston, Mass.: Shambhala Publications, 1990), 129.

25. Jean Piaget, "Intellectual Evolution from Adolescence to Adulthood," *Human Development* 15 (1972), pp. 1–12.

26. Charles D. Laughlin, John McManus, and Eugene G. d'Aquili, "Introduction," in *The Spectrum of Ritual: A Biogenetic Structural Analysis*, ed. Eugene G. d'Aquili, Charles D. Laughlin, and John McManus (New York: Columbia University Press, 1979), 1–50.

27. Laughlin, McManus, and d'Aquili, *Brain, Symbol & Experience*, 141.

28. Laughlin, McManus, and d'Aquili, *Brain, Symbol & Experience*, 129–30.

29. Laughlin, McManus, and d'Aquili, *Brain, Symbol & Experience*, 213–14.

30. Laughlin, McManus, and d'Aquili, "Introduction," 175–76.

31. Laughlin, McManus, and d'Aquili, "Introduction," 177.

32. Richard Schechner, *The Future of Ritual: Writings on Culture and Performance* (New York: Routledge, 1993), 233.

33. See *Faith-Based Diplomacy: Trumping Realpolitique*, ed. Douglas Johnston (New York: Oxford University Press, 2003), and Marc Gopin, *Between Eden and Armageddon: The Future of World Religions, Violence* (New York: Oxford University Press, 2000).

34. Lorne Todd Holyoak, "The Good Red Road: Relations Between Native Elders and Non-Native Seekers" (Ph.D. diss., Calgary: University of Calgary, 1993).

35. *Looking Forward, Looking Back*, in *A Report of the Royal Commission on Aboriginal Peoples* (Ottawa: Canada Communications Group, 1993), 629.

36. *Looking Forward, Looking Back*, 629.

37. Paula Gunn Allen, *The Sacred Hoop: Recovering the Feminine in American Indian Traditions* (Boston: Beacon Press, 1992), 80.

38. Allen, *The Sacred Hoop*, 29.

39. Allen, *The Sacred Hoop*, 68.

40. Allen, *The Sacred Hoop*, 69.

41. Allen, *The Sacred Hoop*, 63.

42. Allen, *The Sacred Hoop*, 29.

43. Basil Johnston, *Ojibway Ceremonies* (Lincoln, Neb.: University of Nebraska Press, 1982), 160.

44. *Gathering Strength*, in *A Report of the Royal Commission on Aboriginal Peoples* (Ottawa: Canada Communications Group, 1993), 211.

45. Mike McTague, interview by the author, February 28, 1995, Toronto, ON.

46. McTague, 1995.

47. Interview by the author, February 27, 1995. Waterloo, ON.

48. Interview by the author, February 27, 1995. Waterloo, ON.

49. Allen, *The Sacred Hoop*, 29.

50. Interview by the author, February 9, 1995. Waterloo, ON.

51. S. M. Stiegelbauer, "What Is an Elder? What Do Elders Do?: First Nation Elders as Teachers in Culture-Based Urban Organizations," *The Canadian Journal of Native Studies* XVI, no. 1 (1996): 57.

52. Riane Eisler, *The Chalice and the Blade* (San Francisco: Harper, 1988).

53. Charlene Spretnak, *The Politics of Women's Spirituality* (Toronto: Doubleday Press, 1982).

54. Batya Podos, "Feeding the Feminist Psyche through Ritual Theater," in *The Politics of Women's Spirituality*, ed. Charlene Spretnak (Toronto: Doubleday, 1982), 307.

55. Podos, "Feeding the Feminist Psyche Through Ritual Theater," 310.

56. Barbara Graber, interview by the author, January 15, 1998. Harrisonburg, Va.

57. Interview by the author. March 7, 1995. Toronto, ON.

58. Mary Belenky, *Women's Ways of Knowing: The Development of Self, Voice, and Mind* (New York: Basic Books, 1997).

59. Quotes are taken from the anonymous final evaluations of the Greek and Turkish Cypriot participants.

60. The Turkish Cypriot average to this question was 3.2. The Greek Cypriot average was 4.05. I have no hypotheses as to why there seems to be such a significant difference in the level of reported transformative experience of the two groups. More research is needed to determine if worldview changes really do occur in two-week experiences such as this, and if the changes in perspective have a lasting impact on participants.

61. Gopin, *Between Eden and Armageddon*, 193.

62. Louis Kriesberg, *International Conflict Resolution: The U.S.–USSR and Middle East Cases* (New Haven: Yale University Press, 1992), 155.

63. Vamik D. Volkan, Joseph Montville, and Demetrios Julius, *The Psychodynamics of International Relationships* (Lexington, Mass.: Lexington Books, 1990), 87.

CHAPTER 8

Forming and Transforming Identities

On a muggy July afternoon, a group of young Greek and Turkish Cypriot women relaxed by a swimming pool in a rustic country camp. Most of their conversation had to do with the upcoming dance party. Girls asked each other which boys would be the best dance partners. Greek and Turkish Cypriot girls usually do not have the opportunity to swim and talk together. This was a unique social context. In this informal, recreational atmosphere, it was possible to view identity through a different lens. These Greek and Turkish Cypriot girls shared a conversation about boys rather than about war. They compared wardrobe plans for the dance party rather than jostling for recognition of their perspectives on the conflict. They spent time as *girls*, rather than Greek or Turkish Cypriots.

These Greek and Turkish Cypriot girls engaged in an informal peacebuilding ritual. They became characters acting out a peacebuilding plot in a decades-long drama. Throughout their lives there has been a cold war between their governments. They have heard gruesome stories about the acts of their enemies. Their history books reinforce the clear distinction between the heroes and the villains.

The dynamic of identity worked in two ways during the camp. First, a common identity of "campers" was established. This peacebuilding workshop allowed the youth to shift characters in the drama. Both Greek and Turkish Cypriots became campers on arrival at the rustic but tranquil camp nestled in the rolling hills of Pennsylvania. The term campers was used to refer to the whole group throughout the two weeks and provided an easy way of creating a common identity for all participants. The campers did everything together. On the first morning, lead trainer Louise Diamond reflected on the group's unique opportunity to form a community for the two weeks the group would be together.

There is something else happening here that is very special and that will take all of our attention. We are now a community together. And I don't mean that word in the sense that you use it in Cyprus, the Greek Cypriot community and the Turkish Cypriot community. Put that out of your mind. I'm talking about a group of people who are living together, eating together, working together, playing together, cleaning up after themselves together, having fun together, fighting together, laughing together, probably crying together. Doing all the things that human beings do, *together*. . . . This is an opportunity to see what we can do, how we can make our community wonderful, enjoyable, [and] caring.

Second, the youth came to realize that they were much more than campers or Greek Cypriots or Turkish Cypriots. A variety of informal activities helped the group explore the great diversity within each ethnic group. The campers who enjoyed playing soccer found themselves competing with each other in mixed ethnic teams. A bicommunal group of girls floated in the pool on a sunny afternoon, comparing notes on which boys were most attractive. In both situations, ethnic identity did not seem to matter. Instead, another identity had become more important in that specific context. Soccer players bonded with their colleagues in sport. Girls shared the ritual of preparing for a romantic evening. Young people joined activities according to their interests rather than their ethnic identities.

These camp activities took on symbolic meaning and enabled the youth to rehumanize each other and move from seeing each other just as Greek or Turkish Cypriots to a more fully human picture of individuals who played sports, sang music with guitars, and had a good sense of humor. Individuals became known to each other by many different identities rather than just the ethnic stereotypical definitions so often used to define the enemy. The longer the campers were together, the more they seemed to become attuned to the unique personal attributes and characteristics of each camper.

Identities are built, protected, and transformed through ritual. This chapter begins by exploring the transformation of identity through ritual, then examines the ways ritual builds, creates, and affirms identities, and the need to protect or heal identities in times of conflict.

Ritual Rehumanizing: Transforming Identity

Identity plays a complicated role in the dynamics of conflict. Issues of identity become so central to many conflicts that it is difficult to imagine the success of a conflict intervention that does not address them. The transformation of identity is necessary to peacebuilding. Identity transformation includes creating new identities and healing identities wounded by or threatened in conflict.

In nonconflict environments, humans perceive themselves and others as having different sources of identity based on their membership in intersecting cultural groups. Figure 3.3 (chapter 3) illustrates that individuals interact in and are defined by multiple cultural groups. In societies without violent identity conflicts, people of different economic classes, ethnicities, and religions establish relationships that cut across these divisions. In peaceful societies, identities do not depend on defining an evil "other."

Conflict threatens both individual and group identity. In conflict situations, people shift from viewing themselves as a complex mix of different identities, all roughly equal. Rather than using multiple groups to define identity, individuals begin to define themselves by a group identity that is threatened. When two people recognize a conflict between them exists, the conflict takes on an additional identity dimension. While the conflict may start out over the issue of office space, for example, the two people in conflict will often look for cultural differences to explain the other's behavior. If the two in conflict are a man and a woman, they may come to see their conflict centered on issues of gender identity. If the two in conflict are African-American and Latino, they may come to see the conflict as race-based. If one is homosexual and the other heterosexual, the conflict may be seen as concerning their sexual identity. In all these cases, people's sense of themselves and others moves from understanding identity as defined by multiple cultural groups toward an emphasis on one form of identity. Figure 8.1 illustrates one such shift, focusing on ethnicity.

The relationship between conflict and identity is potentially dangerous, as people's understanding of themselves and others may become increasingly rigid and centered on one aspect of their identity. Dehumanization, the removal of the humanity of an individual or group, occurs when people strip themselves and others of other sources of identity beside the one in conflict. Name-calling and the use of animal descriptors for the enemy affirm that the enemy is no longer human: they are perceived as evil monsters that must be killed. When groups of people dehumanize one another, the concept of good versus evil dominates people's understanding of identity. The good people believe they must kill or contain the bad people to rid the world of evil. Peacebuilders can respond to this process of dehumanization through increasing the flexibility of identity, rehumanizing, and confirming the complexities of understanding humanity. Ritual can assist in these tasks.

People who are able to identify themselves in multiple ways, even in the midst of a conflict, have a flexible sense of identity. They see themselves and others as belonging to a number of different cultural groups. Identifying oneself and others in multiple ways confirms the nature of each individual as a complex mixture of sameness and diversity and even good and evil, thus allowing people to rehumanize their visions of themselves and others.[1]

Figure 8.1 Identity Transformation in Conflict

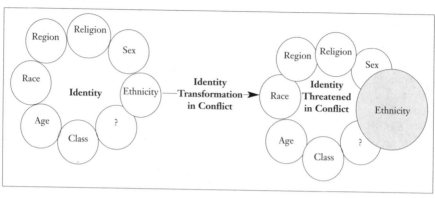

Humans are complex creatures who interact with other multiple, complex cultural groups each day.

A flexible sense of identity allows people to find some shared identities even with their enemies. Recognizing shared identities enables people to more effectively build peace in their communities. In the Middle East, Bosnia, Burundi, and Canada, people who have found shared identities with people across the conflict lines are doing the most to bring about reconciliation and peaceful coexistence in their regions. Religious leaders, for example, who have met each other and discussed the many shared aspects of their lives have gone through a process of rehumanizing their sense of self and other. Together, they are in a stronger position to build peace in the region. People who share identities are able to form crosscutting groups to break down the psychological walls that perpetuate conflict.

Ritual transforms identity by offering a humanizing space. Because identity is defined in context, perceptions of identity change according to both physical and relational situations. When people are at their workplace, they relate to others through their professional identity. When in their own home, they interact with others according to their family role as father, mother, daughter, or son. As discussed in chapter 4, symbols in the physical environment help people know how to relate to each other and how to think and act in any particular context. A ritual context can help people find common identities and recognize the complex identities each person holds.

While conflicts tend to create identities focused on one aspect, ritual transforms people's identities back to an emphasis on multiple cultural groups. Ritual rites of passage literally take people from one concept of identity to another. An individual who defines him or herself mostly through the lens of ethnicity may transform that image of identity through rituals that allow for a rehumanizing and complexifying of identity (see Figure 8.2).

Figure 8.2 Identity Transformed through Ritual

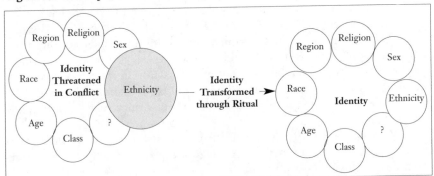

Ritual transforms the focus of identity and locus of conflict from one identity, such as ethnicity, to a more inclusive, complex, and varied set of identities. During a peacebuilding workshop, the Greek and Turkish Cypriot youth, for example, move from defining themselves purely in terms of ethnicity toward an understanding of self and other that includes the multiple cultural groups that shape each person. The informal rituals of eating, drinking, dancing, and playing together assist this process.

Peacebuilders need to construct ritualized contexts conducive to transforming perceptions of identity. Individuals engaged in conflict can be encouraged to strengthen other sources of identity by bringing the conflicted parties into contexts where they can more clearly see what they have in common. Processes aimed at dealing with identity perceptions in conflict could include placing antagonistic groups in a new situation where their old assumptions and perceptions about the identity of the enemy are challenged and transformed.

Transforming Identity through Rites of Passage

Rites of passage act as a lubricator to help move people from one identity to another. Arnold Van Gennep coined the term rites of passage to describe the universal existence of ceremonies to mark the needed passages between identities in times of great change such as birth, marriage, death, and conflict.[2] Rites of passage often occur on the brink of change, such as the dramatic change from childhood to adulthood. Coming of age ceremonies and wedding services are examples of the rituals humans construct in times of change. Rites of passage both mark and help transform identities while helping group members make the psychological adjustments needed to adapt to new social constellations. Rites of passage mark shifts in identity by taking people across physical space. People move across bridges, through doors or gates, or into water to signify inner change.

There are three steps of transformation in rites of passage. Joseph Campbell describes the "heroic journey" in traditional societies that prepares boys and girls to become men and women. It is a journey in which you separate from your known way of being, initiate into a new way of being, and then return to your original context as a changed person.[3] In rites of passage, participants leave behind their former selves and become "born again."

Worldview transformation and identity transformation are intimately related. Participants in a rite of passage are provided with a new, more complex worldview, as well as a new perspective of themselves. Transforming identity, also known as initiation, begins with stressors that break down the existing worldview of the initiate by isolating, harassing, and prohibiting coping behaviors. The created stress, lack of social structure, and physical arousal induced by those guiding the ritual act on the individual to produce uncertainty, which lowers the initiates' ability to resist changing their worldview. As the initiate's cognitive functioning continues to deteriorate and reality becomes increasingly confusing and intolerable, he or she seeks a new model of reality. This is the point at which the individual begins to experience a transformation of identity. "The individual is now ready for rebirth and a new identity."[4] After the initiate's old self is destroyed, the individual is introduced to new rituals and myths that assist in the process of making a meaningful world. The community plays an important role in supporting the initiate's new identity.[5]

These reflections on rites of passage describe formal, traditional rituals that may seem drastic or overly dramatic in today's world. However, informal, improvised rituals can perform some of the same functions in the midst of conflict. Peacebuilding workshops, such as the Cypriot example, illustrate how informal, improvised, secular rites of passage channel people toward a fuller sense of shared humanity. Rites of passage are particularly important for peacebuilding. Ritual assists parties in conflict in the process of changing from being enemies to fellow problem-solvers, warriors to peacebuilders, and victims to survivors. Rituals can also create shared identities for people in conflict or heal identity wounds that may result from conflict.

Forming Identities

Ritual is also used to build group identities. Groups develop their own rituals to initiate and energize their members. Groups assert themselves symbolically through creating names, dress codes, and common ways of acting. Ritual helps individuals within groups understand cultural expectations so that they may more easily belong to and fit in with the group. Groups such as the Ku Klux Klan use elaborate rituals to create the identity of a Klansman and to maintain group identity. Wearing white robes, chanting, and burning crosses serve as rituals that set off their group meetings from the rest of society.[6]

Ritual dramatizes identity, demonstrating the basic values held by a group. Barbara Myerhoff calls rituals "definitional ceremonies," or a "collective autobiography" whereby the group performing the ritual tells a story about itself so as to bring itself into being.[7] Driver uses the term "confessional performance" to describe how humans explain to themselves, their communities, and the world the "veiled truths of their existence" and their identity. He asserts that ritual is a confession of identity, a "coming out of a closet."[8]

Groups experiencing conflict with others need to educate and raise awareness about the issues in conflict. Public rituals are a strategy to both raise awareness and increase power for oppressed groups. In the civil rights movement, nonviolent resisters needed to symbolically create their identity to demonstrate their full humanity to the rest of US society. Kertzer describes how the public rituals of the civil rights movement served to connect local activities and people with the identity of the larger movement. Common chants, freedom songs, symbolic gestures, and specific clothing were used in vigils, demonstrations, and other nonviolent actions. The symbols and rituals of the larger movement tied the nonviolent resisters in small towns across the United States together.[9] Ritual demonstrations at lunch counters, on Greyhound buses, and in Washington, DC gave physical form to the civil rights movement. These rituals provided an identity for the movement itself and for those who participated in it.

Rituals can also be used to encourage and mark the creation of shared identities for people in conflict. Formal ceremonies can mark new identities that groups develop through negotiation, mediation, or other peace-building processes. In the Cyprus peacebuilding workshop graduates of bicommunal workshops were formally presented with certificates and were dubbed "bicommunal peacebuilders" by the US ambassador to Cyprus. These types of graduation ceremonies from peacebuilding workshops create a new, common, shared identity for former adversaries.

People in conflict may be able to use ritual to legitimize or reinvent their identities in ways that express their interdependence and common ground. Peacebuilders can use ritual to create and affirm the identities of groups in conflict in ways that do not denigrate other groups. Positive identities define an "in-group" without negative charges against an "out-group." Overcoming this dualism between an in-group and an out-group is significant, as it makes it more difficult to blame all evil on the out-group and easier to build constructive relationships between groups. In this situation, peacebuilders have the task of using ritual both to create new, shared identities and to heal identity wounds resulting from the conflict.

Definitions of what it means to be male and female are usually framed in opposite terms. Gender-based conflicts reflect the antagonism men and women may hold for each other's styles and ways of behaving. In North America, there is a men's movement and a women's movement that seeks to define masculinity and femininity in positive terms, without comparing or denigrating the other. Both movements use ritual to redefine and strengthen the male or female identity on its own. These movements potentially have a de-escalating effect on the level and number of gender conflicts experienced by their members.[10]

Healing and Protecting Identity

Conflict often threatens identity. Refugees fleeing conflict lose their families, communities, religious places, and other important symbols of their identity. Victims of violence and their families also lose important ways of understanding themselves through their relationships with former family members. Genocidal conflicts, which advocate the destruction of an entire cultural group, threaten whole populations of people based on one aspect of their identity that is correlated with evil. The Hutus and Tutsis in Rwanda and Burundi and the Serbs, Croats, and Muslims in the former Yugoslavia provide ugly reminders of the brutal attacks on identity that occur during ethnic conflicts. Peacebuilders can address the damaged sense of identity in the victims of violence through healing rituals.

Ritual can prevent destructive conflict from occurring by meeting the need for identity and encouraging a healthy, secure sense of self. In the United States, African-Americans struggle to define themselves in a society that often imposes an identity upon them. While they share the same skin color as newer immigrants from Africa and many of the same economic and social concerns as other US minority groups, the historical experience and the collective trauma of slavery create a unique sense of identity for many black Americans. Kwanzaa, Black History Month, and other rituals that celebrate African-American identity may increase the self-esteem and self-respect of African-Americans without denigrating the identity of other racial groups.

Again drawing on the civil rights movement for examples, Driver says that oppressed groups can use "confessional performance" to affirm their identity as complex humans, identify their struggle for liberation, and promote self-esteem within the group. The civil rights movement is an important example of ritual's power both to communicate a common identity of resisters, as noted above, as well as assert the basic humanity of African-Americans. Driver describes the civil rights movement as a series of mass rituals in which "African-Americans demonstrated their equal and full humanity through demonstrations, lunch counter sit-ins and other non-violent actions."[11] Driver claims African-Americans and their supporters enacted a confessional performance as Freedom Riders and, most importantly, as human beings with the capacity to act out a new, more equal society. The ritual actions of demonstrations played important roles in creating, revealing, validating, and demonstrating the humanized identity of free and equal African-Americans.

In the United States, race is a core identity and a lens for understanding both self and other. Many people wrongly assume that Americans need to become color-blind as a way of acknowledging the full humanity of blacks and whites. Rehumanizing black and white Americans does not include forgetting about race. The goal of peacebuilding in this case is not to rid people of their color consciousness. Ignoring race will not solve the historical problems that race consciousness has fostered over the last several hundred years. The goal is to end prejudice and racism against people who do not have white skin, not to shed the perception that race matters. Peacebuilders can transform perceptions of race rather than decreasing the focus on this historically important identity.

Peacebuilders can also help groups develop rituals to heal identity wounds that may have resulted from conflict or violence. If there are no existing or traditional rituals that can provide a healing force to affirm identities threatened by conflict, peacebuilders can improvise new rituals that fulfill these functions. For example, Kwaanza was intentionally created by African-American leaders who sensed the need for this special holiday based on African cultural values.

The Smudging Ceremony as Confessional Performance

The general policy throughout the United States and Canada to crush Native culture and figuratively bleach Native people into cultural whiteness created an identity crisis that still wreaks havoc with Native self-esteem. The Canadian Royal Commission on Aboriginal Rights report notes the importance of Native cultural identity to the well-being of Native peoples. One scholar testified that "a small but growing number of Aboriginal people have created positive new identities in response to the challenges and opportunities of urban life."[12] This includes a transformation of identities from "victims . . . noble savages, or primitive beings to their national Native identities including Cree, Ojibway, Mohawk, and other nationalities which deserve respect, dignity, and can contribute to society."[13]

Themes of cultural identity are found everywhere in Native ceremonies, literature, myths, and stories. Cayuga Elder Jake Thomas said,

"Who I am, and where I am coming from are the two big questions. If you know your nation, who you are, your language—that's what makes you who you are."[14] Mohawk Elder Tom Porter noted, "If we find liberation, we have found who we are. My objective in my life is to be real: no alcohol, marijuana, cocaine, drugs. We need to free ourselves from colonial entrapment and find who we are. . . ."[15] The smudging ceremony and other Native rituals affirm Native identity, reminding Native people today of their ancestors before them who have practiced this exact ceremony for hundreds if not thousands of years.

All the Native people I interviewed in my research shared an affinity for the smudging ceremony as identity-maker. Mike McTague of Spirit of the People noted, "It brings me closer to my culture and together with my people." He uses the smudging ceremony to help Native inmates and ex-offenders remember their cultural and spiritual heritage.[16] Carleen Elliot noted that performing the smudging ceremony is part of "a cultural revival"; a sign that "people are coming back to their culture."[17] While Christians take communion to remind themselves of their relationship with Jesus, Native people purify themselves in the smoke of sacred herbs to remind themselves of their relationships with everything in the world around them.

Vine Deloria, Jr., in *God is Red*, warns that ceremonies should not be seen solely as expressions of tribal identity. "This attitude undercuts the original function of the ceremony and prevents people from reintegrating community life on a religious basis."[18] The Native people I interviewed were all very clear that the smudging ceremony was a sacred, spiritual process. It affirms Native cultural identity through reestablishing a spiritual way of relating to the world.

Identity Transformation in Women's Ritual: From Victim to Survivor

Each March, universities and communities across North America hold Take Back the Night activities to recognize and protest violence against women. One Take Back the Night event at a Christian university campus provided a ritual for survivors of domestic violence or sexual abuse.

A group of ten to fifteen women and men formed a circle in the middle of the room in a round building on a hill behind the main campus. Inside the circle of people, there was an altar that included candles, about two dozen decorative cloth bags, and statues of two women holding their hands up to the sky, symbolizing their power. The candlelit setting announced the ritual space to the participants.

The leader started by talking about the ritual's goal: to recognize the pain of domestic violence and to provide a space for creating healing relationships with others. The leader then asked each person to take his or her neighbor's hand and raise them together, leaning forward to form a sheltered space for victims and survivors of violence. The leader invited anyone who wanted to come into the center of the circle. Several women entered the circle and the safe space that had been created by the outer circle of people. The group read poems and prayers with opportunities for people to respond to the lines that had meaning for them. Everyone read and spoke aloud, overlapping with each other and creating an echo of powerful lines from the Bible that described when and how God is with people in times of need.

Next, people were invited to take a colorful cloth bag from the center of the circle. Paper and pens were available for people to write what they wanted to take out of their baggage, that part of the abuse that is heavy and burdensome for people to carry with them in their lives. Then people wrote down on a piece of paper what they wanted in their luggage to help them be survivors rather than victims. Each person in the circle put the new piece of luggage (symbolized by the cloth bag) on their shoulder with their words of strength inside and rejoined the circle for several rounds of singing the African-American spiritual "There is a Balm in Gilead."

This ritual shows a rite of passage for women who have suffered violence. The transformation from the identity of a victim to a survivor is a powerful journey. The transformation requires the support of a community and the lubrication that ritual provides in moving from one identity to another.

Kay Turner notes that undergoing a shift in identities is a dangerous and frightening experience, as women may feel caught between the destructive, but familiar victim identity, and a new more empowered identity that may be asked to address conflicts with patriarchal values more directly. Feminist ritual helps this transition by recognizing the painful dimensions of transformation and continually supporting and helping each woman recognize on an ongoing basis that "she is new, that she is one of many, that she is welcome."[19] This change in identities is applicable both to women who have experienced violence directly and to those who see themselves as victims of patriarchal society at large. The transformation moves women from seeing themselves as isolated victims toward a vision of themselves as empowered survivors in a community of women.

Feminist rituals provide an opportunity for women to transform themselves in a number of different ways. One of the women I interviewed stated that feminist rituals performed in her women's group

transform me essentially from someone who is acted upon and in the worst cases a victim, to someone who is autonomous and powerful and who is very much part of the universe and all of its pieces . . . it transforms my sense of myself.[20]

Another woman noted that developing rituals based on the lives and experiences of women in the group created a profound change in each woman. This woman's story of using ritual in her women's group to overcome abuse shows the transformation many women experience.

> . . . a lot of us experienced our power being taken away specifically by men. Men that we trusted, so we felt very vulnerable, very powerless, and there were a lot of us who experienced guilt . . . [Ritual] had a profound effect on us, on our sense of selves as powerful.[21]

Yet another woman told of a ceremony created to transform a woman's perception of herself from a victim into a survivor of abuse. With a group of friends, she created a funeral service where she buried a childhood dress, representing her childhood of abuse. She declared herself a survivor of abuse in the ritual and celebrated this new identity with her friends.

In addition to using ritual as a rite of passage from being the victims of specific men or patriarchy at large, feminist rituals are also used to mark and give value to important stages in women's lives. Feminist ritual scholar Starhawk notes:

> Ritual affirms the value of any transition. . . . When we undergo a change uncelebrated and unmarked, that transition is devalued, rendered invisible. If we wish to restore value to the body, we can celebrate its changes with ritual. If we value a new relationship we can publicly celebrate our commitment. . . ."[22]

Birthdays, the onset of menstruation or the arrival of menopause, births, deaths, and new relationships are among the many life transitions marked in women's rituals. In each case, ritual is used to lubricate the movement of identities.

Driver notes that patriarchy has largely prohibited woman's ability to ritually perform and transform their identities. He claims women's groups have provided an opportunity for women to "confess" their new, liberated identities. These confessional performances where women share their own personal stories of empowerment and disempowerment in the world today are often difficult and painful. Driver aptly notes that the telling of the stories helps women "distinguish between a familiar but deceitful story of their lives easily accepted—nay, fostered—by society, and a more shameful, disorienting, anger-producing, yet more truthful story, the telling of which amounted to the first stage of a conversion.[23]

This conversion toward the identity of communally-empowered women is at the heart of the goal and purpose of women's groups in general and their specific use of improvised rituals. Transforming women's identities is a much-needed first step in a long-term peacebuilding process that must also include a transformation of patriarchal society and the relationships between men and women.

Shifting Characters

This chapter explored the ways ritual aids in creating, healing, and transforming the characters in conflict dramas. Rituals assist people in conflict in the process of changing from being enemies to fellow problem-solvers and peacebuilders and in moving from identifying as a victim to seeing oneself as a survivor. The Cypriot peacebuilding workshop rehumanized the identities of Greek and Turkish Cypriot youth. The smudging ceremony affirms Native identity in a country where it is constantly denigrated. Feminist ritual similarly affirms female identity in a patriarchal culture. Rituals that reaffirm or create identities assist the healing that is necessary for reconciliation and peacebuilding.

Peacebuilders can use rites of passage to encourage creation of joint, shared identities for people in conflict. Like theater directors, peacebuilders can plan rituals specifically geared toward transforming, creating, and healing identity. Both formal rites of passage and more informal and improvisational "confessional performances" relate to the peacebuilding process. Activities such as sharing family pictures or childhood stories and visiting each other's homes create opportunities for people to see the full humanity of self and other. These types of rituals help heal the identity wounds suffered in conflict. More formal rituals or ceremonies can be created to assist and mark changes in identity to recognize shifts in the ways people identify themselves and others or to create new, joint identities that build bridges between adversaries.

Peacebuilders can use the following questions as reflection tools when working with people in conflict to help think about the role of ritual and identity in peacebuilding.

1. How is identity a key dynamic in the conflict? In what ways do people in conflict see themselves and others through a one-dimensional aspect of identity?
2. How could ritual be used to transform people's perceptions of their identity? How can ritual be used to transform identities entrenched in the dynamics of a conflict and help people see each other as more fully human, with a complex set of identities?
3. How can ritual be used in a healing way, to affirm the integrity of people's identities?
4. How can ritual be used to create and mark new, joint identities?

The next chapter explores how rites of passage that transform identity can also provide insight and guidance to the relational transformation that is essential to peacebuilding.

Notes

1. Lisa Schirch, "Ritual Reconciliation: Transforming Identity/Reframing Conflict," in *Reconciliation, Coexistence, and Justice in Interethnic Conflicts: Theory and Practice*, ed. Mohammed Abu-Nimer (New York: Rowman and Littlefield, 2001).

2. Arthur Van Gennep, *The Rites of Passage* (Chicago: University of Chicago Press, 1960).

3. *Joseph Campbell: The Power of Myth with Bill Moyers*, ed. Betty Sue Flowers (New York: Doubleday, 1988).

4. John McManus, "Ritual and Human Social Cognition," in *The Spectrum of Ritual: A Biogenetic Structural Analysis*, ed. Eugene G. d'Aquili, Charles D. Laughlin, and John McManus (New York: Columbia University Press, 1979), 216–48.

5. John McManus, "Ritual and Human Social Cognition."

6. David I. Kertzer, *Ritual, Politics, and Power* (New Haven: Yale University Press, 1988).

7. Victor Turner, "Are There Universals of Performance in Myth, Ritual and Drama?" in *By Means of Performance: Intercultural Studies of Theatre and Ritual*, ed. Richard Schechner and Willa Appel (Cambridge: Cambridge University Press, 1993), 8–18.

8. Tom Faw Driver, *The Magic of Ritual: Our Need for Liberating Rites That Transform Our Lives and Our Communities* (San Francisco: Harper San Francisco, 1991).

9. Kertzer, *Ritual, Politics, and Power.*

10. *After Eden: Facing the Challenge of Gender Reconciliation*, ed. Mary Stewart Van Leeuwen (Grand Rapids, Mich.: W. B. Eerdmans, 1993).

11. Driver, *The Magic of Ritual.*

12 A Report of the Royal Commission on Aboriginal Peoples. *Gathering Strength* (Ottawa: Canada Communications Group, 1993).

13. A Report of the Royal Commission on Aboriginal Peoples.

14. Jake Thomas, interview by the author, February 19, 1995, London, ON.

15. Tom Porter, interview by the author, February 9, 1995, Toronto, ON.

16. Mike McTague, interview by the author, February 28, 1995, Toronto, ON.

17. Carleen Elliot, interview by the author, February 22, 1995, Toronto, ON.

18. Vine Deloria, *God is Red: A Native View of Religion* (Golden, Colo.: Fulcrum, 1994).

19. Kay Turner, "Contemporary Feminist Rituals," in *The Politics of Women's Spirituality*, ed. Charlene Spretnak (Toronto: Doubleday, 1982).

20. Interview by the author, March 1, 1995, Toronto, ON.

21. Interview by the author, March 3, 1995, Toronto, ON.

22. Starhawk, *Truth or Dare: Encounters with Power, Authority, and Mystery* (San Francisco: Harper & Row, 1987).

23. Driver, *The Magic of Ritual.*

CHAPTER 9

Forming and Transforming Relationships

A cheerful, outgoing, middle-aged Native man saw me taking notes at a Native gathering. After scolding me for not being able to remember what I hear and having to write things down, he told me what smudging was all about. "People bring the smoke to the eyes to see others better, to the ears to hear good intentions in the words of others, to the mouth to speak kind words that may be understood by others, to the mind to purify people's intentions about how they want to interact with others."[1] The prayer for healing and good relationships floats upward in the smoke and permeates the air around the smudging circle. Every breath is a reminder of the intentions symbolized in the smudging.

The smudging ceremony choreographs relational change among participants. It sets the stage for peaceful, inclusive, and respectful social interactions. An Elder advised the group:

> [W]e should put conflict ahead of us and bring people together in ceremonies; the smudge ceremonies open up people's minds to each other and helps them to listen to each other so they hear the opposition in a meeting and get the whole picture, the whole part of the truth. . . . The ceremonies bring people together in that unity.

The smudging ceremony creates a model for how to relate to others. Participants assert their constructive intentions to interact with others in equal, respectful relationships. One Native person stated that, in the smudging circle, "there is equality, all humans are equal. No one is more or less than anyone else; the circle allows everyone to communicate better and everyone can be involved in communication. . . ." Ideally, people remove signs of their wealth before the smudging ceremony to create more sense of equality. "Before you smudge, you are supposed to take off all your worldly items, all the things you've gotten in this world, like jewelry and glasses."[2]

The smudging ceremony is an intentional symbolic act. By participating in the ritual, participants agree to its message. The smudging ceremony acts as a conflict prevention mechanism by encouraging participants in a circle to listen, speak, see, and feel respectful during a gathering. Diversity is welcomed while destructive forms of conflict are banished, for conflict that creates divisions between people has no place in a circle that has joined them. The smudge tells participants that diversity exists and encourages acceptance of multiple truths. By drawing attention to each participant's subjective experience, the smudging ceremony creates an atmosphere in which people share experiences rather than dominate or win a debate.

The relational functions of the smudging ceremony are profound. The lack of any such relational frame in most meetings to orient participants and set the tone for good relationships likely contributes to the current abundance of aggressive, competitive relationships. Rituals such as the smudging ceremony could have a tremendous impact on the quality of relationship and the tone of meetings between diplomats, grassroots leaders, and religious figures.

The smudging ceremony serves both as socialization and transformation. These two forces choreograph relationships, acting sometimes as a social lubricant and sometimes as a pathway for change. Ritual is socializing when it builds, protects, preserves, and supports existing relational patterns and structures in a community. Ritual is transforming when it helps change a relationship from one way of behaving, pattern of interaction, or social structure to another.

Building Relationships with Ritual

People use rituals to create meaningful relationships. Ritual's relationship with religion can shed some light on its social functions. The roots of the word religion come from the same root as ligament. *Ligare* means to bind together. Religion binds people together. Similarly, the word holy is etymologically connected with the words whole and health.[3]

The world is a system of relationships. People experience wholeness and holiness in relationship to others. Ritual is an essential element of religion because it binds people together; ritual is a tool for building relationships. Participating in rituals helps people experience a fuller sense of health, wholeness, and holiness. Every religion uses ritual to strengthen relationships both between humans and God and among human followers of the religion. Buddhist meditation, Catholic Mass, Muslim prayers, and Native dancing are all examples of these social functions.

Ritual, however, is not limited to these religious relational functions. Many of the early ritual theorists focused on the social functions of secular, informal rituals. Many scholars credit Fustel de Coulanges for first describing the social functions of ritual. Coulanges claimed that early Greek and Roman rituals were used as "boundary maintaining mechanisms" to express and sustain group identities. Rituals such as eating together establish relationships and send messages about who belongs to a group. Coulanges argued that in Roman times the social rituals of eating together took on religious importance. Munn claims the symbol of a meal was a "holy communion" and produced the social bond better than having common interests in or agreement on issues.[4]

Other scholars also examine the ritual dynamics at play in the act of eating together. Alfred Radcliffe-Brown claims eating together symbolically joins people in a shared activity. People share their trials and tribulations with others over food. People depend on others for providing food. The act of eating communicates that a relationship exists between participants in the meal. Ritual thus came to be defined as an informal public drama in which people act out their relationships with each other in activities such as eating together.[5] People conduct business over meals; they talk about marriage, birth, plans for the future, and the latest gossip. These social dramas of public eating define "who's who" in a community. In peacebuilding settings, eating together is a symbolic social drama, one that says, "These people are in relationship with each other" and possibly, "These people get along well enough to eat together."

Other ritual theorists such as Emile Durkheim claimed more formal ritual spaces were used to define group identity, create internal solidarity, and permit individuals to engage in and express relationships with others. He claims, "It is by uttering the same cry, pronouncing the same word, or performing the same gesture in regard to some object that [ritual participants] become and feel themselves to be in unison."[6] Formal and traditional rituals are more easily choreographed as they usually have a ritual leader and possibly even written instructions to help participants know when it is time to speak in unison, drink the cup of wine, light the candle, or engage in some other symbolic activity. Performing an action simultaneously with others has the effect of creating a sense of rhythm and synchronicity among a group of people. Doing something together helps them feel "as one."

These social qualities of formal and informal, and secular and religious rituals led Roy Rappaport to argue that ritual is "the basic social act." Rappaport notes that people tend to lose their sense of self and gain a feeling of union with others through doing common actions together. When people sing, dance, or speak in unison with others, they begin to feel less like an individual and more like an essential part of a larger group. The community itself takes on an identity.[7] Humans use ritual to create a shared culture together. In drawing the circle around a group of people who feel a sense of union with each other, rituals also create a boundary that excludes people outside the circle.

Ritual Boundaries

Ritual has a role in creating both ties and boundaries in human relationships. In his study of the role of ritual in school education, education theorist Peter McLaren highlights the paradox that the rituals of life in a school setting can both divide and unite students.[8] The relative amount of distance in relationships, whether individuals have a sense of being united with or separate from others, is communicated through ritual. As with conflict, ritual neither solely brings people together nor separates them. It does both, by regulating and negotiating relationships. It assists in making explicit the degree of relationship among individuals. Rituals provide spaces, meanings, rules, and order for social relationships.

Ritual provides social rules and guidelines that help people know how to treat each other. In *Interaction Ritual*, Erving Goffman describes how everyday rules about social interaction are ritualized. These informal rituals are used to make boundaries or mark degrees of separation in relationships, providing a social lubricant for face to face interactions.[9] Informal, traditional rituals provide unspoken rules, for example, of the kinds of acceptable conversations to have while eating and the physical distance between people sitting at a table.

Moore and Myerhoff reflect on Goffman's work, agreeing on the significance of these everyday rituals for interaction. They see the "allegedly empty ritual behaviors" of handshaking and physical spacing between people as containing "a wealth of social agreements" needed to maintain and bring order to social relationships.[10] By informing the participants about the rules of the game for interacting with others, and in identifying the boundaries of a relationship, rituals enable individuals to interact more comfortably with each other.

A variety of scientific research enters into the discussions of ritual's role in maintaining relational boundaries. Neurobiologists claim that most vertebrates require physical or relational space or distance from others. Boundaries establish physical limits and distinctions of hierarchy between humans and many other vertebrates.[11] Biologist Konrad Lorenz believes human rituals perform the same functions as animal rituals, creating mechanisms for establishing both relationships and boundaries between the historic and ever-present social identities of us and them. "The triple function of suppressing fighting within the group, of holding the group together, and of setting it off as an independent entity against other, similar units, is performed by the developed ritual. . . ."[12] Ethologist Julian Huxley claims that the enormous social violence seen today is due, at least in part, to people's failure to use ritual effectively through the last century's massive social change.[13]

Rituals of separation or boundaries between groups in conflict may be just as important as rituals that bring groups together. Many authors in the peacebuilding field talk about building relationship without detailing the many different degrees and kinds of relationships. In a marriage, a degree of separation between and individuality of spouses is essential for the functioning of the partnership. If the marriage ends in divorce, and there are children involved, structured guidelines or boundaries around the time each parent spends with the children may enable the relationship between the spouses to function more smoothly. In an ethnic conflict peace settlement, groups may need a sense of separation as well as clarity about the nature of their relationship. Serbs, Croats, and Muslims in the former Yugoslavia, for example, need ritual spaces to build their relationship as well as nonviolent ritual mechanisms to express their differences.

Theologians refer to the loss of ritual pathways to create space between groups and to bind them together. Tom Driver defines ritual as a "moral territory" that creates a boundary between life-giving community and the "moral desert" where no relationships exist.[14] Peacebuilders underuse ritual's ability to communicate complicated messages about social ties, shared humanity, and the dangers of using violence to solve problems in a world increasingly marked by failed social relations between identity groups.

Communal Rites of Passage: Structure and Communitas

Ritual's role in fostering peaceful relationships among people also includes a structural component. Relationships between people come to be structured and consistent as some people and groups gain legitimacy or wield authority to make decisions about community life. Community rituals can maintain structures by affirming the existing social order or can revolutionize a social order.

Building on Van Gennep's description of rites of passage at the individual level, Victor Turner elaborated on the social revolutions that can occur through ritual. He claimed social or community rites of passage provide a pathway for moving between structural positions.[15] Turner's theory of the balance between communitas (community life) and structure provides another language to talk about how ritual regulates relationships. Turner sees life as composed of phases in and out of communitas.[16] In other words, humans need to be in close, free flowing community with one another *and* to have structures that set boundaries between them.

Turner's *The Ritual Process* suggests that life in the structural realm is full of challenges and difficulties.[17] Hierarchical community structures are always rife with conflict between individuals and groups competing to climb the social ladder that gives some people more privileges than others. Structure, according to Turner, creates an "us" versus "them." When people experience conflict, some social norms have failed to bring the community together. Conflict can affirm or test the hierarchical order of communities. As this crisis of social order escalates, people try to make the situation better by using ritual to bring the community together again. While nonritual time structures human relationships, ritual provides the experience of community with others. This ritual phase of communitas is mainly pleasurable and a comparatively egalitarian time and space. Ritual creates a unified "us." This social drama is played out again and again.

Ritual's liminal space allows transformation and transition to take place. Figure 8.2 showed ritual's role in moving between different perceptions of identity. Figure 9.1 siimilarly attests to ritual's role in social transformation.

Ritual can affirm or significantly alter existing social structure. Turner claimed that ritual assisted the process of social change by removing its participants from everyday social structure, allowing ambiguous social status and the possibility of egalitarian interchanges.

In Israel and Palestine, political, economic, and social structures divide people. Yet there are also rituals of communitas that bring them together. Marc Gopin notes the important symbolic meaning when Palestinian and Israeli families share the vital organs of their lost loved ones with others who need transplants. These symbolic acts cross the lines of conflict, show how people can live together, and are profoundly antiracist in portraying the true and full humanity of each side.[18]

Turner also describes "rituals of status elevation" that raise a person on a social hierarchy of positions.[19] In these rituals, oppressed peoples "exercise ritual authority over their superiors" by verbally and physically abusing their superiors. "The stronger are made weaker; the weak act as though they were strong."[20] Usually, those who hold power in a community are the guides for the new ritual subjects who will increase their social status through the ritual.

Turner's writings on "ritual anti-structure" portray ritual as a form of protest against societal structures. In ritual, social structures and roles are temporarily suspended, creating a passageway to a new reality in which

Figure 9.1 Social Transformation of Conflict through Ritual

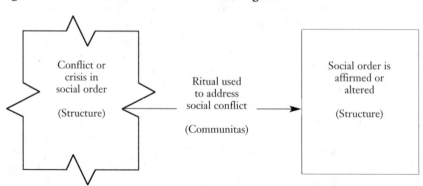

new social structures, relationships, and roles can take hold. In ritual's liminal space, "the possibility exists of standing aside not only from one's own social position but from all social positions, and of formulating a potentially unlimited series of alternative social arrangements."[21]

Others have built on Turner's concept of ritual as social transformation. Bobby Alexander, reflecting on Turner's work in *Victor Turner Revisited: Ritual as Social Change*, gives a variety of examples of informal and formal rituals used by oppressed peoples to overcome structural oppression and concludes, "Ritual often acts as a form of protest against the existing social structure and contributes to social change."[22]

Ritual theorists debate whether ritual really creates permanent new relational patterns or whether it simply acts as a cathartic, feel-good experience that allows the status quo of relationships to continue after the ritual is over. Systems theory provides a deeper analysis of how and why ritual becomes either socializing or transforming through the concept of feedback processes. The terms positive feedback and negative feedback are not used in systems theory to make judgments about whether change is good or bad. Rather, positive feedback indicates that an intervention into the system by one of its parts sustains current relational patterns within a system.[23,24] Socializing rituals use positive feedback to affirm existing social structure. Negative feedback refers to an intervention into the system by one of its parts in a way that creates real change between system components. Transforming rituals challenge and change existing social structures through negative feedback in the larger social system.

Status Quo–Preserving Rituals

Positive feedback reinforces existing system patterns. Social systems seek to protect themselves, even if many people within the social system are hurt by the prevailing values and structures. Rituals can act as positive feedback in a social system when the result perpetuates existing social values and structures. Ritual scholars from the functionalist academic camp looked for ritual's equilibrating, ordering, status quo–maintaining qualities. Many early anthropological scholars such as Malinowski,[25] Firth,[26] and Gluckman[27] examined how ritual acts as a catharsis or safety valve against rapid or violent social change. The cathartic functions of ritual suggest that it acts as a form of positive feedback, allowing the system to maintain itself, even to its own detriment. Just as a safety valve releases just enough pressure to keep a tank from exploding, cathartic rituals relieve just enough pressure on a system to keep it from collapsing, or revolutionizing and bringing new relational patterns.

Cathartic rituals can offer a short-term or confined transformation of social hierarchy. The cathartic release allows the social structure to continue post-ritual. These rituals are socializing in that they support and confirm status quo values and structures by allowing frustrations to vent in a specific, ritualized space. Some status quo–preserving rituals may be constructive and beneficial to a community. Others appear to be destructive.

People in conflicts often perpetuate relational patterns in a way that escalates conflict. John Paul Lederach outlines the patterns social conflict typically follows. Beginning with an original issue in a relationship, a conflict often grows to include more issues, more people involved in the conflict, increasingly violent escalation of reaction and retaliation between parties, and finally polarization of social groups.[28] One form of positive feedback occurs in conflicts when an "eye for an eye" relationship pattern occurs. This mutual escalation is a form of positive feedback. In the pursuit of perceived justice, aggression breeds aggression, violence gives birth to violence, and the structure of hostile relationships become increasingly difficult to transform.

Rene Girard's classic works on ritual violence demonstrate the ways bloody rites, sacrifices, and public carnage can act as communal catharsis. He notes the important role sacrificial violence played in many societies to strengthen community bonds. One individual is plucked out of their family and sacrificed in the name of maintaining the existing social structure. The scapegoat, the literal substitute for the sacrificial goat, is loaded with all of the community's potential violence before he or she is sacrificed. The community thus rids itself of its own violence, at least temporarily, and the social order is sustained by the blood of its own member. People use ritual violence, which is comparatively controlled and small relative to open warfare, cathartically to prevent more widespread destruction.[29]

People often use violence in the hope of changing relational patterns. Israelis and Palestinians both use violence to make the other group stop doing something that it is doing. In reality, one of the effects of each side's violence is to reinforce the belief in the brutality and inhumanity of the other side, allowing for and justifying an increase in violence. Interventions designed to change the system or help the system adapt to changing circumstances may inadvertently reinforce existing patterns of relationship. Even social revolution can maintain current patterns and act as positive feedback. Laurent Kabila's Democratic Republic of Congo looked very much like Mobuto Sese Seko's Zaire. Rather than stopping violence, using violence—either to keep the status quo or to force others to change—almost always leads to more violence.

The Waco conflict between the US Federal Bureau of Intelligence (FBI) and the Branch Davidians provides another example of how an intervention designed to change a system may in fact end up supporting existing relational patterns. The intervention and bombing of the Waco compound did not change the number of armed standoffs between militia groups and the federal government. In fact, some felt increased fervor to resist state and federal authorities after the debacle at Waco. Timothy McVeigh's reaction to the Waco bombing seems to have been a primary factor in his own retaliation toward the federal government in Oklahoma. FBI interventions actions intended to correct the system ended up reinforcing the exact patterns of relationship that are symptomatic of the conflict within the system.

Not all status quo–preserving rituals are violent or destructive. Rituals such as Brazil's Carnival appear able to overcome the social power hierarchies that divide people, if only for the length of the ritual. These rituals fall on the constructive end of the spectrum if they allow people to see everyone's full humanity and treat each other slightly more kindly the next time they interact. Roberto Da Matta describes rituals such as Carnival as a "process of inversion," a time and place where social structures and roles that divide people in everyday life evaporate. Ritual turns social structures inside out, bringing together people who normally do not interact.

> The context which we call "ritual" is therefore created when the thief and the policeman, the prostitute and the housewife, the convict and the diplomat, the transvestite and the macho, are placed side by side. . . . Thus, during Carnival, the social classes of Brazil, "from top to toe," can enter into association.[30]

Da Matta says that during rituals such as Carnival, the mediating element in social relationships moves away from traditional notions of power-over based on status and class toward a power-with expressed in singing, dancing, dressing in costumes, and playing together. "What is being said at this time is that differences do indeed exist, but at the same time everyone is fundamentally the same in that they are all human beings."[31]

On the other hand, these cathartic rituals could simply allow an unjust and hierarchical social system to continue. Even when there are status reversal rituals, when "the powerless switch places with the powerful" and "the Dickensian dream becomes a ritual reality," the reversals may actually undermine change.[32] Burns and Laughlin give an excellent example from Robert Dirks (1978). During Christmas celebrations in the British West Indies during the 1700s,

> the absolute barrier between slaves and plantation owners was dissolved. Slaves felt free to don their finery and eat at the table, speak with planters on equal terms, commit crimes with impunity, and openly ridicule the planters. Runaway slaves who returned during this period were granted amnesty.[33]

The authors conclude that this type of blatantly controlled revolutionary ritual created a safe space for dramatizing contradictions and conflicts within a social system, without requiring the social system to change. Status reversal rituals enabled the hierarchical slave system to continue unchanged for most of the year. Thus they were a form of positive feedback that sustained rather than challenged the underlying relationship patterns.

Eva Hunt argues that ritual is often used *instead* of violence to deal with conflict when real social change seems impossible.

> Ritualism tends to appear where there are no dynamic structural outlets for the open expression of conflict, that is, when social relations cannot be restructured by open battle, and where the possibility of social revolution, rather than balanced rebellion, is not forthcoming. In a sense, behaviors are formalized when potential hostility is accompanied by the impossibility of breaking relations or interactions permanently, or of permanently changing their power balances.[34]

When no other options for dealing with a social problem are attractive, ritual seems to adjust the relationship imbalances within a social hierarchy to allow the system to continue to function "as is" rather than completely collapse. Yet cathartic rituals often prevent the real social change that could bring about healthier relational patterns. Breaking the cycle of violence requires interventions that interrupt existing relational patterns. True social change toward more peaceful and just societies requires interventions that cause negative feedback in the social system.

Transforming Structures

According to Bateson, systems that are flexible in response to stress or conflict can survive longer. Flexible systems are self-corrective or self-balancing and constantly seek equilibrium between extremes.[35] A living body's ability to maintain a constant temperature is an example of a system that works by negative feedback. The human body has the ability both to heat and cool itself. When the body is hot, for example, it tries to cool itself with perspiration. When it is cool, it tries to warm itself by shivering. The body thus maintains a steady temperature by its flexibility to respond to information from parts of the body that are experiencing heat or cold.[36]

Negative feedback in a social system occurs as individuals or groups within the structure break destructive relational patterns such as the cycle of violence. Driver notes that most traditional societies develop complex rituals that prevent warfare because they know that violence often destroys the very system it seeks to protect. He argues that one of the causes for the recent plethora of wars is the loss of "ritual pathways" for dealing with conflict.[37]

From his study of industry-labor union conflicts, Murray Edelman concludes that ritualization is a process to which "a conflicted relationship is subjected in order to facilitate both the escalation and resolution of a struggle that otherwise would destroy the relationship."[38] Edelman describes a process in which ritual acts as a way to change system patterns before the system is destroyed by its unhealthy conflict.

Roy Rappaport reached similar conclusions in his anthropological study of the Maring peoples in Papua New Guinea. In his ecological, systems-oriented analysis of ritual in *Pigs for the Ancestors: Ritual in the Ecology of a New Guinea People*, Rappaport says that ritual negotiates relationships both between groups of people and between people and the natural environment.[39] Rappaport reports that the Maring peoples of New Guinea use ritual to limit the nature and amount of interethnic warfare, facilitate trade between communities, and create ecological balance and sustainability in the overall environment.

He critiques other functionalists for looking at ritual only as equilibrating, ordering, and status quo-maintaining without looking at how ritual functions to allow needed systematic changes to occur. Rappaport uses a systems analysis to describe how rituals in the Maring culture are a form of negative feedback that preserves, sustains, and affirms the system—even as it changes relational patterns within a system. He also describes ritual as a set of regulating mechanisms. Maring ritual functions to adjust and finely tune their total system, including social, economic, and environmental factors. Rather than inhibiting real change, Maring ritual creates a pathway for improvisation and change to occur. When systems begin to experience pressure or conflict, people use ritual to facilitate the needed changes in worldview, identity, and relationships between different social groups and between people and the environment.[40]

Rituals help systems maintain themselves by creating a way to transform the system without destroying it. In ritual, humans recreate themselves by acting out new relational patterns. The rituals of marching, holding vigils, singing, riding buses, and sitting at lunch counters during the civil rights movement established a new, empowered identity for African-Americans and permanently transformed the relationships between all Americans. This is radically different from cathartic rituals that bring only temporary change, returning to the same world they left before entering ritual's time and space.

Tom Driver states that groups use ritual as the principal technique in transforming oppressive contexts.[41] According to Driver, ritual is not simply a "cornucopia of inventiveness or a factory of fantasies . . . [Ritual has real power to affect the] powers and structures of society."[42] Ritual transforms relationships by inventing ways for people to break through the rigidity of social structures. As Driver says, ritual "embodies the principle of growth or dynamic process through which society transcends itself, praising, evaluating, rebuking, and remolding life as it is presently lived."[43] He continues:

> To ritualize is to make (or utilize) a pathway through what would other-
> wise be uncharted territory. . . . The necessity to act or rehearse the way
> into a new state of being seems to be as imperative for our entire species
> in its not-yet-finished evolution as it is for specific cultures in their devel-
> opment, and . . . We become what we learn by doing—or what we do
> while learning.[44]

Ritual symbolic, sensual, emotional, and physical performance communicates and teaches people to overcome structures that are oppressive. Ritual
can be a plow that turns over the soil, allowing us to plant new seeds to
sustain ongoing growth in a system. It changes our worldviews, identities,
and social relationships. Examples from the smudging ceremony, feminist
rituals, and the Cypriot youth camp attest to these dynamic functions.

All My Relations: Smudging Together

The smudging ceremony exemplifies the ways ritual fosters and transforms
relationships and serves as a vehicle for Native people to express their relationships with each other and the Creator. People transform the orientation of their heart and mind, and prepare to change the way they speak,
listen, and look at others. They affirm and re-create themselves as Native
people and as human beings who are related to and interdependent with
each other. The quality of their relationships shift as they sit in a circle,
prepared to strip off any of the external social structures or trappings that
may divide or separate them into hierarchical relationships.

An emphasis on relationships is found throughout Native literature
and was explicitly stated in each of the smudging ceremonies I observed.
People often use the term "all my relations" at the start and close of a ceremony. The prayers that begin a smudge often emphasize the familial relationships humans have with the nonhuman world around them. In a
Native-produced film, *Healing the Hurts,* a Native person reports, "When
we are able to make everyone we know a mother, father, grandmother,
grandfather, aunt or uncle, nephew, niece, then we'll know exactly how to
treat them."[45] The smudging ceremony appears to have a profound way of
fulfilling these functions.

Smudging connects people to the physical world around them, to
other people, and to their Creator. Native scholar Vine Deloria writes that
Native people seek to "locate our species within the fabric of life that con-
stitutes the natural world, the land and all its various forms of life."[46] Paula
Gunn Allen also affirms, "The purpose of a ceremony is to integrate: to
fuse the individual with his or her fellows, the community of people with
that of the other kingdoms, and this larger communal group with the
worlds beyond this one."[47] Allen notes that all Native ceremonies, "whether
for war or healing, create and support the sense of community that is the

bedrock of tribal life."[48] Native elders such as Black Elk confirm the important role ritual plays in fostering relationships. For example, the pipe ceremony is how Native people

> make relatives and peace. . . . By making this rite we shall carry out Thy will upon this earth, and we shall make a peace that will last to the end of time. The smoke from this sweet grass will be upon everything in the universe.[49]

Black Elk makes it clear that peace is intimately related to having intentional relationships with other parts of creation.

Native scholars document the history of dealing with difficult relationships and problematic social structures through Native ritual. Sweat lodges and the pipe ceremony marked the "termination of conflicts between nations or confirmed trading alliances . . . governing public obligations."[50] Native and European peoples also used ritual to address their conflicts. The two-row Wampum Treaty symbolized and ritually sealed a deal between whites and Natives that the two groups of people would never govern one another, interfere with one another, and would hold "peace, friendship and a good mind" as qualities of their relationship. Former First Nations Grand Chief of Canada Anthony Mercredi testified in the Royal Commission on Aboriginal People's in Canada report that the use of ceremonies in the treaty making process between white governments and Native peoples was important.

> The fact that our ceremonies were used tells us that the basis of our relationship with non-Aboriginal governments is one that respects the fact that we are different. It respects the fact that we have our own cultures, political systems, spirituality, and that these are not inferior to those of European peoples.[51]

Given the history of deceptive intentions on the part of white authorities, the approach of white people to the use of Native ceremonies today is important. When approached with seriousness and reverence, the smudging ceremony and other Native rituals may be important resources for moving Native/non-Native relationships into a more equal, respectful, and just relationship. Further research should collect more case studies using Native ceremonies in the political process of land claims and Aboriginal rights, but it appears that ritual can be used as a significant form of negative feedback that instigates a lasting change in the quality and quantity of relationships between Native and non-Native peoples and the Canadian social and political system.

On the other hand, the smudging ceremony is not the only tool Native communities need in today's complex and conflicted world. Native communities and organizations face incredible pressures and it is not surprising that many internal Native conflicts seem to be destructive, despite the practice of cultural traditions such as the smudging ceremony. Other methods of addressing conflict, such as Western forms of conflict resolution that focus on the material and social dimensions of conflict, may also be appropriate and helpful for Native people.

Transforming Patriarchy with Feminist Ritual

Feminist rituals change women's perspectives on patriarchy, affirm their identity as women, and empower them. Feminist ritual also builds and transforms relationships, changing the way women interact in the world—the way they relate to others and the world itself. The conflict between women and the patriarchal societies they live within is invisible to many people who ignore or trivialize the inequalities in the lives of men and women. Feminists have worked for decades to raise awareness of these issues. Feminist ritual offers an opportunity to build relationships with other women and to begin creating the ideal world so many women and men long for, in which social relationships reflect more egalitarian principles.

Feminists use systems thinking to express the belief that women share similar experiences in the world, and to articulate how spirituality is connected to politics, how humans are connected to the environment, and how each woman is a reflection of the Divine. One woman interviewed noted that ritual for her was an "expression of a connection with God, with the Universe, with people. . . . I certainly felt that I could get closer to people that I didn't necessarily think that I ever would."[52] Change begins within each woman as she heals the wounds of patriarchy that have told her that she is not good enough, strong enough, or smart enough to contribute to society.

While transformation in women's ritual is centered on the individual, women use their newfound sense of empowerment and cultural knowledge to change the world around them.

> Power-within grows exponentially and women together set about to right the wrongs of modern civilization. . . . A group of five such like-minded women then will set out to clean up a stream bed or a park in their neighborhood; a group of twenty-five will join a protest march for women's reproductive rights; a group of a hundred will set up a peace encampment.[53]

Women's rituals create opportunities for women to re-envision the world. Women use ritual as a visionary tool to move beyond current cultural beliefs on a path toward cultural discovery and creativity. Women begin to create new cultural values and respect for their sex within the circle of feminist ritual. Kay Turner describes feminist ritual as "a potent source of invention because the participants feel the extreme intensity, sometimes the ecstasy, of openness to possibility and revelation."[54] Feminist ritual promotes and sanctions a move from existing social structures to new patterns of relationship. Diane Stein describes feminist ritual as a "training ground to end the patriarchy and to learn to work together."[55] A small circle of women can remake the world within their own ritual.

Feminist ritual is not designed as a temporary cathartic release of the pressures of patriarchy. Many women's groups and individual women act socially to begin spreading the cultural values lived out in the microcosm of women's ritual into the larger world. Their aim is to produce lasting change that will affect the lives of the women involved, and hopefully their family, friends, churches, and communities as well.

The Take Back the Night ritual described in earlier chapters raised awareness of media images of women and increased the sense of agency and urgency to do something about it. Participants learned about an issue in their society through a film, named the way it negatively impacted them, and then engaged in a form of cultural resistance by burning their written response in a public place. The organizers designed the public condemnation of the messages given in the film to inspire a social transformation in each participant and in the university community. The goal of this ritual is a transformation in the way the media mythologizes the relationships between men and women. This ritual provided a space to educate and mobilize people for long-term social change where women and men relate as equals.

Relational Transformation: The Heart of Peacebuilding

Building relationships between people in conflict is the heart of peacebuilding. It requires a basic value orientation that encourages respect for and recognition of other human beings and empowerment of individuals to manage conflict peacefully.[56] The smudging ceremony and feminist rituals described in this book are distinctly different from the Cypriot peacebuilding rituals. Many women and Native people recognize that interacting in today's world can be a toxic experience and a one-time healing approach to social problems is not enough. Both Native people and women's groups regularly return to their respective ritual circles for healing and purifying from their interactions in a sick, violent world.

The Cypriot camp, like other conflict resolution workshops, is a different kind of ritual atmosphere. It is an improvised, one-time event. The workshop's three-step process of "know where you stand, meet the other, and see what you can do" created new ways of thinking about relationships and conflict during the workshop. The camp rituals offered participants a forum for integrating the new cultural values of mutual respect, recognition of the other, and empowerment into their social relationships.

According to current theories about how people learn and communicate through ritual action (see chapter 6), these social activities are significant to the process of learning and communicating with an "other" in an indirect, nonverbal way. The informal rituals at the Cypriot camp, for example, helped the youth relate to each other in harmonious ways, serving as a social lubricant for their interactions. Again, this underscores that ritual plays a uniting, harmonizing function for groups, particularly groups experiencing conflict. In the Cypriot camp, the informal rituals reframed the interaction. Rather than acting as adversaries, hammering out dogmatic political statements passed down by their parents, these youth engaged each other as potential friends, and playmates—as young men and young women.

The campers spent one whole day at a ropes course where teams had to work together to travel between trees on ropes that were twenty to thirty feet off the ground. The campers raved about the experience in interviews and the final evaluation:

> "It taught us many things: cooperation, planning, safety."

> "It built trust among us. It tested our courage and it improved the helping relationships among us."

> "It was challenging and risky . . . challenges make good friends."

Business executives, school systems, universities, law firms, and many other groups use ropes courses to improve trust and cooperation among team members. In this situation, the ropes course contributed to the development of more trusting relationships among these ethnically divided youth. Several of the campers also noted that the ropes course "made it easier to discuss [the conflict] because it built trust between us." Evidently, the ropes course made a significant impact on the group, as nearly every camper commented on its significance during the final evaluation.

During the evenings, the trainers planned cultural activities. The group went to a fourth of July fireworks display, had campfires with marshmallow and chocolate s'more sandwiches, played folk guitar music, held a talent show for the campers to display their talents, went shopping at a local mall, cooked shish kebabs outside, saw two American movies, and held two dances. The campers remarked that during many of these evenings, they realized the similarities between their cultures. During the shish kebab and souvlaki cookouts, the Greek and Turkish Cypriots relished the familiar tastes together. (They also complained about the American food together during the rest of the camp.) During the talent show, they laughed at the same kinds of jokes and shared similar tastes in musical styles. On the shopping trips, one camper noted, "We found out we had a lot of common tastes."

From an observer's standpoint, the dancing and party nights were the most significant social events. During the pool party, almost everyone was dancing. Nearly every boy-girl couple was bicommunal during the slow songs. One camper commented, "Now that's what I call bringing the two communities together!" Another said, "Dancing is the most important thing for youth. While dancing, every problem is forgotten, feelings become more important." Looking in on this scene of Greek and Turkish Cypriots dancing together, an outsider would have no way of knowing the deep divisions that have plagued their communities. On these evenings, there was no outward evidence of conflict.

The Greek and Turkish Cypriot youth first met at the Ledra Palace along the Green Line that divides Cyprus several weeks before arriving at the camp. I asked small groups of campers to reflect on what it would have been like if they had not come to a camp to share in all these other activities. What would have happened if they had continued to meet along the Green Line for a three-hour conflict resolution workshop and then returned to their homes without an opportunity to play and interact socially with each other? A control group that followed this pattern would have been the most insightful and rigorous way to gather this data. However, the camper's comments on this question provide some insight into the importance of the rituals. One camper remarked that the imaginary recreationless conflict resolution workshop would be "worse" because people would not be friends—they would be afraid of each other, and nobody would talk.

One group tie-dying T-shirts during arts and crafts time one afternoon shared their opinions on the importance of the recreational time. One boy said, "Yes, of course!" these activities are important, "because you see different things . . . [and] you are not pushed by your own community." One girl added, "In this way we become friends, and no one wants to break anyone's heart." Arguing for the inclusion of social activities in the camp schedule, one camper noted, "We have fun together, so it is easier to do more serious things together." Another camper offered more justification for the recreational activities. "You learn everything about the other side [when doing social activities]. We've never seen them, and they've never seen us . . . we always hear everything about this other side, and you want to know . . . and you get to know each other more during the activities. . . ." Finally, a camper stated, "All of the activities were very good for conflict resolution because they have all increased communications."

The written evaluations at the end of the camp affirmed the value of these activities as well.[57] "We were closer to each other because of the activities and we spoke to each other more freely. Many activities built trust. . . ." Another noted that the activities "were important because we got close to each other, we worked together and we experienced some of the greatest moments of our lives. . . . We built some strong friendships."

In the campers' minds, the social activities and the conflict resolution workshop had the same aim: to help them find ways of relating to each other. Social activities were not just recreational times without any significance. Playing soccer, going swimming, boating together, and other social activities had an important impact on the relationship between the Greek and Turkish Cypriot youth.

Toward Peaceful and Just Relationships

Ritual's ability to change and transform social systems is important to the study of conflict. Relationships between humans often suffer most in conflicts that have escalated out of control because there are no processes to prevent the destruction of the social and environmental system. The case studies show how ritual challenges and changes existing social structures. Native people reconnect with their Native identity and their Creator. Feminist rituals bring women together to celebrate their common experiences. The informal rituals in the Cypriot youth camp helped build relationships between Greek and Turkish Cypriot youth.

These rituals of inversion create an interesting possibility for peacebuilders to either mute the impact of power on social relationships entirely or actually turn the power structures upside down, if only for the length of the ritual. The examples above indicate that the power inversion that happens in ritual is often temporary, and needs to be repeated. Even though ritual itself is a time-specific event, people in conflict may gain new perspectives and relationships through participating in this type of ritual, which may then carry over into nonritual time and space. Further research on rituals of inversion and their long-term impact on social structure and relationships may shed light on ways practitioners can encourage these types of rituals in conflict situations.

Many of the current forms of conflict intervention advocated in the West rely on short-term, quick-fix solutions that lack an appreciation for the potential societal transformation that is possible through peacebuilding. *The Promise of Mediation* by Folger and Bush outlines different Western approaches to the mediation process. Some see mediation as a transformative tool for real social change through empowering people to deal with their own conflicts and helping them recognize their interdependence with others. Others see it as a more limited tool for solving problems. A third approach to mediation describes it as an oppressive tool of the powerful to dissipate the brewing conflicts in society. Instead of dealing with race, class, and gender issues in public, mediation solves these problems by putting band-aids on individual wounds in the private context of mediation, where no one else has to know that the same conflicts keep appearing over and over again. In other words, some people believe mediation is a form of positive feedback, acting as a cathartic mechanism for the social system.[58] Peacebuilders need to reflect on their practice in terms of the systemic principles of negative and positive feedback. It is crucial to discuss whether the processes advocated to deal with conflict create merely cathartic mechanisms or encourage significant and real social change.

The same type of question is also applicable in international peacebuilding efforts such as the problem-solving workshop format that brings together mid- to upper-level actors from opposite sides of a conflict for an extended period of time to analyze their conflict and build relationships with one another.[59] While the individuals who participate in these relationship-building efforts may build strong relationships with the other participants in the process and may develop ways of resolving some of the issues in conflict, it has been difficult for these individuals to reintegrate into their family, community, and nations after short-term interventions. This short-term approach to peacebuilding pulls individuals out of their larger relational systems. Transferring transformation at the interpersonal level to real change at the group, community, and national levels has been much more difficult.

It is unclear whether the social change experienced during these peacebuilding workshops creates temporary or lasting change. While there does seem to be some lasting change, the ritual inversion that the Cypriot youth experienced during the camp may or may not last in the years to come as they are completely surrounded by their own ethnic group.

A variety of peacebuilding researchers are conducting quantitative and qualitative research to determine the effectiveness of conflict resolution or peacebuilding workshops. The question of whether peacebuilding workshops create temporary or lasting change is heavily debated. The long-term efficacy of the informal rituals sometimes included in these workshops thus also need analysis.

There is not nearly enough research on material, social, or symbolic approaches of addressing conflict to suggest that any of them definitely produces constructive results in the long term. However, research on ritual approaches to conflict faces particular challenges. Ronald Grime's *Research in Ritual Studies*[60] and "Ritual Criticism and Infelicitous Performances"[61] outline the dangers and challenges of researching ritual. First, he notes that the category of ritual "resists criticism." People do not like to have their rituals critiqued, analyzed, or even described. Rituals are often personal and sacred, making them private and therefore difficult for a researcher to gain access to observe them. Second, rituals may succeed or fail in many different ways. Third, judging the success or failure of a ritual is "inescapably religiocentric or ethnocentric." Grimes appropriately asks, "By what criteria do participants judge rites? Are there any cross-culturally valid ways to assess a rite?"[62]

Much of the peacebuilding field thrives on the informal, qualitative storytelling from practitioners about their own observations about what seems to work. John Paul Lederach's significant contribution to the field is the most obvious example. Ultimately, my belief in the usefulness of using ritual in peacebuilding developed from my own peacebuilding practice. In a world full of seemingly intractable conflicts, any apparent relational transformation between groups in conflict, even if it is temporary, provides hope.

Lessons from the study of ritual social change and identity transformation can shed light on how to create real, constructive, lasting transformation of conflicted relationships. While rituals operate as positive or negative feedback, both types can limit the amount of violence in a social system. Peacebuilders need tools to interrupt the cycle of violence with interventions such as ritual that can provide negative feedback to the conflict system. Ritual is able to interrupt violence partly due to its socializing, harmonizing role. Ritual becomes transformative mainly due to its liminal space, which creates equality, inverts hierarchies, invites intentional relationship, opens channels (symbolic, sensory, and emotional) for feedback, and shapes new actions that in turn feed into the larger system. As in previous chapters, the questions below guide peacebuilding practitioners in the application of ritual in conflicts.

1. How are relationships important to the conflict? Do new relationships need to be made? Do existing relationships and social structures need transformation?
2. How can rituals be used in peacebuilding processes to encourage participants to highlight and strengthen their relationships?
3. How can ritual be used to symbolically mark boundaries between groups in conflict?
4. How can ritual provide a pathway for the nonviolent expression of differences between groups in conflict?
5. How can peacebuilders use rituals to remove participants from a hierarchical social structure that is central to the conflict?
6. Can formal, improvised rituals mark the shift in relationships that occurs in peacebuilding processes?
7. Can rituals include the negative feedback needed to bring change to the system without destroying it?

This chapter concludes the exploration of ritual's functions in peacebuilding. The next chapter synthesizes these key ideas into practical applications for peacebuilders.

Notes

1. Interview by the author, February 13, 1995, Toronto, ON.
2. Interview by the author, February 13, 1995, Toronto, ON.

3. Roy A. Rappaport, *Ecology, Meaning, and Ritual* (Richmond, Calif.: North Atlantic Books, 1979).

4. Nancy D. Munn, "Symbolism in a Ritual Context: Aspects of Symbolic Action," in *Handbook of Social and Cultural Anthropology*, ed. John J. Honigmann (Chicago: Rand McNally, 1973), 579–612.

5. Alfred Radcliffe-Brown, *The Andaman Islanders* (New York: Free Press, 1964).

6. Emile Durkheim, *The Elementary Forms of the Religious Life* (Glencoe, Ill.: Free Press, 1915).

7. Roy A. Rappaport, *Ecology, Meaning, and Ritual.*

8. Peter McLaren, *Schooling as a Ritual Performance: Towards a Political Economy of Educational Symbols and Gestures* (London; New York: Routledge, 1993).

9. Erving Goffman, "Interaction Ritual: Deference and Demeanor," in *Readings in Ritual Studies*, ed. Ronald L. Grimes (Upper Saddle River, N.J.: Prentice Hall, 1996), 268–78.

10. Sally F. Moore and Barbara Myerhoff, "Introduction: Secular Ritual: Forms and Meanings," in *Secular Ritual*, ed. Sally F. Moore and Barbara Myerhoff (Amsterdam: Van Gorcum, 1977), 3–24.

11. Charles D. Laughlin, John McManus and Eugene G. d'Aquili (Eds.), *The Spectrum of Ritual: A Biogenetic Structural Analysis* (New York: Columbia University Press, 1979).

12. Konrad Lorenz, *On Aggression* (New York: Harcourt, Brace, and World, 1966).

13. Julian Huxley, "A Discussion on Ritualization of Behavior in Animals and Man," *Philosophical Transactions of the Royal Society* Series B, no. 251 (1966): 247–525.

14. Tom Faw Driver, *The Magic of Ritual: Our Need for Liberating Rites That Transform Our Lives and Our Communities* (San Francisco: Harper San Francisco, 1991).

15. Victor Witter Turner, *Dramas, Fields, and Metaphors: Symbolic Action in Human Society* (London: Cornell University Press, 1974).

16. Victor Witter Turner, *The Ritual Process: Structure and Anti-Structure* (Chicago: Aldine, 1969).

17. Victor Turner, "Are There Universals of Performance in Myth, Ritual and Drama?" in *By Means of Performance: Intercultural Studies of Theatre and Ritual*, ed. Richard Schechner and Willa Appel (Cambridge: Cambridge University Press, 1993), 8–18.

18. Marc Gopin, *Holy War, Holy Peace* (New York: Oxford Press, 2002).

19. Turner, *The Ritual Process.*

20. Turner, *The Ritual Process.*

21. Victor Witter Turner, *Dramas, Fields, and Metaphors.*

22. Bobby Chris Alexander, *Victor Turner Revisited: Ritual as Social Change* (Atlanta, Ga.: Scholars Press, 1991).

23. Norbert Wiener, *Collected Works with Commentaries*, trans. P. Masani (Cambridge, Mass.: MIT Press, 1976).

24. Gregory Bateson, *A Sacred Unity: Further Steps to an Ecology of Mind* (San Francisco: Harper San Francisco, 1991).

25. Bronislav Malinowski, *Sex, Culture, and Myth* (New York: Harcourt, Brace, and World, 1962).

26. Raymond Firth, *The Work of the Gods in Tikopia* (London: Athlone Press, 1967).

27. Max Gluckman, *Essays on the Ritual of Social Relations* (Manchester: Manchester University Press, 1962).

28. John Paul Lederach, *Building Peace: Sustainable Reconciliation in Divided Societies* (Washington, DC: United States Institute for Peace, 1997).

29. Rene Girard, "Violence and the Sacred: Sacrifice," in *Readings in Ritual Studies*, ed. Ronald L. Grimes (Upper Saddle River, N.J.: Prentice Hall, 1996), 239–56.

30. Roberto da Matta, "Constraint and License: A Preliminary Study of Two Brazilian National Rituals," in *Secular Ritual*, ed. Sally F. Moore and Barbara G. Myerhoff (Amsterdam: Van Gorcum, 1977), 244–64.

31. Roberto da Matta, "Constraint and License."

32. David I. Kertzer, *Ritual, Politics, and Power* (New Haven: Yale University Press, 1988).

33. Tom Burns and Charles D. Laughlin, "Ritual and Social Power," in *The Spectrum of Ritual: A Biogenetic Structural Analysis*, ed. Eugene G. d'Aquili, Charles D. Laughlin, and John McManus (New York: Columbia University Press, 1979), 249–79.

34. Eva Hunt, "Ceremonies of Confrontation and Submission: The Symbolic Dimension of Indian-Mexican Political Interaction," in *Secular Ritual*, ed. Sally F. Moore and Barbara G. Myerhoff (Amsterdam: Van Gorcum, 1977), 124–150.

35. T. Downing Bowler, *General Systems Thinking: Its Scope and Applicability* (New York: North Holland, 1981).

36. Gregory Bateson, *Steps to an Ecology of Mind* (New York: Ballantine Books, 1972).

37. Driver, *The Magic of Ritual.*

38. Catherine M. Bell, *Ritual Theory, Ritual Practice* (New York: Oxford University Press, 1992).

39. Roy A. Rappaport, *Pigs for the Ancestors: Ritual in the Ecology of a New Guinea People* (New Haven: Yale University Press, 1967).

40. Rappaport, *Pigs for the Ancestors.*

41. Driver, *The Magic of Ritual.*

42. Driver, *The Magic of Ritual.*

43. Driver, *The Magic of Ritual.*

44. Driver, *The Magic of Ritual.*

45. Phil Lucas Productions, *Healing the Hurts* (Four Worlds Development Project, 1989).

46. Vine Deloria, *God is Red: A Native View of Religion* (Golden, Colo.: Fulcrum Publishing, 1994).

47. Paula Gunn Allen, *The Sacred Hoop: Recovering the Feminine in American Indian Traditions* (Boston: Beacon Press, 1992).

48. Gunn Allen, *The Sacred Hoop.*

49. Joseph Epes Brown, "Becoming Part of It," in *I Become Part of It: Sacred Dimensions in Native American Life*, ed. D. M. Dooling and Paul Jordan-Smith (New York: HarperCollins, 1989), 9–20.

50. A Report of the Royal Commission on Aboriginal Peoples. *Looking Forward, Looking Back* (Ottawa: Canada Communications Group, 1993).

51. A Report of the Royal Commission on Aboriginal Peoples.

52. Interview by the author, March 5, 1995, Toronto, ON.

53. Diane Stein, "Introduction," in *The Goddess Celebrates: An Anthology of Women's Rituals*, ed. Diane Stein (Freedom, Calif.: The Crossing Press, 1991).

54. Kay Turner, "Contemporary Feminist Rituals," in *The Politics of Women's Spirituality*, ed. Charlene Spretnak (Toronto: Doubleday, 1982).

55. Diane Stein, *Casting the Circle: A Women's Book of Ritual* (Freedom, Calif.: The Crossing Press, 1990).

56. Robert A. Baruch Bush and Joseph Folger, *The Promise of Mediation: Responding to Conflict Through Empowerment and Recognition* (San Francisco: Jossey-Bass, 1994).

57. All quotations are taken from the anonymous final evaluations of the Greek and Turkish Cypriot participants.

58. Baruch Bush and Folger, *The Promise of Mediation*.

59. Christopher Mitchell and Michael Banks, *The Handbook of Conflict Resolution: The Analytical Problem-Solving Approach* (New York: Pinter, 1996).

60. Ronald L. Grimes, *Beginnings in Ritual Studies* (Columbia: University of South Carolina Press, 1995).

61. Ronald L. Grimes, "Ritual Criticism and Infelicitous Performances," in *Readings in Ritual Studies*, ed. Ronald L. Grimes (Upper Saddle River, N.J.: Prentice Hall, 1996), 279–92.

62. Grimes, "Ritual Criticism and Infelicitous Performances."

CHAPTER 10

Dancing in the Dragon's Jaws: Designing Peacebuilding Rituals

Building peace with ritual is like dancing in a dragon's jaws. Ritual is a brave ballerina eluding the grip of Nazi fangs. Ritual is a smoke-washed Native person cleaning off generations of oppression. Ritual is a circle of women standing firm against the tides of patriarchy. Ritual is a group of ethnically divided girls swimming together while political winds try to blow them apart. Ritual empowers people to be free even while in the grips of conflict.

This book connects the work of ritual studies scholars, particularly what they have written about ritual's role in conflict, to the field of conflict studies and peacebuilding. As noted earlier, in writing this book I often felt as if I were writing down the obvious. For many of us, Fisher and Ury's *Getting to Yes*, conflict resolution's most widely known and recognized book, fills the same task. There is a place for articulating what we know intuitively. This book provides words, theoretical frameworks, definitions, and lists of functions to the capacity for using ritual in peacebuilding. It moves peacebuilding scholars from an intuitive sense that ritual is important to their work toward an academic and conceptual justification of the need to include ritual spaces and dramas. Peacebuilders, and the funding community that sponsors peacebuilding programs, have barely begin to recognize the potential of ritual in their crucial work.

These pages are not the last word on ritual's use in peacebuilding. They are only the beginning. The exploratory research in this chapter needs to be followed by more rigorous research over a longer time to discover ritual's lasting capacity to create space, communicate symbolic messages, and to socialize and transform worldviews, identities, and relationships toward more peaceful, human needs–oriented societies. Long-term evaluations of all forms of peacebuilding (which are beyond the scope of this book) face the same challenge. What are the lasting impacts of peace settlements, community mediation programs, truth and reconciliation commissions, peacekeeping forces, and economic development initiatives geared toward a peacebuilding vision? Do they make a difference twenty, thirty, or even a hundred years later? Peacebuilding rituals must face the same evaluation standards as other peacebuilding processes.

The Future of Ritual Peacebuilding

When I started writing this book in the fall of 1994, I had never heard anyone mention the words ritual and conflict in the same sentence. I thought the use of ritual as a form of peacebuilding would be radically new to the field and that a book on this topic would make a significant contribution. In the years that have passed since that autumn, I have increasingly seen and heard of others in the field noting the importance of ritual. When I presented some of the frameworks covered in these chapters at a conference at American University in February 1999, seven of the other presenters mentioned the importance of ritual in the process of reconciliation and conflict resolution. I am stunned at how far the field has come since the light went on in my own head. Ritual peacebuilding is a good idea whose time has come.

Yet the ability to talk about the roles and functions of ritual in peacebuilding, from both an academic and practitioner's perspective, is still emerging. Future research into ritual peacebuilding may help describe and evaluate the effectiveness of ritual approaches more thoroughly. Some of the remaining questions include:

- How much ritual should peacebuilders use compared to direct, verbal approaches to conflict? What is the appropriate balance between ritual and direct, verbal methods of peacebuilding?
- What happens if groups in conflict only experience ritual together without using any of ritual's other problem-solving, communication, analytical, and social skills?
- Is ritual subject to a conflict's "ripeness" or readiness of a conflict to intervention and change? If so, when is the best time to use ritual within the cycles and stages of conflict?
- What kinds of rituals are currently being used in peacebuilding around the world?[1]
- Are there dangers in using ritual? How do peacebuilders help prevent negative use of ritual (such as ritual being used to feed hysteria) in peacebuilding processes?

- How effective are mass rituals for peace?[2] How do these rituals create a movement toward peace?

These research questions are just a sample of directions for future research. There are endless opportunities to explore the use of ritual in the journey toward learning how to build peace in a world in which scarce resources, oppressive social structures, lack of communication skills, and vastly different worldviews keep most peacebuilders overemployed. Ritual peacebuilding must be both validated and harnessed by people building peace.

I dream of the day when negotiators, mediators, trainers, nonviolent activists, community developers, and others use the term "ritual peacebuilding" without explanation, justification, or looking over their shoulder to see who might be listening. Validating the important role of ritual in conflict intervention will come through practice.

Many peacebuilders will ask where to start in designing peacebuilding rituals. As an experimenter in the alchemy of ritual peacebuilding, one lesson learned in my own practice is that there are no recipes. While the general ingredients and techniques of rituals can be described, the timing and combination of ingredients is up to the people involved. Reverting to the theater metaphors used throughout this book, there are no existing scripts, no director instructions, no drama classes for peacebuilders wanting to use ritual in their work.

A number of recent books try to help people create rituals and ceremonies. *Healing Ceremonies: Creating Personal Rituals for Spiritual, Emotional, Physical and Mental Health* is written by two doctors who testify to the use of ritual in the healing process and describe how to develop rituals.[3] *The Art of Ritual: A Guide to Creating and Performing Your Own Ceremonies for Growth and Change* also provides a number of general steps for creating ritual.[4]

While some general principles exist for creating rituals that are interesting, effective, and transformative, rituals look very different depending on the cultural context. Peacebuilders cannot "give" people rituals unless they come from the same cultures as the groups in conflict. Ritual is rooted in the unique ways individuals view and experience the world. Peacebuilders from within a cultural context may develop meaningful peacebuilding rituals, as they will likely know how far they can push the boundaries of comfort in experimenting with new symbols and rituals. Outside interveners, however, must find ways of making space for people to create and participate in rituals themselves. In my own use of ritual peacebuilding, I have noted three key principles of developing rituals. First, attention needs to go toward designing a space for peacebuilding. Second, the peacebuilding process should use multiple ways of knowing and communicating. Third, it is important to recognize the potential for ritual to form and transform identities and worldviews.

Create an Oasis for Peace

Peacebuilders should pay as much attention to the *context* as to the *content* of their interventions. Space is symbolic. The typical negotiation room is filled with adversarial images and symbols such as square or rectangular tables that force people to sit on opposite sides. Other contexts, such as eating a meal or sitting at a round table with candles and flowers, hold more cooperative images and connotations. Creating a "safe space," a symbolically-supportive environment or an atmosphere conducive to transformation, may help people feel more comfortable and open in a peacebuilding process.

Peacebuilders can also create a safe space, an "oasis for peacebuilding," through constructing a ritual environment that is set aside or separated from everyday time and space. The smudging ceremony case study outlined how ritual space is carved out from normal time through special sensual stimuli or unique combinations of people. The smudging ceremony became a safe space to "be Native" and to interact respectfully with other people. In feminist rituals, composing a ritual space with special symbols and actions that represented and encouraged the empowerment of women created "patriarchy-free zones." Peacebuilders can create ritual spaces where new ways of being can be tried out without the normal pressures and strains of everyday life (see Box 10.1). Peacebuilders should pay close attention to the kinds of contexts they shape for bringing together people in conflict. What symbolic ways does the negotiating room hold people together? How will people relate to each other? What are the specific values that are communicated to the people in conflict to help set the tone for their interactions?

Engage People's Bodies, Senses, and Emotions

For centuries, people have used ritual communication when words alone were not sufficient. Peacebuilding processes should include pedagogies that engage people through multiple ways of learning and knowing. Peacebuilding rituals allow people to eat, drink, smell, dance, laugh, cry, and

---

Box 10.1 Places for Peacebuilding

- Religious spaces such as holy sites and buildings
- Home spaces such as the kitchen, dining room table, or living room
- Outdoor spaces at parks or in the wilderness
- Recreational spaces such as resorts, parks, boats, or restaurants

express the full range of human emotions and activity as they communicate their humanity, learn to rehumanize their adversary, and develop new and creative ways of understanding their conflict.

Peacebuilders need to conceptualize learning as more than just a transfer of knowledge. They need to involve symbols, emotions, senses, and people's bodies in the learning process. A first step is to plan activities that encourage people to interact physically and emotionally with each other, and to act out new ways of being with each other is a first step. Peacebuilders can engage people's senses and make channels or ritual spaces where emotions are both allowed and valued. Repetition, rhythm, and pattern have a physical impact on the brain and can enable people to think and see differently. Symbols, metaphors, myths, and symbolic actions remind participants of who they are, where they are, and what they are doing in a peacebuilding process.[5] "Performatives"—words and actions that are declared to be true by their context—also help people believe that real change is happening in peacebuilding.

Box 10.2 and 10.3 list common symbols and actions that can help create rituals.

Recognize Ritual's Role in Socialization and Transformation

Change is an inherent part of conflict. Ritual, like conflict, can be constructive or destructive. Peacebuilders need to be aware of the power of

Box 10.2 Sensual Stimuli in Peacebuilding

Sight = flowers, colorful scarves, circles, smoke
Touch = textured fruit, fabric, water, sand
Smell = burning incense, candles, home-baked bread
Taste = salt water, fruit, bread, herbs
Hearing = bells, falling water, drums, music, spoken word

Box 10.3 Common Peacebuilding Symbols

Fire (candles)
Water (ice, steam, warm and cold)
Earth (sand, rocks, dirt, ashes)
Plants (flowers, tree branches, leaves)
Foods (milk, honey, bread, salt, fruit)

ritual to create further destructive dynamics in a conflict, or to create a pathway out of the violent expression of conflict toward relationships based on coexistence.

Ritual can be used to socialize people, confirming cultural values that support peace and that may be threatened in a time of conflict or war. Ritual can also be used to heighten cultural anxiety around particular chosen traumas or chosen glories from a community's generational memory, which can escalate conflict.

Likewise, ritual's role in the transformation of worldview, identity, and relationships can assist the change process in both positive and negative ways. Peacebuilders can create ritual that enables groups to see each other as fully human and find mutually satisfying ways of meeting their human needs. Ritual also has the destructive potential to turn civilians into warriors, or to polarize and make enemies out of ethnic groups.

Peacebuilding rituals can help neutralize or overcome destructive rituals that fan the flames of hatred. Box 10.4 shows ritual-like activities that can prompt a reaffirmation of positive cultural values in peace and coexistence, or constructive changes in worldview, identity, and relationships. These could be used with participants during any mediation, high-level diplomatic effort, conflict resolution training, or peacebuilding workshop.

In addition to these three principles of peacebuilding, the following concepts relate to designing peacebuilding rituals.

Planning Informal Rituals

Peacebuilders beginning their experiments with using ritual might want to start with informal rituals, such as the ones used during the Cypriot workshops or the South African trout fishing weekend. Peacebuilders working with cultural groups they do not belong to will need to plan informal rituals (see Box 10.5) along with a local planning committee, ideally made up of people from all sides of the conflict. Informal rituals such as drinking

---

Box 10.4 Peacebuilding Actions

Burying	Breaking	Affirming	Drawing
Drinking	Washing	Burning	Denouncing
Passing	Holding	Cutting	Playing games
Walking	Tying	Cleaning	Playing sports
Singing	Eating	Planting	Playing music
Lifting	Folding	Naming	Cooking
Dancing	Smoking	Fishing	Watching movies

> **Box 10.5 Informal Rituals for Peacebuilding**
>
> • Share family pictures
> • Tell childhood stories
> • Prepare meals together
> • Eat meals together
> • Visit participants' homes
> • Create spaces for participants to live together temporarily
> • Provide musical instruments for participants to play

coffee or tea, eating hummus and pita, playing guitar and singing, kicking a soccer ball at breaks, or even a day-long safari can provide a radically different context for participant interaction. These rituals can also relieve the emotional stress caused by other parts of a peacebuilding workshop.

To communicate, especially across cultural divides, the symbolic activities in rituals should include symbols that provide meaning to many people. Some rituals reflect basic common symbols of humanity. For example, although eating and dancing are done in culturally specific ways, the basic concepts are the same in each culture. Food is eaten in social groups to provide both sustenance and community. Dancing involves moving one's body to music with others. Peacebuilders can develop rituals that are culturally accessible to peoples in conflict and therefore serve to bridge different cultures.

Informal rituals used in peacebuilding processes also should be as interactive as possible. The Cypriot campers placed more value on some informal rituals than others, according to their final evaluation. Activities that required little interaction, such as arts and crafts and going to a carnival, were rated lowest; the campers reported that these activities were not very helpful in building relationships. The ropes course and building the egg tower rated highest. Campers commented that these activities required teamwork, built trust, and increased their ability to communicate about other issues after the activities were complete. Sleeping in cabins together, cleaning together, and free time for singing and other improvisational activities were also rated highly in terms of their importance to building relationships. Ritual spaces that required the campers to converse with each other, figure out how to do something (such as cleaning a rustic cabin with a lot of spiders), and develop activities themselves during free time were also important.

Consciously introducing more informal ritual may be the place to start for those who are convinced of the academic argument for using ritual, but are wary about using symbols to develop new rituals. Others may be ready at this point to try their hand at the task of all religious and spiritual leaders around the world: creating and leading formal rituals.

Creating Formal Ritual

The previous examples of feminist ritual demonstrate how groups can develop their own rituals to address issues in their lives. The act of creating a ritual with affirming messages is empowering for women who, as a group, are often excluded from traditional rituals. While not all feminist rituals are developed in a group, group planning or participation in ritual creation is an important characteristic of feminist ritual.

Participating in the creation of new, improvised formal rituals (see Box 10.6) is important to their success. Rituals imposed on people without their input or consent have a high failure rate—they are seen as boring or irrelevant, and have no function for the group doing the ritual.

On the last night of the Cypriot youth camp, I worked with several of the trainers to come up with a final ritual. The youth sat in a circle around an altar of candles. Each camper walked to the front of the room to light a candle and share a wish or dream for the future. The campers came forward one at a time, saying, "I wish equality." "I wish friendship." "I wish everyone could understand each other one day." When all the campers had finished, the group sang John Lennon's song "Imagine," arms around each other: "You may say I'm a dreamer . . . but I'm not the only one. I hope some day you'll join us, and the world will live as one." The song and the ritual ended in giggles, a few claps, and people straggling away. Then one camper asked everyone to stand up and shout "WE WANT PEACE!" together three times in a row. Excited clapping, hoots, hollers, and laughter followed, ending the ritual on a positive note. While the singing and shouting in this final ritual had eager participation, the first half of the ritual did

---

Box 10.6 Formal, Improvised Peacebuilding Rituals

- Use fire to purify or transform pictures, objects, papers, or other symbols
- Create a quilt of patches representing the conflict or peacebuilding efforts
- Build an altar in the center of the room to which people can bring objects with significant symbolic value and share with the group
- Pass a bowl of salt water around a circle of people for them to dip their fingers into and mark their neighbor's forehead or cheek, either to cleanse or remember tears shed in the conflict
- Weave a web between people in a circle by having each participant hold a piece of the yarn and throw the ball of yarn to another person in the circle while sharing a story or emotion to represent their shared journey into conflict
- Create an ordination ceremony for people who have made it through a peacebuilding training, workshop, or mediation
- Create an arbor for people to walk through to symbolize their new identities

not engage the youth. Most of the youth yawned with boredom, talked with friends about things that had happened earlier in the day that were irrelevant to this final closing ceremony, and seemed unmoved by the candle lighting symbolism.

There is very little ritual theory to explain the nuances that seem to make or break a ritual. This story attests to the clumsy, awkward beginnings of including formal, improvised rituals in peacebuilding. Ritual's applications to peacebuilding need more flesh, more case studies of how peacebuilders use formal ritual in their work.

Ideally, the campers should have developed the closing ritual on their own. A camper rather than a trainer initiated the one action that seemed to be meaningful and significant, when everyone shouted "WE WANT PEACE!" The campers may have been more attentive to a final ritual that they had created themselves to communicate to each other what the experience had meant to them and what they wanted to take home. To be meaningful and effective, improvised, formal rituals usually need to be developed by the people participating in them. Perhaps under the name of a closing ceremony or a final celebration participants could have developed a way of marking their own transformation during the week. Campers could have "graduated" each other, a rite of passage to mark their new identities and relationships. A presentation by each community to their new friends from the other community may have had significant symbolic, transformative value for the group.

Participating in the creation of ritual may be particularly empowering for groups who historically have been oppressed or excluded from formal ritual making. Peacebuilders can assist people in creating rituals that empower and affirm their identity. Since so many conflicts result from perceptions of threatened identity, creating empowering rituals can profoundly affect the conflict behavior of a group. Improvised ritual offers an alternative method for approaching a conflictual issue that gives the people in conflict the power to author the means for transforming their conflict, allowing them to create an idealized world that moves beyond the anger and frustration that prohibits conflictual relationships from changing.

Adapting Other People's Rituals

While the smudging ceremony appears to be a powerfully transforming ritual for some Native people, it is rarely appropriate for non-Natives to use the smudging ceremony or other Native rituals. Many Native writers and leaders condemn this modern form of piracy in which culture rather than land is expropriated by non-Natives.[6] The smudging ceremony is a part of Native culture and makes sense in relation to broader cultural values and ways of being. Many Native people feel offended when non-Natives practice Native culture without sharing this broader cultural framework. Of course, culture has always been traded and exchanged throughout human history, with groups of people borrowing ideas and rituals from each other; but the act of taking a Native ritual is painfully reminiscent of North America's imperialist past.

There are, however, principles from the smudging ceremony that translate into non-Native contexts. For example, Native cultures use rituals such as the smudging ceremony as a way of healing relationships that have been broken. The smudging ceremony purifies and cleanses people physically, emotionally, spiritually, and mentally of whatever prevents them from having relationships with others. The smudging ceremony appears to reweave the web of relationships, set the universe in order, and bind people to their community and to the world around them. There are several important lessons here for non-Natives. First, viewing conflict as a state of brokenness implies that peace is a state of health, wholeness, and holiness. Second, transforming conflict involves healing, purifying, and cleansing. Third, healing is a sacred task involving our spirituality, emotions, intellect, and physical selves. These teachings are important for non-Natives to learn. In the end, peacebuilders need to find a careful balance between respectful learning and cultural piracy.

Alternating Structure and Ritual Communitas

Peacebuilders need to think about the time they allow for informal rituals during peacebuilding. Ritual complements rather than replaces existing peacebuilding components such as teaching communication and problem-solving skills. Figure 10.1 illustrates how peacebuilders can allow space for structured activities where traditional forms of learning and communication take place and for ritual activities where nonverbal, symbolic communication occurs. The central line represents a peacebuilding workshop. The wavy line shows how trainers can alternate between traditional training and ritual activities to provide the benefits of both to participants.

People can use ritual in many different types of peacebuilding, including mediations, dialogues, business or political negotiations, or training.

Figure 10.1 Designing Ritual Spaces in a Peacebuilding Workshop

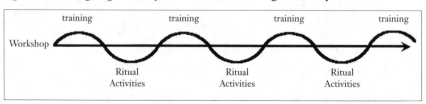

Regardless of the form of verbal peacebuilding, ritual's symbolic, nonverbal communication adds depth to the peacebuilder's message.

Using Ritual within and between Groups in Conflict

Peacebuilding rituals are important for use both within groups experiencing conflict and between groups in conflict. Native communities use the smudging ceremony to deal with issues related to living in a state of conflict with the larger Canadian society. Likewise, women's groups use feminist rituals to address the experience of living in a patriarchal world. These peacebuilding rituals assist groups in conflict in maintaining a healthy self-identity and in addressing the effects of conflict. The rituals used by the Greek and Turkish Cypriots attest to ritual's role in building relationships across communal lines. At the same time, there were important rituals throughout the Cypriot Camp that occurred within the Greek or Turkish Cypriot groups of youth. They ate their meals with their own ethnic community. The groups seemed to need some time to themselves to process what was happening during the camp. Mealtime became an important check-in time for each group.

Reentry after intense periods of transformation, such as the Cypriot youth camp, is always challenging. Designing times for groups to meet with their own side during the process may be an important way of creating space for digesting the experience. It will be more difficult to process a peacebuilding workshop with friends and family who were not part of the process and may even ostracize those who participated if their beliefs change more than nonparticipants can tolerate.

Ritual Intention: Planning Transformation?

As a non-Native observer of and participant in the smudging ceremony, I was fascinated by the intentional construction of a context conducive to transformation. The smudging ceremony was explicit, yet artistic in its transforming capacity. No one said, "Okay, now we're going to transform your worldviews and the way you see each other." I carry with me the lesson that peacebuilders need to be intentional in their desire to transform, but need to encourage transformation through ritual rather than words.

Intention is an important concept in feminist ritual. Each of the women I interviewed spoke of the power of intention, the belief that if we intend for something to happen in ritual, it will happen. A new reality takes shape when people *will* something to happen, when they actually create a ritual to bring a new reality into being. The three levels of intention are thinking, speaking, and doing. Thinking new thoughts enables a dream to begin. Talking about the dream lets others know about it and starts to spread the dream. Acting out the dream makes it a reality.

In feminist ritual, participants bring their hopes and dreams of the ideal world and set about to create it within ritual space. Feminist ritual requires participants to be explicit in their intention to gain awareness of their power and to change patriarchal society. Women create rituals where they enact a new, changed reality. An individual's intention to be transformed in a ritual is linked to his or her participation in the creation of ritual. While peacebuilders are often aware of the need for transformation in the perceptions and worldviews of the individuals and groups in conflict, the latter are usually resistant to change.

Intentionally creating a ritual adds momentum to the possibility of being transformed in ritual. An expectation and desire for change contributes to ritual's transformative capacity. Again, peacebuilders should think about how to *engage* participants in planning and designing a ritual for their conflict rather than planning a ritual *for* people in conflict. The power of intention is more evident when people create a ritual to do something for themselves.

Planning and carrying out an improvised ritual can be an anxious experience, especially for people used to a sense of control and predictability. Barbara Graber explains that in both drama and ritual, spontaneity and improvisation are important for the success of the transformation. She described the role of intention in feminist ritual as a creative act, and her advice is particularly savvy for peacebuilders accustomed to leading processes.

> There is a need to step back and let the group energy [take over] and really intuit and send out feelers for what is coming at you rather than what you need to act on or do. Theoretically, I think the most important aspect is that the leader follows the follower. Instead of thinking that you have to make something happen, move yourself energetically way back and wait, watch, and ask "what's next?" There really is a spirit that wants us to celebrate and enjoy and love and nurture and when you start giving that spirit its way, when you are willing to step back and put the ego and need to be perfectly organized and processed away, then something else takes over and you are just in awe of what is happening with this group of people. . . . It's trusting the spontaneous, it's interactive, its not "I'm here delivering the goods to you," and you receive them and are better for it . . . no one knows what is going to happen next . . . including the leader.[7]

Theater directors train for years to be able to see and feel group dynamics on the stage. Ritual can feel more natural and less forced if the leader is willing to carefully let a process unfold while being aware of how to lead a group's energy toward their intended goal.

Setting the Stage for Peace

This book opened with nine stories about the use of ritual in peacebuilding. Two more stories here will pull it all together.

On cliffs overlooking the Atlantic, just miles away from Protestant and Catholic tensions in the cities of Northern Ireland, a community of peacebuilders lives and invites others into their space. The Corrymeela Reconciliation Center provides workshops, weekend retreats, and ongoing structured dialogues for Catholics and Protestants. Emily Stanton lived, worked, and researched the functions of ritual at Corrymeela as a graduate student in the Conflict Transformation Program at Eastern Mennonite University. Her final report "A Space in Your Heart You Never Knew You Had" details the unique space, symbolic communication, socialization, and transformation that take place at Corrymeela.[8]

Stanton describes Corrymeela as a "safe haven away from the tensions and divisions of the city." She documents four key ways the community creates safe space. First, people are welcomed into the community with a "buzz of affirmation." Smiles, handshakes, hugs, cups of tea, and a warm sense of hospitality are the first act in this peacebuilding drama. Second, Stanton identifies an atmosphere of acceptance and nonjudgment. Protestants and Catholics—middle class and less wealthy, male and female, gay and straight—experience equal treatment and acceptance. The third element in the drama is the physical space, inside and out. Participants are asked to feel at home and are given access to the fireplace, kitchen, and living room. On the outside, Corrymeela is "isolated and beautiful." It is surrounded by fields and overlooks crashing waves. A circular church in the center provides a particularly liminal space for joint worship between the groups.[9]

Stanton's interviews with participants in Corrymeela peacebuilding dialogues, workshops, and retreats reveal a profound sense of personal growth and increased self-esteem, a new awareness of their relationship to others, and a breaking down of stereotypes of others. In addition to this personal growth, people improvise new ways of acting and relating to members of the opposite religious and ethnic group, and adopting an identity of a peacebuilder by committing their lives to working toward social change in Northern Ireland.[10]

Across the Atlantic Ocean, the Summer Peacebuilding Institute (SPI) at Eastern Mennonite University (EMU) creates another type of ritual space. Each May and June, hundreds of people from more than sixty different countries come to EMU to take academic classes rooted in experiential teaching methods and the real-world practice of peacebuilding. Most participants already have extensive experience in peacebuilding processes and organizations.

Participants share dorm rooms, cook meals together, and spend their time outside of the classroom braiding each other's hair, sharing stories of conflict where they come from, crying over events reported on CNN, and dancing to music from around the world. According to qualitative research conducted by an SPI research methods class, participants report that time spent in class and time spent in informal rituals are equally important.[11] A participant might take a class during the day on mediation, and ponder how they might practically implement the ideas in their home context. In the evening, after eating a meal of Thai spring rolls, West African ground-nut stew, and Latin American rice pudding, participants might find themselves mediating a conversation between Israeli and Palestinian participants. The interplay between informal and formal learning, bodies, cultures, and ways of thinking about peace creates a potent brew for participants. As the field of peacebuilding progresses, funders, strategists, scholars, and practitioners need to join together to create more of these "theaters" where creative dramas engage whole people in a journey toward a culture of peace.

Notes

1. Efforts to document peacebuilding rituals indigenous to ethnic groups across Africa include Kana Roba Duba et al., *Honey and Heifer, Grasses, Milk and Water: A Heritage of Diversity in Reconciliation* (Nairobi, Kenya: Mennonite Central Committee, 1997) and William Zartman (Ed.), *Traditional Cures for Modern Conflicts: African Conflicts: African Conflicts "Medicine"* (Boulder, Colo.: Lynne Rienner Publishers, 1999).

2. For example, the mass rituals such as people across South Africa simultaneously singing a national song to mark the transformation of that country's social values.

3. Carl A. Hammerschlag and Howard D. Silverman, *Healing Ceremonies: Creating Personal Rituals for Spiritual, Emotional, Physical and Mental Health* (New York: Perigee, 1997).

4. Renee Beck and Sydney Barbara Metrick, *The Art of Ritual: A Guide to Creating and Performing Your Own Rituals for Growth and Change* (Berkeley, Calif.: Celestial Arts, 1990).

5. Barbara Myerhoff, "We Don't Wrap Herring in a Printed Page: Fusion, Fictions and Continuity in Secular Ritual," in *Secular Ritual*, ed. Sally F. Moore and Barbara G. Myerhoff (Amsterdam: Van Gorcum, 1977), 199–226.

6. Laurie Anne Whitt, "Cultural Imperialism and the Marketing of Native America," in *Natives and Academics: Researching and Writing About American Indians*, ed. Devon Mihesuah (Lincoln, Neb.: University of Nebraska Press, 1998).

7. Barbara Graber, interview by the author, January 15, 1998. Harrisonburg, Va.

8. Emily Stanton, "A Space in Your Heart You Never Knew You Had" (Eastern Mennonite University, Harrisonburg, Va., October 1, 2000).

9. Stanton, "A Space in Your Heart You Never Knew You Had."

10. Stanton, "A Space in Your Heart You Never Knew You Had."

11. Qualitative Research for Social Change, "Research on the SPI Community: Class Project" (Eastern Mennonite University, Harrisonburg, Va., June 18, 2002).

Bibliography

Abu-Nimer, Mohammed. *Dialogue, Conflict Resolution, and Change: Arab-Jewish Encounters in Israel.* New York: State University of New York Press, 1999.

Achterberg, Jeanne, and Barbara Montgomery Dossey. *Rituals of Healing: Using Imagery for Health and Wellness.* New York: Bantam Books, 1994.

Agnew, John. "Beyond Reason: Spatial and Temporal Sources of Ethnic Conflicts." In *Intractable Conflicts and Their Transformation*, eds. Louis Kriesberg, Terrell A. Northrup, and Stuart J. Thorson. Syracuse: Syracuse University Press, 1989.

Alexander, Bobby Chris. *Televangelism Reconsidered: Ritual in the Search for Human Community.* Atlanta, Ga.: Scholars Press, 1994.

———. *Victor Turner Revisited: Ritual as Social Change.* Atlanta, Ga.: Scholars Press, 1991.

Allen, Paul Gunn. "Special Problems in Teaching Leslie Marmon Silko's Ceremony." In *Native and Academics: Researching and Writing About American Indians*, ed. Devon Mihesuah, 23–26. Lincoln, Neb.: University of Nebraska Press, 1998.

Allen, Paula Gunn. *The Sacred Hoop: Recovering the Feminine in American Indian Traditions.* Boston: Beacon Press, 1992.

Amiotte, Arthur. "Eagles Fly Over." In *I Become Part of It: Sacred Dimensions in Native American Life*, eds. D. M. Dooling and Paul Jordan-Smith, 206–32. New York: HarperCollins, 1989.

———. "Our Other Selves." In *I Become Part of It: Sacred Dimensions in Native American Life*, eds. D. M. Dooling and Paul Jordan-Smith, 161–72. New York: HarperCollins, 1989.

———. "The Road to the Center." In *I Become Part of It: Sacred Dimensions in Native American Life*, eds. D. M. Dooling and Paul Jordan-Smith, 246–54. New York: HarperCollins, 1989.

"Ancient Indian Rite Performed by Police." *Toronto Globe and Mail*, May 31, 1991, A10.

Artigiani, Robert. "From Epistemology to Cosmology: Post-Modern Science and the Search for New Cultural Cognitive Maps." In *The Evolution of Cognitive Maps*, ed. Ervin Laszlo et al., 29–60. Philadelphia: Gordon and Breach, 1993.

Augsburger, David W. *Conflict Mediation Across Cultures: Pathways and Patterns.* Louisville, Ky.: Westminster/John Knox Press, 1992.

177

Austin, J. L. *How To Do Things With Words.* Cambridge, Mass.: Harvard University Press, 1962.

Avruch, Kevin. *Culture and Conflict Resolution.* Washington, DC: US Institute of Peace, 1998.

Avruch, Kevin, and Peter Black. *Conflict Resolution: Cross-Cultural Perspectives.* New York: Greenwood Press, 1991.

Bakhurst, David, and Christine Sypnowish. *The Social Self.* Thousand Oaks, Calif.: Sage, 1995.

Banathy, Bela H. "The Cognitive Mapping of Societal Systems: Implications for Education." In *The Evolution of Cognitive Maps,* ed. Ervin Laszlo et al., 205–20. Philadelphia: Gordon and Breach, 1993.

Barrie, Thomas. *Spiritual Path, Sacred Place: Myth, Ritual, and Meaning in Architecture.* Boston: Shambhala, 1996.

Barstow, Anne Llewellyn. *Witchcraze: A New History of the European Witch Hunts.* London: Pandora, 1994.

Bateson, Gregory. *Mind and Nature: A Necessary Unity.* New York: Dutton, 1979.

———. *A Sacred Unity: Further Steps to an Ecology of Mind.* San Francisco: Harper San Francisco, 1991.

———. *Steps to an Ecology of Mind.* New York: Ballantine Books, 1972.

Bateson, Gregory, and Mary Catherine Bateson. *Angels Fear: Towards an Epistemology of the Sacred.* New York: Macmillan, 1987.

Bateson, Mary Catherine. "Ordinary Creativity." In *Social Creativity.* Cresskill, N.J.: Hampton Press, 1999.

———. *Peripheral Visions: Learning Along the Way.* New York: HarperCollins, 1994.

———. "Ritualization: A Study in Texture and Texture Change." In *Religious Movements in Contemporary America,* eds. Irving I. Zaretsky and Mark P. Leone, 150–65. Princeton, N.J.: Princeton University Press, 1974.

Beck, Renee, and Sydney Barbara Metrick. *The Art of Ritual: A Guide to Creating and Performing Your Own Rituals for Growth and Change.* Berkeley, California: Celestial Arts, 1990.

Belenky, Mary. *Women's Ways of Knowing: The Development of Self, Voice, and Mind.* New York: Basic Books, 1997.

Bell, Catherine. "Constructing Ritual." In *Readings in Ritual Studies,* ed. Ronald L. Grimes, 21–32. Upper Saddle River, N.J.: Prentice Hall, 1996.

———. *Ritual: Perspectives and Dimensions.* New York: Oxford University Press, 1997.

———. *Ritual Theory, Ritual Practice.* New York: Oxford University Press, 1992.

Berger, Peter L., and Thomas Luckmann. *The Social Construction of Reality: A Treatise in the Sociology of Knowledge.* Garden City, N.Y.: Doubleday, 1966.

Berman, Morris. *Coming to Our Senses: Body and Spirit in the Hidden History of the West.* New York: Simon and Schuster, 1989.

Bewley, Anne R. "Re-Membering Spirituality: Use of Sacred Ritual in Psychotherapy." *Women and Therapy* 16, no. 2/3 (1995): 201–13.

Blau, Herbert. "Universals of Performance; or Amortizing Play." In *By Means of Performance,* eds. Richard Schechner and Willa Appel, 250–72. New York: Cambridge University Press, 1993.

Blechman, Frank, et al. *Finding Meaning in a Complex Environment Policy Dispute: Research Into Worldviews in the Northern Forest Lands Council Dialogue 1990–1994.*

George Mason University Working Paper Series (no. 14). Fairfax, Va.: Institute for Conflict Analysis and Resolution, 2000.

Bocock, Robert. *Ritual in Industrial Society; A Sociological Analysis of Ritualism in Modern England.* London: Allen & Unwin, 1974.

Bond, Michael Harris (ed.). *The Cross-Cultural Challenge to Social Psychology.* Newbury Park, Calif.: Sage, 1988.

Borris, Eileen R. "Spirituality and the Psychological Components in Conflict Resolution." Peace Initiatives Paper, 1993.

Bouissac, Paul. "The Profanation of the Sacred in Circus Clown Performances." In *By Means of Performance,* eds. Richard Schechner and Willa Appel, 194–207. New York: Cambridge University Press, 1993.

Boulding, Kenneth. *The Image: Knowledge in Life and Society.* Ann Arbor, Mich.: University of Michigan Press, 1956.

Boulding, Kenneth Ewart. *The World as a Total System.* Beverly Hills, Calif.: Sage, Publications, 1985.

Bourdieu, Pierre. *Language and Symbolic Power.* Cambridge, Mass.: Harvard University Press, 1991.

Bowen, Murray. *Family Therapy in Clinical Practice.* New York: Jason Aronson, 1978.

Bowler, T. Downing. *General Systems Thinking: Its Scope and Applicability.* New York: North Holland, 1981.

Boyer, Pascal. "Cognitive Aspects of Religious Symbolism." In *Cognitive Aspects of Religious Symbolism,* ed. Pascal Boyer, 4–47. Cambridge: Cambridge University Press, 1993.

Broner, E. M. "Honor and Ceremony in Women's Ritual." In *The Politics of Women's Spirituality,* ed. Charlene Spretnak. Toronto: Doubleday, 1982.

Brown, Joseph Epes. "Becoming Part of It." In *I Become Part of It: Sacred Dimensions in Native American Life,* eds. D. M. Dooling and Paul Jordan-Smith, 9–20. New York: HarperCollins, 1989.

———. *The Sacred Pipe: Black Elk's Account of the Seven Rites of the Oglala Sioux.* Norman, Okla.: University of Oklahoma Press, 1989.

Brown, Lyn Mikel, and Carol Gilligan. *Meeting at the Crossroads: Women's Psychology and Girls' Development.* Cambridge, Mass.: Harvard University Press, 1992.

Bruchac, Joseph. *The Native American Sweat Lodge.* Freedom, Calif.: The Crossing Press, 1993.

Budapest, Z. "Teaching Women's Spirituality Rituals." In *The Goddess Celebrates: An Anthology of Women's Rituals,* ed. Diane Stein. Freedom, Calif.: The Crossing Press, 1991.

Burke, Kenneth. "The Human Actor: Definition of Man." In *Kenneth Burke: On Symbols and Society,* ed. Joseph R. Gusfield, 56–75. Chicago: University of Chicago Press, 1989.

———. "The Symbol as Formative." In *Kenneth Burke: On Symbols and Society,* ed. Joseph R. Gusfield, 107–13. Chicago: University of Chicago Press, 1989.

———. "Symbolic Action." In *Kenneth Burke: On Symbols and Society,* ed. Joseph R. Gusfield, 77–85. Chicago: University of Chicago Press, 1989.

Burns, Tom R., and Helena Flam. *The Shaping of Social Organization: Social Rule System Theory with Applications.* Beverly Hills, Calif.: Sage Publications, 1987.

Burns, Tom, and Charles D. Laughlin. "Ritual and Social Power." In *The Spectrum of Ritual: A Biogenetic Structural Analysis,* eds. Eugene G. d'Aquili, Charles D.

Laughlin, and John McManus, 249–79. New York: Columbia University Press, 1979.

Burton, John W. *Conflict: Human Needs Theory.* New York: St. Martin's Press, 1990.

Bush, Robert A. Baruch, and Joseph Folger. *The Promise of Mediation: Responding to Conflict Through Empowerment and Recognition.* San Francisco: Jossey-Bass, 1994.

Bynum, Caroline Walker. "Women's Stories, Women's Symbols: A Critique of Victor Turner's Theory of Liminality." In *Readings in Ritual Studies,* ed. Ronald L. Grimes, 71–85. New Jersey: Prentice Hall, 1996.

Cairns, Alan. "Restoring the Spirit." *Toronto Sun,* December 21, 1996, 28.

Caley, Michael T., and Daiyo Sawada. *Mindscapes: The Epistemologies of Magoroh Maruyama.* New York: Gordon and Breach, 1994.

Calhoun, Craig. *Social Theory and the Politics of Identity.* Oxford, UK; Cambridge, Mass.: Blackwell, 1994.

Campanella, Miriam. "The Cognitive Mapping Approach to the Globalization of World Politics." In *The Evolution of Cognitive Maps,* ed. Ervin Laszlo et al., 237–54. Philadelphia: Gordon and Breach, 1993.

Campbell, Joseph. *Myths to Live By.* New York: Bantam Books, 1973.

Capra, Fritjof. *The Web of Life.* New York: Anchor Book, 1996.

Carlson, J. G., and E. Hatfield. *Psychology of Emotion.* Ft. Worth, Tex.: Harcourt Brace Jovanovich, 1992.

Carnes, Robin Deen, and Sally Craig. *Sacred Circles: A Guide to Creating Your Own Women's Spirituality Groups.* San Francisco: Harper, 1998.

Caron, Charlotte. *To Make and Make Again: Feminist Ritual Thealogy [Sic].* New York: Crossroads, 1993.

Champagne, Duane. "American Indian Studies Is for Everyone." *American Indian Quarterly* 20, no. 1 (Winter 1996): 77–85.

Chapple, E. D. *Culture and Biological Man.* New York: Holt, Rinehart, and Winston, 1970.

Chase, Rob. "Healing and Reconciliation for War-Affected Children and Communities." In *International Development Research Center, Canada,* 2000. June 22, 2002, http://www.hri.ca/children/conflict/srilanka2000paper.htm.

Cheal, David. "Ritual: Communication in Action." *Sociological Analysis* 53, no. 4 (1992): 363–74.

Clark, Mary. "Meaningful Social Bonding as a Universal Human Need." In *Conflict: Human Needs Theory,* ed. John Burton, 34–59. New York: St. Martin's Press, 1990.

———. "Symptoms of Cultural Pathologies: A Hypothesis." In *Conflict Resolution Theory and Practice,* eds. Dennis J. D. Sandole and Hugo van der Merwe, 43–54. New York: Manchester University Press, 1993.

Clark, Mary E. *Ariadne's Thread: The Search for New Modes of Thinking.* New York: St. Martin's Press, 1989.

Clarke, David D., and Jill Crossland. *Action Systems: An Introduction to the Analysis of Complex Behaviour.* London; New York: Methuen, 1985.

Clemmer, Dennis. "On the Nature of Families: Bowen Family Systems Theory." *Conciliation Quarterly* 8, no. 2 (Spring 1989): 2–4.

Cobb, Sara. "Empowerment and Mediation: A Narrative Perspective." *Negotiation Journal* 9, no. 3 (1993): 245–59.

Cohen, Abner. "Political Anthropology: The Analysis of the Symbolism of Power Relations." *Man* 4, no. 2 (1969): 215–35.

———. "Political Symbolism." *Annual Review of Anthropology* (1979): 87–113.

———. *Two-Dimensional Man: An Essay on the Anthropology of Power and Symbolism in Complex Society.* Los Angeles: University of California Press, 1974.

Collins, Sheila D. "The Personal is Political." In *The Politics of Women's Spirituality*, ed. Charlene Spretnak. Toronto: Doubleday, 1982.

Colson, Elizabeth. "The Least Common Denominator." In *Secular Ritual*, eds. Sally F. Moore and Barbara G. Myerhoff, 189–98. Amsterdam: Van Gorcum, 1977.

Comte, Auguste. "Introduction to Positive Philosophy," trans. F. Ferre. Indianapolis, Ind.: Bobbs-Merrill, 1970.

Cook-Lynn, Elizabeth. "American Indian Intellectualism and the New Indian Story." *American Indian Quarterly* 20, no. 1 (Winter 1996): 57–76.

Corbin, Jane. *The Norway Channel: The Secret Talks That Led to the Middle East Peace Accord.* New York: Atlantic Monthly Press, 1994.

Corsini, Raymond J. *Current Personality Theories.* Ithaca, N.Y.: F. E. Peacock Publishers, Inc., 1977.

Coser, Lewis A. *The Functions of Social Conflict.* Glencoe, Ill., Free Press, 1956.

Cragan, John F., and Donald C. Shields. *Symbolic Theories in Applied Communication Research: Borman, Burke, and Fisher.* Cresskill, N.J.: Hampton Press, 1995.

Crocker, Christopher. "Ritual and the Development of Social Structure: Liminality and Inversion." In *The Roots of Ritual*, ed. James D. Shaughnessy. Grand Rapids, Mich.: Eerdmans, 1973.

Crum, Thomas. *The Magic of Conflict.* New York: Simon and Schuster, 1987.

Csanyi, Vilmos. "The Biological Bases of Cognitive Maps." In *The Evolution of Cognitive Maps*, ed. Ervin Laszlo et al., 23–28. Philadelphia: Gordon and Breach, 1993.

Da Matta, Roberto. "Constraint and License: A Preliminary Study of Two Brazilian National Rituals." In *Secular Ritual*, eds. Sally F. Moore and Barbara G. Myerhoff, 244–64. Amsterdam: Van Gorcum, 1977.

Daly, Mary. "Be-Friending: Weaving Contexts, Creating Atmospheres." In *Weaving the Visions: New Patterns in Feminist Spirituality*, eds. Judith Plaskow and Carol P. Christ. San Francisco: Harper, 1989.

Davis, Laura. *The Courage to Heal Workbook: For Women and Men Survivors of Child Sexual Abuse.* New York: Harper and Row, 1990.

de Coulanges, Fustel. *The Ancient City.* Trans. Willard Small. New York: Doubleday, 1963.

Deloria, Vine. *God is Red: A Native View of Religion.* Golden, Colo.: Fulcrum Publishing, 1994.

DeMarinis, Valerie. "A Psychotherapeutic Exploration of Religious Ritual as Mediator of Memory and Meaning." In *Religious and Social Ritual: Interdisciplinary Explorations*, eds. Michael B. Aune and Valerie DeMarinis. New York: State University of New York Press, 1996.

Descartes, Rene. *The Philosophical Works of Descartes.* Trans. E. S. Haldane and G. R. T. Ross. New York: Dover, 1955.

Diamond, Louise. *The Four Basic Needs.* Washington, DC: Institute for Multi-Track Diplomacy, 1993.

Diamond, Louise, and John W. McDonald. *Multi-Track Diplomacy: A Systems Approach to Peace.* West Hartford, Conn.: Kumarian Press, 1996.

Diesing, Paul. *Patterns of Discovery in the Social Sciences.* Chicago: Aldine, Atherton, 1971.

———. *Science & Ideology in the Policy Sciences.* Hawthorne, N.Y.: Aldine, 1982.

Docherty, Jayne Seminare. *Learning Lessons from Waco: When the Parties Bring Their Gods to the Negotiation Table.* Syracuse, N.Y.: Syracuse University Press 2001.

Douglas, Mary. *Purity and Danger: An Analysis of Concepts of Pollution and Taboo.* New York: Praeger, 1966.

Drewal, Margaret Thompson. *Yoruba Ritual: Performers, Play, Agency.* Bloomington: Indiana University Press, 1992.

Driver, Tom F. "Transformation: The Magic of Ritual." In *Readings in Ritual Studies,* ed. Ronald L. Grimes, 170–87. Upper Saddle River, N.J.: Prentice Hall, 1996.

Driver, Tom Faw. *The Magic of Ritual: Our Need for Liberating Rites That Transform Our Lives and Our Communities.* San Francisco: Harper San Francisco, 1991.

Duba, Kana Roba, et al. *Honey and Heifer, Grasses, Milk and Water: A Heritage of Diversity in Reconciliation.* Nairobi, Kenya: Mennonite Central Committee, 1997.

Durkheim, Emile. *The Elementary Forms of the Religious Life.* Glencoe, Ill: Free Press, 1915.

———. "Ritual, Magic, and the Sacred." In *Readings in Ritual Studies,* ed. Ronald L. Grimes, 188–93. New Jersey: Prentice Hall, 1996.

Duryea, Michelle LeBaron. *Conflict and Culture: Research in Five Communities in Vancouver, British Columbia.* Victoria, BC: University of Victoria Institute for Dispute Resolution, 1993.

d'Aquili, Eugene G., and Charles D. Laughlin, Jr. "The Neurobiology of Myth and Ritual." In *Readings in Ritual Studies,* ed. Ronald L. Grimes, 132–45. New Jersey: Prentice Hall, 1996.

Echols, Alice. *Same Difference: Feminism and Sexual Difference.* London: Allen and Unwin, 1990.

Eisler, Riane. *The Chalice and the Blade.* San Francisco: Harper, 1988.

———. "Technology, Gender and History: Toward a Nonlinear Model of Social Evolution." In *The Evolution of Cognitive Maps,* ed. Ervin Laszlo et al., 181–204. Philadelphia: Gordon and Breach, 1993.

Eliade, Mircea. *Patterns in Comparative Religion.* Trans. Rosemary Sheed. New York: New American Library, 1963.

———. "Ritual and Myth." In *Readings in Ritual Studies,* ed. Ronald L. Grimes, 194–200. Upper Saddle River, N.J.: Prentice Hall, 1996.

Erikson, Erik H. "The Development of Ritualization." In *Readings in Ritual Studies,* ed. Ronald L. Grimes, 201–11. Upper Saddle River, N.J.: Prentice Hall, 1996.

Ewen, Robert. *An Introduction to Theories of Personality.* Orlando, Fla.: Academic Press, 1984.

Faithful Women: Harmony and Balance. Canadian Broadcasting Corporation, 1989.

Feldman, S. *Cognitive Consistency.* New York: Academic Press, 1966.

Festinger, Leonard. *A Theory of Cognitive Dissonance.* Stanford, Conn.: Stanford University Press, 1957.

Firth, Raymond. *The Work of the Gods in Tikopia*. London: Athlone Press, 1967.

Fischer, Edward. "Ritual as Communication." In *The Roots of Ritual*, ed. James D. Shaughnessy. Grand Rapids, Mich.: Eerdmans, 1973.

Fisher, Jennifer. "Symbol in Mediation." *Mediation Quarterly* 18, no. 1 (Fall 2000): 87–107.

Fisher, Roger, and Scott Brown. *Getting Together: Building a Relationship That Gets to Yes*. Boston: Houghton Mifflin, 1988.

Fisher, Roger, and William Ury. *Getting to Yes: Negotiating Agreement Without Giving In*. Boston: Houghton Mifflin, 1983.

Fisher, Roger, Elizabeth Kopelman, and Andrea Kupfer Schneider. *Beyond Machiavelli: Tools for Coping with Conflict*. Cambridge, Mass.: Harvard University Press, 1994.

Fisher, Ronald J. "Needs Theory, Social Identity and an Eclectic Model of Conflict." In *Conflict: Human Needs Theory*, ed. John Burton. New York: St. Martin's Press, 1990.

Fitzgerald, Thomas K. *Metaphors of Identity: A Culture-Communication Dialogue*. Albany: State University of New York Press, 1993.

Fixico, Donald L. "Ethics and Responsibilities in Writing American Indian History." In *Natives and Academics: Researching and Writing about American Indians*, ed. Devon Mihesuah. Lincoln, Neb.: University of Nebraska Press, 1998.

Flowers, Betty Sue. (ed.). *Joseph Campbell: The Power of Myth with Bill Moyers*. New York: Doubleday, 1988.

Frankl, Victor. *Man's Search for Meaning: An Introduction to Logotherapy*. Boston: Beacon Press, 1963.

Freidman, Edwin H. *Generation to Generation: Family Process in Church and Synagogue*. New York: The Guilford Press, 1985.

Frese, Pamela (ed.). *Celebrations of Identity: Multiple Voices in American Ritual Performance*. Westport, Conn.: Bergin & Garvey, 1993.

Freud, Sigmund. *The Complete Psychological Works*. Trans. J. Strachey. New York: Norton, 1922.

———. "Obsessive Actions and Religious Practices." In *Readings in Ritual Studies*, ed. Ronald L. Grimes, 212–16. Upper Saddle River, N.J.: Prentice Hall, 1996.

Friedman, Edwin H. *Generation to Generation: Family Process in Church and Synagogue*. New York: Guilford Press, 1985.

Gadon, Elinor. *The Once and Future Goddess*. San Francisco: Harper, 1989.

Gathering Strength. In *A Report of the Royal Commission on Aboriginal Peoples*. Ottawa: Canada Communications Group, 1993.

Geertz, Clifford. *The Interpretation of Cultures: Selected Essays*. New York: Basic Books, 1973.

Gennep, Arnold van. *The Rites of Passage*. Chicago: University of Chicago Press, 1960.

Gergen, Kenneth J. *The Saturated Self: Dilemmas of Identity in Contemporary Life*. New York: Basic Books, 1991.

Gibson, Kimberly Denise Barnett. "Weaving a New World: The Rhetoric of Reorientation in Contemporary Women's Spirituality Rituals." Ph.D. diss., Ohio State University, 1993.

Gilbert, Roberta M. *Extraordinary Relationships: A New Way of Thinking About Human Interactions*. Minneapolis, Minn.: Chronimed, 1992.

Gill, Sam. "It's Where You Put Your Eyes." In *I Become Part of It: Sacred Dimensions in Native American Life*, eds. D. M. Dooling and Paul Jordan-Smith. New York: HarperCollins, 1989.

Gilligan, Carol. *In a Different Voice: Psychological Theory and Women's Development.* Cambridge, Mass.: Harvard University Press, 1982.

Girard, Rene. "Violence and the Sacred: Sacrifice." In *Readings in Ritual Studies*, ed. Ronald L. Grimes, 239–56. Upper Saddle River, N.J.: Prentice Hall, 1996.

Gluckman, Max. *Essays on the Ritual of Social Relations.* Manchester, UK: Manchester University Press, 1962.

———. *Rituals of Rebellion in Southeast Africa.* Manchester, UK: Manchester University Press, 1954.

Goffman, Erving. *Frame Analysis: An Essay on the Organization of Experience.* New York: Harper & Row, 1974.

———. "Interaction Ritual: Deference and Demeanor." In *Readings in Ritual Studies*, ed. Ronald L. Grimes, 268–78. Upper Saddle River, N.J.: Prentice Hall, 1996.

———. *Presentation of Self in Everyday Life.* New York: Doubleday, 1959.

Goody, Jack. "Against 'Ritual': Loosely Structured Thoughts on a Loosely Defined Topic." In *Secular Ritual*, eds. Sally F. Moore and Barbara G. Myerhoff, 25–35. Amsterdam: Van Gorcum, 1977.

Gopin, Marc. *Between Eden and Armageddon: The Future of World Religions, Violence.* New York: Oxford University Press, 2000.

———. *Holy War, Holy Peace.* New York: Oxford Press, 2002.

Greisdorf, Karen Elliot. "The City That Dares to Talk." *For a Change* 15, no. 1, pp. 4–9 (February/March 2002).

Grimes, Ronald L. *Beginnings in Ritual Studies.* Columbia: University of South Carolina Press, 1995.

———. *Research in Ritual Studies: A Programmatic Essay and Bibliography.* Chicago: American Theological Library Association; Metuchen, N.J.: Scarecrow Press, 1985.

———. "Ritual Criticism and Infelicitous Performances." In *Readings in Ritual Studies*, ed. Ronald L. Grimes, 279–92. Upper Saddle River, N.J.: Prentice Hall, 1996.

———. *Ritual Criticism: Case Studies in Its Practice, Essays on Its Theory.* Columbia: University of South Carolina Press, 1990.

Gurr, Ted. *Minorities at Risk.* Washington, DC: United States Institute of Peace, 1993.

Hammerschlag, Carl A., and Howard D. Silverman. *Healing Ceremonies: Creating Personal Rituals for Spiritual, Emotional, Physical and Mental Health.* New York: Perigee, 1997.

Hammond, Sue Annis. *The Thin Book of Appreciative Inquiry.* Thin Book Publishing Company, 1998.

Hanson, Barbara Gail. *General Systems Theory: Beginning with Wholes.* Washington, DC: Taylor and Francis, 1995.

Harries-Jones, Peter. *Ecological Understanding and Gregory Bateson.* Toronto: University of Toronto Press, 1995.

Heider, F. "Attitudes and Cognitive Organization." *Journal of Psychology* 21 (1946): 107–12.

Heller, Jeffrey. "Israeli Cabinet Minister/Holocaust Survivor Condemns Rafah Demolitions." *Reuters* (Jerusalem), May 23, 2004.

Hewitt, John P. *Self and Society: A Symbolic Interactionist Social Psychology.* Boston: Allyn and Bacon, 1997.

Hocker, Joyce L., and William W. Wilmot. *Interpersonal Conflict.* Dubuque, Iowa: Wm. C. Brown, 1995.

Holyoak, Lorne Todd. "The Good Red Road: Relations Between Native Elders and Non-Native Seekers." Ph.D. diss., University of Calgary, 1993.

Honwanda, Alcinda. "Sealing the Past, Facing the Future: Trauma Healing in Rural Mozambique." *Accord* 3 (1998), pp. 75–80.

Hultkrantz, Ake. "Ritual in Native North American Religions." In *Native Religious Traditions,* eds. Earle H. Waugh and K. Dad Prithipaul. Waterloo, ON: Wilfred Laurier Press, 1977.

Humphrey, Caroline, and James Laidlaw. *The Archetypal Actions of Ritual: A Theory of Ritual.* New York: Oxford, 1994.

Hunt, Eva. "Ceremonies of Confrontation and Submission: The Symbolic Dimension of Indian-Mexican Political Interaction." In *Secular Ritual,* eds. Sally F. Moore and Barbara G. Myerhoff, 124–150. Amsterdam: Van Gorcum, 1977.

Huxley, Julian. "A Discussion on Ritualization of Behavior in Animals and Man." *Philosophical Transactions of the Royal Society* Series B, no. 251 (1966): 247–525.

Ibrahim, Dekha, and Jannice Jenner. "Breaking the Cycle of Violence in Wajir." In *Transforming Violence: Linking Local and Global Peacemaking,* eds. Robert Herr and Judy Zimmerman Herr. Scottdale, Pa.: Herald Press, 1998.

Imber-Black, Evan, and Janine Roberts. *Rituals for Our Times: Celebrating, Healing, and Changing Our Lives and Our Relationships.* New York: HarperPerennial, 1992.

James, William. *The Principles of Psychology.* New York: Smith, 1890.

Jennings, Theodore W., Jr. "On Ritual Knowledge." In *Readings in Ritual Studies,* ed. Ronald L. Grimes, 324–34. Upper Saddle River, N.J.: Prentice Hall, 1996.

Johnston, Douglas (ed.). *Faith-Based Diplomacy: Trumping Realpolitique.* New York: Oxford University Press, 2003.

Johnson, Douglas, and Cynthia Sampson. *Religion, The Missing Dimension of Statecraft.* New York: Oxford University Press, 1994.

Johnson, Mark. *The Body in the Mind: The Bodily Basis of Meaning, Imagination, and Reason.* Chicago: University of Chicago Press, 1987.

Johnston, Basil. *Ojibway Ceremonies.* Lincoln, Neb.: University of Nebraska Press, 1982.

———. *Ojibway Heritage.* Toronto: McClelland and Steward Limited, 1976.

Kant, Immanuel. *Critique of Pure Reason.* Trans. N. Kemp Smith. New York: Humanities, 1781.

Kapferer, Bruce. "First Class to Maradana: Secular Drama in Sinhelese Healing Rites." In *Secular Ritual,* eds. Sally F. Moore and Barbara G. Myerhoff, 91–123. Amsterdam: Van Gorcum, 1977.

Kavanagh, Aidan. "Introduction." In *The Roots of Ritual,* ed. James D. Shaughnessy. Grand Rapids, Mich.: Eerdmans, 1973.

———. "The Role of Ritual in Personal Development." In *The Roots of Ritual,* ed. James D. Shaughnessy. Grand Rapids, Mich., Eerdmans, 1973.

Kertzer, David I. *Ritual, Politics, and Power.* New Haven, Conn.: Yale University Press, 1988.

Kierkegaard, Soren. *A Kierkegaard Anthology*. Trans. Robert Bretall. New York: Modern Library, 1959.

Kleinman, Seymour (ed.). *Mind and Body: East Meets West*. Champaign, Ill.: Human Kinetics Publishers, 1986.

Kochman, Thomas. *Black and White Styles in Conflict*. Chicago: University of Chicago Press, 1981.

Kriesberg, Louis. *International Conflict Resolution: The US–USSR and Middle East Cases*. New Haven, Conn.: Yale University Press, 1992.

Kuhn, Thomas S. *The Structure of Scientific Revolutions*. Chicago: University of Chicago Press, 1979.

Laird, Joan. "Women and Ritual in Family Therapy." In *Readings in Ritual Studies*, ed. Ronald L. Grimes, 353–67. Upper Saddle River, N.J.: Prentice Hall, 1996.

Lakoff, George, and Mark Johnson. *Metaphors We Live By*. Chicago: University of Chicago Press, 1980.

Langer, Susanne. *Philosophy in a New Key: A Study in the Symbolism of Reason, Rite, and Art*. New York: Penguin Books, 1948.

Laszlo, Ervin. *Changing Visions: Human Cognitive Maps: Past, Present, and Future*. Westport, Conn.: Praeger, 1996.

———. *The Relevance of General Systems Theory*. New York: George Braziller, Inc., 1972.

Laszlo, Ervin, et al. *The Evolution of Cognitive Maps: New Paradigms for the Twenty-First Century*. Philadelphia: Gordon and Breach, 1993.

Laue, James. "Conversation on Peacemaking with Jimmy Carter: Interview with James Laue." Presented at the National Conference on Peacemaking and Conflict Resolution. Charlotte, N.C., June 1991.

Laughlin, Charles D., John McManus, and Eugene G. d'Aquili. *Brain, Symbol & Experience: Toward a Neurophenomenology of Human Consciousness*. Boston: Shambhala, 1990.

Laughlin, Charles D., John McManus, and Eugene G. d'Aquili. *The Spectrum of Ritual: A Biogenetic Structural Analysis*. New York: Columbia University Press, 1979.

Lawson, E. Thomas. "Cognitive Categories, Cultural Forms and Ritual Structures." In *Cognitive Aspects of Religious Symbolism*, ed. Pascal Boyer, 188–206. Cambridge: Cambridge University Press, 1993.

———. *Rethinking Religion: Connecting Cognition and Culture*. Cambridge, UK; New York: Cambridge University Press, 1990.

Lazarus, R. S. *Emotion and Adaptation*. New York: Oxford University Press, 1991.

Leach, Edmund. *Culture and Communication: The Logic by Which Symbols Are Connected*. New York: Cambridge University Press, 1976.

———. "Ritual." In *International Encyclopedia of Social Sciences*, ed. Claude Levi-Strauss, 520–26. New York: MacMillan, 1968.

———. "The Structure of Symbolism." In *The Interpretation of Ritual: Essays in Honor of I. A. Richards*, ed. J. S. La Fontaine, 239–75. London: Tavistock, 1972.

Lederach, John Paul. *Building Peace: Sustainable Reconciliation in Divided Societies*. Washington, DC: United States Institute for Peace, 1997.

———. "Conflict Transformation: A Working Definition." In *Mediation and Facilitation Training Manual*, ed. Mennonite Conciliation Service, 48–49. Akron, Pa.: Mennonite Conciliation Service, 1995.

———. *Preparing for Peace: Conflict Transformation Across Cultures.* Syracuse, N.Y.: Syracuse University Press, 1995.

Levi-Strauss, Claude. *The Savage Mind.* Chicago: University of Chicago Press, 1966.

Levine, M. W., and J. M. Shefner. *Fundamentals of Sensation and Perception.* Pacific Grove, Calif.: Brooks/Cole, 1992.

Lex, Barbara W. "The Neurobiology of Ritual Trance." In *The Spectrum of Ritual: A Biogenetic Structural Analysis*, eds. Eugene G. d'Aquili, Charles D. Laughlin, and John McManus, 117–51. New York: Colombia University Press, 1979.

Looking Forward, Looking Back. In *A Report of the Royal Commission on Aboriginal Peoples.* Ottawa: Canada Communications Group, 1993.

Lorenz, Konrad. *On Aggression.* New York: Harcourt, Brace, and World, 1966.

MacLean, Paul D. *A Triune Concept of the Brain and Behaviour.* Toronto: University of Toronto, 1972.

———. "Women: A More Balanced Brain?" *Zygon* 31, no. 3 (September 1996): 421–39.

Malinowski, Bronislav. *Magic, Science, and Religion and Other Essays.* Glencoe, Ill.: Free Press, 1974.

———. *Sex, Culture, and Myth.* New York: Harcourt, Brace, and World, 1962.

Mander, Jerry. *In the Absence of the Sacred.* San Francisco: Sierra Club Books, 1991.

Martin, John Hilary. "Bringing the Power of the Past Into the Present." In *Religious and Social Ritual: Interdisciplinary Explorations*, eds. Michael B. Aune and Valerie DeMarinis, 23–48. New York: State University of New York Press, 1996.

Maruyama, Magoroh. "Introduction." In *Mindscapes: The Epistemology of Magoroh Maruyama*, eds. Michael T. Caley and Daiyo Sawada, xiii–xx. Langhorne, Pa.: Gordon and Breach, 1994.

———. "Most Frequently Found Mindscape Types." In *Mindscapes: The Epistemology of Magoroh Maruyama*, eds. Michael T. Caley and Daiyo Sawada, 1–29. Langhorne, Pa.: Gordon and Breach, 1994.

———. "Some African and Asian Epistemologies." In *Mindscapes: The Epistemology of Magoroh Maruyama*, eds. Michael T. Caley and Daiyo Sawada, 47–63. Langhorne, Pa.: Gordon and Breach, 1994.

Marx, Karl. *Economic and Philosophical Manuscripts.* Trans. R. C. Tucker. New York: Norton, 1972.

Masulli, Ignazio. "Cognitive Maps and Social Change." In *The Evolution of Cognitive Maps*, ed. Ervin Laszlo, et al., 169–80. Philadelphia: Gordon and Breach, 1993.

Maturana, Humberto, and Francisco J. Varela. *Autopoiesis and Cognition: The Realization of the Living.* Dordrecht, Holland: D. Reidel Publishing, 1980.

———. *The Tree of Knowledge: The Biological Roots of Human Understanding.* Boston: Shambhala, 1987.

May, Rollo. *Existence: A New Dimension in Psychiatry and Psychology.* New York: Basic Books, 1958.

McLaren, Peter. *Schooling as a Ritual Performance: Towards a Political Economy of Educational Symbols and Gestures.* London; New York: Routledge, 1993.

McLaughlin, Corinne, and Gordon Davidson. *Spiritual Politics: Changing the World from the Inside Out.* New York: Ballantine Books, 1994.

McLuhan, Marshall. *Understanding Media.* Cambridge, Mass: MIT Press, 1994.

McManus, John. "Ritual and Human Social Cognition." In *The Spectrum of Ritual: A Biogenetic Structural Analysis,* eds. Eugene G. d'Aquili, Charles D. Laughlin, and John McManus, 216–48. New York: Columbia University Press, 1979.

———. "Ritual and Ontogenetic Development." In *The Spectrum of Ritual: A Biogenetic Structural Analysis,* eds. Eugene G. d'Aquili, Charles D. Laughlin, and John McManus, 183–215. New York: Columbia University Press, 1979.

McManus, John, Charles D. Laughlin, and Eugene G. d'Aquili. "Concepts, Methods and Conclusions." In *The Spectrum of Ritual: A Biogenetic Structural Analysis,* eds. Eugene G. d'Aquili, Charles D. Laughlin, and John McManus, 342–62. New York: Columbia University Press, 1979.

Mead, George Herbert, and Charles William Morris (eds.). *Mind, Self & Society from the Standpoint of a Social Behaviorist.* Chicago, Ill: University of Chicago Press, 1934.

Mead, Margaret. "Ritual and Social Crisis." In *The Roots of Ritual,* ed. James D. Shaughnessy. Grand Rapids, Mich.: Eerdmans, 1973.

Metrick, Sydney Barbara. *Crossing the Bridge: Creating Ceremonies for Grieving and Healing from Life's Losses.* Berkeley, Calif.: Celestial Arts, 1994.

Middleton, John. "Ritual and Ambiguity in Lugbara Society." In *Secular Ritual,* eds. Sally F. Moore and Barbara G. Myerhoff, 73–90. Amsterdam: Van Gorcum, 1977.

Mihesuah, Devon A. "Voices, Interpretations, and the 'New Indian History'." *American Indian Quarterly* 20, no. 1 (Winter 1996): 91–107.

Mitchell, C. R. *The Structure of International Conflict.* New York: St. Martin's Press, 1981.

Mitchell, Christopher, and Michael Banks. *Handbook of Conflict Resolution: The Analytical Problem-Solving Approach.* New York: Pinter, 1996.

Montville, Joseph. *Conflict and Peacemaking in Multiethnic Societies.* Lexington, Mass.: Lexington Books, 1990.

———. "The Healing Function in Political Conflict Resolution." In *Conflict Resolution Theory and Practice,* eds. Dennis J. D. Sandole and Hugo van der Merwe, 112–28. Manchester: Manchester University Press, 1993.

———. "Psychoanalytic Enlightenment and the Greening of Diplomacy." In *The Psychodynamics of International Relationships,* eds. Vamik Volkan, Joseph Montville, and Demetrios Julius, 177–92. Toronto: Lexington Books, 1991.

Moore, Sally F. "Political Meetings and the Simulation of Unanimity: Kilimanjaro 1973." In *Secular Ritual,* eds. Sally F. Moore and Barbara G. Myerhoff, 151–72. Amsterdam: Van Gorcum, 1977.

Moore, Sally F., and Barbara Myerhoff. "Introduction: Secular Ritual: Forms and Meanings." In *Secular Ritual,* eds. Sally F. Moore and Barbara Myerhoff, 3–24. Amsterdam: Van Gorcum, 1977.

Moore, Thomas. *The Re-Enchantment of Everyday Life.* New York: HarperCollins, 1996.

Moravia, Sergio. *The Enigma of the Mind: The Mind-Body Problem in Contemporary Thought.* Cambridge; New York: Cambridge University Press, 1995.

Mountainwater, Shekhinah. "Writings on Rituals and Spells." In *The Goddess Celebrates: An Anthology of Women's Rituals,* ed. Diane Stein. Freedom, Calif.: The Crossing Press, 1991.

Moyers, Bill. *Healing and The Mind.* New York: Doubleday, 1993.

Munn, Nancy D. "Symbolism in a Ritual Context: Aspects of Symbolic Action." In *Handbook of Social and Cultural Anthropology,* ed. John J. Honigmann, 579–612. Chicago: Rand McNally, 1973.

Myerhoff, Barbara. "The Transformation of Consciousness in Ritual Performances: Some Thoughts and Questions." In *By Means of Performance,* eds. Richard Schechner and Willa Appel, 245–49. New York: Cambridge University Press, 1993.

———. "We Don't Wrap Herring in a Printed Page: Fusion, Fictions and Continuity in Secular Ritual." In *Secular Ritual,* eds. Sally F. Moore and Barbara G. Myerhoff, 199–226. Amsterdam: Van Gorcum, 1977.

Myers, Bethany. "Public Ritual." *Citizen Forum* 8 (1922): 221–29.

Neu, Diann L. "Women's Empowerment through Feminist Ritual." *Women and Therapy* 16, no. 2/3 (1995): 185–200.

Newbury, J. W. E. "The Universe at Prayer." In *Native Religious Traditions,* eds. Earle H. Waugh and K. Dad Prithipaul. Waterloo, ON: Wilfred Laurier Press, 1977.

Nobeck, E. "African Rituals of Conflict." *American Anthropologist* 65 (1963): 1254–79.

Northrup, Terrel A. "The Dynamic of Identity in Personal and Social Conflict." In *Intractable Conflicts and Their Transformation,* eds. Louis Kriesberg, Terrell A. Northrup, and Stuart J. Thorson. Syracuse, N.Y.: Syracuse University Press, 1989.

Nudler, Oscar. "On Conflicts and Metaphors: Toward an Extended Rationality." In *Conflict: Human Needs Theory,* ed. John Burton, 177–204. New York: St. Martin's Press, 1990.

Obeyesekere, Ranjini. "The Significance of Performance for Its Audience: An Analysis of Three Sri Lankan Rituals." In *By Means of Performance,* eds. Richard Schechner and Willa Appel, 118–30. New York: Cambridge University Press, 1993.

Obomsawin, Alanis. *Poundmaker's Lodge: A Healing Place.* Canadian Broadcasting Corporation, 1987.

Ornstein, R. *The Psychology of Consciousness.* San Francisco: Freeman.

Oshry, Barry. *Seeing Systems.* San Francisco: Berrett-Koehler, 1995.

Paper, Jordan. "Cosmological Implications of Pan-Indian Sacred Pipe Ritual." *The Canadian Journal of Native Studies* 2 (1987): 297–306.

Papero, Daniel. *Bowen Family Systems Theory.* Boston: Allyn and Bacon, 1990.

Parsons, Talcott. *Toward a General Theory of Action.* Cambridge, Mass.: Harvard University Press, 1951.

Payne, Richard K. "Realizing Inherent Enlightenment: Ritual and Self-Transformation in Shingon Buddhism." In *Religious and Social Ritual: Interdisciplinary Explorations,* eds. Michael B. Aune and Valerie DeMarinis. New York: State University of New York Press, 1996.

Pearson d'Estree, Tamra. "The Role of 'Symbolic Gestures' in Intergroup Conflict Resolution: Addressing Group Identity." Ph.D. diss., Harvard University, 1990.

Peirce, Charles. *Selected Writings.* Trans. J. Buchler. New York, 1940.

Perspectives and Realities. In *A Report of the Royal Commission on Aboriginal Peoples.* Ottawa: Canada Communications Group, 1993.

Phil Lucas Productions. *Healing the Hurts.* Four Worlds Development Project.

Piaget, Jean. "Intellectual Evolution From Adolescence to Adulthood." *Human Development* 15 (1972).

Podos, Batya. "Feeding the Feminist Psyche Through Ritual Theater." In *The Politics of Women's Spirituality*, ed. Charlene Spretnak. Toronto: Doubleday, 1982.

Popper, Karl Raimund, Sir. *Knowledge and the Body-Mind Problem: In Defence of Interaction.* London; New York: Routledge, 1994.

Pottebaum, Gerard A. *The Rites of People: Exploring the Ritual Character of Human Experience.* Washington, DC: Pastoral Press, 1992.

Poundmakers Lodge/Nechi Institute: Part 2. Magic Lantern Communications.

Qualitative Research for Social Change. "Research on the SPI Community: Class Project." Eastern Mennonite University, Harrisonburg, Va., June 18, 2002.

Radcliffe-Brown, Alfred. *The Andaman Islanders.* New York: Free Press, 1964.

Rapoport, Anatol. *General System Theory: Essential Concepts and Applications.* Cambridge, Mass.: Abacus Press, 1986.

Rappaport, Roy A. *Ecology, Meaning, and Ritual.* Richmond, Calif.: North Atlantic Books, 1979.

———. "The Obvious Aspects of Ritual." In *Readings in Ritual Studies*, ed. Ronald L. Grimes, 427–49. Upper Saddle River, N.J.: Prentice Hall, 1996.

———. *Pigs for the Ancestors: Ritual in the Ecology of a New Guinea People.* New Haven, Conn.: Yale University Press, 1967.

———. *Ritual and Religion in the Making of Humanity.* Cambridge, UK: Cambridge University Press, 1999.

Reason, Peter (ed.). *Participation in Human Inquiry.* London; Thousand Oaks, Calif.: Sage Publications, 1994.

Reason, Peter and John Rowan (eds.). *Human Inquiry: A Sourcebook of New Paradigm Research.* New York: J. Wiley, 1981.

Redekop, Vern Neufeld. *From Violence to Blessing.* Ottawa: Novalis, 2002.

Richling, Barnett. "Labrador Nalujuk: The Transformation of an Aboriginal Ritual Complex in a Post-Contact Setting." In *The Power of Symbols: Masks and Masquerade in the Americas*, eds. N. Ross Crumrine and Marjorie Halpin, 21–29. Vancouver: University of British Colombia, 1983.

Ross, Marc Howard. "Psychocultural Interpretations and Dramas: Identity Dynamics in Ethnic Conflict." *Political Psychology* 22, no. 1 (2001): 157–78.

Ruether, Rosemary Radford. "Feminist Metanoia and Soul-Making." *Women and Therapy* 16, no. 2/3 (1995): 33–44.

Ruether, Rosemary Radford. *In Memory of Her: A Feminist Theological Reconstruction of Christian Origins.* New York: Crossroad, 1985.

Rupesinghe, Kumar. (ed.). *Conflict Transformation.* New York: St. Martin's Press, 1995.

Rush, Anne Kent. "The Politics of Feminist Spirituality." In *The Politics of Women's Spirituality*, ed. Charlene Spretnak. Toronto: Doubleday, 1982.

Sampson, Cynthia et al. (eds.). *Positive Approaches to Peacebuilding.* Washington, DC: Pact Publications, 2003.

Sartre, Jean-Paul. *Existentialism and Humanism.* Trans. P. Mairet. London: Methuen, 1948.

Saunders, Peter T. "Evolution Theory and Cognitive Maps." In *The Evolution of Cognitive Maps*, ed. Ervin Laszlo et al., 105–18. Philadelphia: Gordon and Breach, 1993.

Schechner, Richard. *The Future of Ritual: Writings on Culture and Performance*. New York: Routledge, 1993.

Schechner, Richard, and Willa Appel. *By Means of Performance: Intercultural Studies of Theatre and Ritual*. Cambridge; New York: Cambridge University Press, 1990.

Scheibe, Karl E. *Self Studies: The Psychology of Self and Identity*. Westport, Conn.: Praeger, 1995.

Schirch, Lisa. *The Little Book of Strategic Peacebuilding*. Intercourse, Pa.: Good Books, 2004.

———. "Ritual and Conflict: The New (Old) Tool in the Conflict Transformer's Toolbox." *Conciliation Quarterly* Summer 1998, pp. 2–4.

———. "Ritual Reconciliation: Transforming Identity/Reframing Conflict." In *Reconciliation, Coexistence, and Justice in Interethnic Conflicts: Theory and Practice*, ed. Mohammed Abu-Nimer. New York: Rowman and Littlefield, 2001.

———. "Transforming and Creating Identity through Ritual." *Conciliation Quarterly* Winter 2000, pp. 8–9.

Seltzer, L. F. *Paradoxical Strategies in Psychotherapy: A Comprehensive Overview and Guide*. New York: Wiley, 1986.

Shaughnessy, James D. *The Roots of Ritual*. Grand Rapids, Mich.: Eerdmans, 1973.

Sherif, Muzafer. *The Robbers' Cave Experiment: Intergroup Conflict and Cooperation*. Norman, Okla.: Oklahoma Book Exchange, 1961.

Smith, Jonathan Z. "The Influence of Symbols Upon Social Change: A Place on Which to Stand." In *The Roots of Ritual*, ed. James D. Shaughnessy. Grand Rapids, Mich.: Eerdmans, 1973.

Solomon, Eva. "The Sacred Pipe." In *Dancing the Drum*, ed. Joyce Carlson. Toronto: Anglican Book Centre, 1995.

Some, Malidoma Patrice. *Of Water and the Spirit: Ritual, Magic, and Initiation in the Life of an African Shaman*. New York: Putnam, 1994.

Sparks, Allister. *Tomorrow is Another Country: The Inside Story of South Africa's Negotiated Revolution*. Sandton, South Africa: Struik Book Distributors, 1994.

The Spirit That Moves. Medical Audio Visual Communication, Inc., Canadian Broadcasting Corporation, 1987.

Spretnak, Charlene. *The Politics of Women's Spirituality*. Toronto: Doubleday, 1982.

Stanton, Emily. "A Space in Your Heart You Never Knew You Had." Eastern Mennonite University, Harrisonburg, Va., October 1, 2000.

Starhawk. "Creating Sacred Space." In *The Goddess Celebrates: An Anthology of Women's Rituals*, ed. Diane Stein. Freedom: California: The Crossing Press, 1991.

———. *Dreaming the Dark: Magic, Sex, and Politics*. San Francisco: Harper & Row, 1988.

———. *Truth or Dare: Encounters with Power, Authority, and Mystery*. San Francisco: Harper & Row, 1987.

Stein, Diane. *Casting the Circle: A Women's Book of Ritual*. Freedom, Calif.: The Crossing Press, 1990.

————. "Introduction." In *The Goddess Celebrates: An Anthology of Women's Rituals*, ed. Diane Stein. Freedom :California: The Crossing Press, 1991.

Stiegelbauer, S. M. "What Is an Elder? What Do Elders Do?: First Nation Elders as Teachers in Culture-Based Urban Organizations." *The Canadian Journal of Native Studies* XVI, no. 1 (1996): 37–66.

Stortz, Martha Ellen. "Ritual Power, Ritual Authority: Configurations and Reconfigurations in the Era of Manifestations." In *Religious and Social Ritual: Interdisciplinary Explorations*, eds. Michael B. Aune and Valerie DeMarinis. New York: State University of New York Press, 1996.

Tajfel, H., and J. C. Turner. "The Integrative Theory of Inter-Group Conflict." In *The Social Psychology of Intergroup Relations*, eds. S. Worchel and W.G. Austin. Monterey, Calif.: Brooks/Cole, 1979.

————. "The Social Identity Theory of Intergroup Behavior." In *The Psychology of Intergroup Relations*, eds. S. Worchel and W. G. Austin. Chicago: Nelson-Hall, 1986.

Tambiah, Stanley Jeyaraja. *Culture, Thought, and Social Action*. Cambridge, Mass.: Harvard University Press, 1985.

————. *Magic, Science, Religion, and the Scope of Rationality*. Cambridge, UK: Cambridge University Press, 1990.

————. *A Performative Approach to Ritual*. London: British Academy, 1981.

Tannen, Deborah. *The Passion of the Western Mind*. New York: Ballentine Books, 1991.

————. *You Just Don't Understand: Women and Men in Conversation*. New York: Morrow, 1990.

Toren, Christina. "Sign Into Symbol, Symbol Into Sign: Cognitive Aspects of a Social Process." In *Cognitive Aspects of Religious Symbolism*, ed. Pascal Boyer, 147–64. Cambridge: Cambridge University Press, 1993.

Traditional Cures for Modern Conflicts: African Conflict 'Medicine.' Edited by William I. Zartman. Sais African Studies Library. Boulder, Colo.: Lynne Rienner, 1999.

Tuan, Yi-Fu. "Space and Context." In *By Means of Performance*, eds. Richard Schechner and Willa Appel, 236–44. New York: Cambridge University Press, 1993.

Turnbull, Colin. "Liminality: A Synthesis of Subjective and Objective Experience." In *By Means of Performance*, eds. Richard Schechner and Willa Appel, 50–81. New York: Cambridge University Press, 1993.

Turner, Edith L. B. *Experiencing Ritual: A New Interpretation of African Healing*. Philadelphia: University of Pennsylvania Press, 1992.

Turner, Kay. "Contemporary Feminist Rituals." In *The Politics of Women's Spirituality*, ed. Charlene Spretnak. Toronto: Doubleday, 1982.

Turner, Terence. "Transformation, Hierarchy and Transcendence: A Reformulation of Van Gennep's Model of the Structure of Rites of Passage." In *Secular Ritual*, eds. Sally F. Moore and Barbara G. Myerhoff, 53–72. Amsterdam: Van Gorcum, 1977.

Turner, Victor. *The Anthropology of Performance*. New York: PAJ Publishers, 1988.

————. "Are There Universals of Performance in Myth, Ritual and Drama?" In *By Means of Performance: Intercultural Studies of Theatre and Ritual*, eds. Richard Schechner and Willa Appel, 8–18. Cambridge: Cambridge University Press, 1993.

————. "Variations on a Theme of Liminality." In *Secular Ritual*, eds. Sally F. Moore and Barbara G. Myerhoff, 36–52. Amsterdam: Van Gorcum, 1977.

Turner, Victor Witter. *Dramas, Fields, and Metaphors: Symbolic Action in Human Society.* Ithaca, N.Y.: Cornell University Press, 1974.

———. *The Forest of Symbols: Aspects of Ndembu Ritual.* Ithaca, N.Y.: Cornell University Press, 1967.

———. *The Ritual Process: Structure and Anti-Structure.* Chicago: Aldine, 1969.

Van der Hart, Onno. *Rituals in Psychotherapy: Transition and Continuity.* Trans. Angie Pleit-Kuiper. New York: Irvington Publishers, 1983.

Van Gennep, Arthur. *The Rites of Passage.* Chicago: University of Chicago Press, 1960.

Van Leeuwen, Mary Stewart, ed. *After Eden. Facing the Challenge of Gender Reconciliation.* Grand Rapids, Mich.: Eerdm ans, 1993.

Varela, Francisco J., Evan Thompson, and Eleanor Rosch. *The Embodied Mind: Cognitive Science and Human Experience.* Cambridge, Mass.: MIT Press, 1991.

Vayrynen, Raimo. *New Directions in Conflict Theory: Conflict Resolution and Conflict Transformation.* London: Sage Publications, 1991.

Volkan, Vamik. *Blood Lines: From Ethnic Pride to Ethnic Terrorism.* Boulder, Colo.: Westview Press, 1997.

———. "Official and Unofficial Diplomacy." In *The Psychodynamics of International Relationships,* eds. Vamik Volkan, Joseph Montville, and Demetrios Julius, 1–16. Toronto: Lexington Books, 1991.

———. "Psychological Processes in Unofficial Diplomacy Meetings." In *The Psychodynamics of International Relationships,* eds. Vamik Volkan, Joseph Montville, and Demetrios Julius, 207–22. Toronto: Lexington Books, 1991.

Volkan, Vamik D. *The Need to Have Enemies and Allies: From Clinical Practice to International Relationships.* Northvale, N.J.: J. Aronson, Inc., 1988.

Volkan, Vamik D., Joseph Montville, and Demetrios Julius. *The Psychodynamics of International Relationships.* Lexington, Mass.: Lexington Books, 1990.

von Bertalanffy, Ludwin. *General System Theory: Foundations, Development, Applications.* New York: George Braziller, 1968.

Walker, Barbara G. *Women's Rituals: A Sourcebook.* San Francisco: Harper & Row, 1990.

Warnock, G. J. *J. L. Austin.* New York: Routledge, 1989.

Webber, Mark, Christopher Stephens, and Charles D. Laughlin. "Masks: A Re-Examination, or 'Masks? You Mean They Affect the Brain?'" In *The Power of Symbols: Masks and Masquerade in the Americas,* eds. N. Ross Crumrine and Marjorie Halpin, 204–18. Vancouver: University of British Colombia Press, 1983.

West, Cornell. *Race Matters.* New York: Vintage Books, 1994.

White, Ralph. *Nobody Wanted War.* New York: Doubleday, 1968.

Whitt, Laurie Anne. "Cultural Imperialism and the Marketing of Native America." In *Natives and Academics: Researching and Writing About American Indians,* ed. Devon Mihesuah. Lincoln, Neb.: University of Nebraska Press, 1998.

Wicker, Brian. "Ritual and Culture: Some Dimensions of the Problem Today." In *The Roots of Ritual,* ed. James D. Shaughnessy. Grand Rapids, Mich.: Eerdmans, 1973.

Wiener, Norbert. *Collected Works with Commentaries.* Trans. P. Masani. Cambridge, Mass.: MIT Press, 1976.

Wink, Walter. *The Powers That Be: Theology for a New Millennium.* New York: Doubleday, 1999.

Wood, Julia. *Spinning the Symbolic Web: Human Communication as Symbolic Interaction.* Norwood, N.J.: Ablex Publishing Corporation, 1992.

Yarbrough, Elaine, and William Wilmot. *Artful Mediation: Constructive Conflict at Work.* Boulder, Colo.: Cairns Publishing, 1995.

Zarrilli, Phillip. "What Does It Mean to 'Become the Character': Power, Presence, and Transcendence in Asian In-Body Disciplines of Practice." In *By Means of Performance,* eds. Richard Schechner and Willa Appel, 131–48. New York: Cambridge University Press, 1993.

Index

About the Author

Lisa Schirch is an associate professor of peacebuilding at Eastern Mennonite University. A former Fulbright Fellow, Schirch has worked in the United States, Taiwan, Fiji, Ghana, Kenya, Brazil, Canada, and in other countries as a researcher, trainer, and facilitator in the fields of conflict transformation and peacebuilding for 15 years. Her areas of expertise include training programs for women in peacebuilding, facilitating dialogue in identity-based conflicts, the use of rituals and ceremonies in peacebuilding, conflict and violence analysis, civil-military relations, and civilian peacekeeping. With her colleagues in the Institute for Justice and Peacebuilding at Eastern Mennonite University, Schirch consults with a network of strategic partner organizations involved in peacebuilding activities throughout the United States, Latin America, Africa, Asia, and Europe.

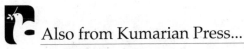

Also from Kumarian Press...

Peacebuilding, Ethics, Conflict Resolution

Buddhism at Work
Community Development, Social Empowerment and the Sarvodaya Movement
George D. Bond

Ethics and Global Politics: The Active Learning Sourcebook
Edited by April Morgan, Lucinda Joy Peach, and Colette Mazzucelli

Not a Minute More: Ending Violence Against Women
UNIFEM

Progress of the World's Women 2002, Volume One
Women, War, Peace: The Independent Expert's Assessment on the Impact of
Armed Conflict on Women and Women's Role in Peace-Building
Edited by Elisabeth Rehn and Ellen Johnson Sirleaf, published by UNIFEM

War and Intervention: Issues for Contemporary Peace Operations
Michael V. Bhatia

World Disasters Report, 2004: Focus on Community Resilience
Edited by Jonathan Walter, Published by International Federation of Red Cross and Red
Crescent Societies

Worlds Apart: Civil Society and the Battle of Ethical Globalization
John Clark

Humanitarianism, Development, Civil Society

Creating a Better World: Interpreting Global Civil Society
Edited by Rupert Taylor

Globalization and Social Exclusion: A Transformationalist Perspective
Ronaldo Munck

Human Rights and Development
Peter Uvin

Nation-Building Unraveled? Aid, Peace and Justice in Afghanistan
Edited by Antonio Donini, Norah Niland and Karin Wermester

The Charity of Nations: Humanitarian Action in a Calculating World
Ian Smillie and Larry Minear

Visit Kumarian Press at **www.kpbooks.com** or
call **toll-free 800.289.2664** for a complete catalog.

Kumarian Press, located in Bloomfield, Connecticut, is a forward-looking, scholarly press that promotes active international engagement and an awareness of global connectedness.